PRAISE FOR *SCORES*

"A fascinating, funny, and, at times, frightening tale of strippers, money, and the mob by one of the FBI's most unlikely informants ever!"

— **Anderson Cooper**

"*Scores* is a compelling true crime book that takes readers on a wild ride. This book has it all—mobsters, strippers, extortion, G-men, and one unlikely FBI informant. Michael Blutrich has told a riveting tale that will keep readers entertained and enthralled."

— **Miles Corwin, author of *Homicide Special***

"In *Scores*, we finally have the definitive insider memoir of the club that changed New York City nightlife forever. The book is a blockbuster ride revealing secrets held close since the 1990s."

— **Harvey Osher, Scores Owner, 1998–2008**

"Michael's story is a riveting window into the secret world of FBI undercover cooperation by a prominent NYC lawyer against the Mafia. As Michael's lawyer, I was present for many of the events he describes, and, unbelievable as it may seem, his story is true. His case is like no other I've encountered in my 40-year career, and his book will become an instant classic. Even knowing how it would end, I couldn't put the book down until the final page."

— **Morris "Sandy" Weinberg, Jr., partner, Zuckerman Spaeder LLP, Tampa, FL, former AUSA in the Southern District of New York, chair-elect of the ABA Criminal Justice Section**

"Michael Blutrich, a smart lawyer from Brooklyn, was feeling pretty good when his new Upper East Side strip club became a must-visit destination for everyone from Leonardo DiCaprio to Donald Trump. Then Blutrich found out he had partners he hadn't known about: John Gotti's crime family. An irrepressible wiseacre, Blutrich's first thought was that he'd seen nothing about that in the lease. Then a couple of hoods whacked two employees and things got very real, very fast. Soon, Blutrich became the least likely undercover agent the FBI ever had, wearing a wire against Gotham's biggest gangsters. But he kept his eyes open and his sense of humor and the result is this great read."

— **Tom Robbins, investigative reporter and coauthor of *Mob Boss***

SCORES

SCORES

How I Opened the Hottest Strip Club in New York City, Was Extorted out of Millions by the Gambino Family, and Became One of the Most Successful Mafia Informants in FBI History

MICHAEL D. BLUTRICH

BenBella Books, Inc.
Dallas, TX

BENBELLA

BenBella Books, Inc.
10440 N. Central Expressway
Suite #800
Dallas, TX 75231
www.benbellabooks.com
Send feedback to feedback@benbellabooks.com

Printed in the United States of America
10 9 8 7 6 5 4 3 2 1

Library of Congress Cataloging-in-Publication Data
Names: Blutrich, Michael D., author.
Title: Scores : how I opened the hottest strip club in New York City, was extorted out of millions by the Gambino family, and became one of the most successful Mafia informants in FBI history / Michael D. Blutrich.
Description: Dallas, TX : BenBella Books, Inc., [2017]
Identifiers: LCCN 2016037690 (print) | LCCN 2016051586 (ebook) (print) | LCCN 2016051586 (ebook) | ISBN 9781942952633 (trade cloth) | ISBN 9781942952640 (electronic)
Subjects: LCSH: Blutrich, Michael D. | Mafia—New York (State) | Informers—New York (State)—New York. | Nightclubs—New York (State)—New York. | Organized crime investigation—New York (State)—New York.
Classification: LCC HV6452.N7 B58 2017 (print) | LCC HV6452.N7 (ebook) | DDC 364.10609747/1—dc23
LC record available at https://lccn.loc.gov/2016037690

Editing by Erin Kelley and Alexa Stevenson
Copyediting by Scott Calamar
Cover design by Faceout Studio, Kara Davison
Jacket design by Sarah Dombrowsky
Text design by Aaron Edmiston

Text composition by Integra Software Services Pvt Ltd.
Proofreading by Brittney Martinez and Sarah Vostok
Printed by Lake Book Manufacturing

Distributed by Perseus Distribution
www.perseusdistribution.com

To place orders through Perseus Distribution:
Tel: (800) 343-4499
Fax: (800) 351-5073
E-mail: orderentry@perseusbooks.com

For my family, who in the darkest of life's times taught me the meaning of unqualified loyalty, unshakable faith, and selfless dedication.

For my dear and true old friends, who never withdrew their love, confidence, or support, even when my own dreams had fled and my hope deserted me.

For the special old friends who welcomed me back into their hearts and lives, and patiently helped me to rediscover a place in a new world. And for the amazing new friends who accepted and healed a bruised and battered spirit.

I have finally learned that a loving family and true friends are the only requirements for a life worth living. With this revelation, coming late in my life, I view myself as the luckiest man in the world.

CONTENTS

PROLOGUE
Murders That Shocked the Big Apple

Scores. The first and most notorious upscale gentlemen's club in New York City. After opening to the derision of its neighborhood residents on Manhattan's fashionable Upper East Side on Halloween night 1991, Scores grew into an unrelenting cauldron of celebrity, publicity, controversy, and profitability.

Unlike any New York club before it, except perhaps Studio 54, Scores' regular patrons included film and television superstars, sports figures, major recording artists, fashion models, comedians, politicians, billionaire business-persons, infamous mafiosos, and every horny New Yorker or tourist with cash or plastic assets. In a city that reveled in its secret adoration of celebrities, Scores was the singular stop where stargazing was matter-of-fact.

The first club of its kind to feature topless lap dancing, Scores attracted the fierce and perverse loyalty of the self-proclaimed "King of All Media," Howard Stern. Tales of Stern's star-studded parties at the club, replete with lurid lesbian exhibitions, were described daily and in excruciating detail on his radio and television programs; Stern's personal endorsement served to vault Scores' reputation into the national and international arenas. The club further attracted the unsolicited and costly "protection" of the Gambino crime family, which, over the years, seasoned its financial demands with every possible form of extortion, threatening beatings, arson, bombings, and even murder.

My name is Michael Blutrich, and I am the club's founding owner. It's very nice to meet you. I will be your guide through this tale: a gay lawyer who found himself owning the most successful den of heterosexuality in the history of the western world. It is a tale of laughter and tears, luck and betrayal—and the beginning of the end of my lifetime of successes began at the club on one warm night in June 1996.

JUNE 22, 1996, SCORES, 4 AM

Scores was closed, the staff winding down from a typical Friday. Business had boomed and Willie Marshall, one of the club's assigned mafia representatives, had acted as the evening's manager. The stale stench of drying beer curdled the air, and ugly carpet stains were visible in the now brazenly overlit premises. Most of the club's principals and senior executives were already with me in Atlantic City for a pay-per-view HBO boxing match between Macho Camacho and Roberto Durán, which I was co-promoting with Donald Trump at Trump's Taj Mahal casino and arena.

Proving the adage, "while the cat's away, the mice will play," the absence of the club's experienced supervisors had resulted in Simon and Victor Dedaj, a pair of Albanian brothers, being accorded unusual freedom to roam around. They were acquaintances of Marshall, and were known for causing serious problems whenever they partied at the club. In the past, Simon and Victor had fired handguns into the club's floor during arguments, stolen tips from bartending staff, touched dancers inappropriately, and refused to pay for drinks and food. Marshall had been under strict directive to issue this duo a lifetime ban from the club and, at the very least, should have placed an immediate tight leash on them, but it was probably easier and less confrontational at that late hour to just let them alone and hope for the best.

One of the club's most popular waiters, Jon Segal, a handsome and athletic college student, was packing up for the night when he began an innocent discussion with Simon about collegiate wrestling. When Jon mentioned he'd competed at school and won countless awards, Simon scoffed and grabbed the unsuspecting young man, quickly applying a dangerous choke hold.

Alarmed, the bar manager, Laurie, tried to diffuse the situation with humor. "Come on, Simon," she said, "you got your hands all over that gorgeous guy. People are gonna think it's like a fag thing."

As Jon desperately struggled, his complexion began to turn a mottled blue. Laurie, now almost hysterical, screamed, "Simon, are you fucking crazy? Let him go, you're killing him!"

Simon tossed Jon to the floor, and walked menacingly toward Laurie. Marshall positioned himself protectively between the two.

"Your girlfriend is a bitch! No one calls me a fag or crazy!" Simon screamed at Marshall, literally frothing at the mouth.

"Simon, calm down, you might've killed him. She saved us all from a big problem."

As the confrontation settled, Segal rose from the carpet and began walking toward Marshall. In the same instant, Michael Greco, a new bouncer and one I'd never met, followed Segal toward the bar.

Marshall attempted to further calm things by separating everyone. "Jon, hit the vestibule, I'll meet you there in a couple minutes." Segal immediately changed direction, and Greco diverted to the far end of the bar.

Simon continued staring down Marshall, and Marshall walked to the end of the bar near Greco, away from Laurie. "Keep talking to me like that, Willie," Simon said, "and I promise I'll kill you or someone else here tonight!"

"You're not gonna kill anyone, Simon."

Just then, Simon's brother Victor approached. The two brothers whispered in Albanian, and Marshall had the sinking feeling he was losing control.

When the whispering between the brothers stopped, Simon brandished a gun and, without warning or provocation, shot Greco between the eyes. The bouncer silently crumpled to the floor and never stirred.

As Greco fell, the brothers ran down the nearby stairs toward the entrance to the street. Segal was in the vestibule and, without missing a step, Simon raised his gun and shot the young man four times in the chest. Victor laughed as he pulled a knife from his waistband and stabbed Jon repeatedly.

And then the perpetrators were gone. The club was silent, only the acrid smell of gunpowder left to hang in the air. It was over in a matter of seconds. Stunned and in shock, Willie picked up a phone and called Andrew Pearlstein, one of my partners.

PART ONE

Please Stop Bugging Me!

CHAPTER ONE

Coping with Murder

JUNE 22, 1996, 5:30 AM—ATLANTIC CITY, NEW JERSEY LEONARDO da VINCI PENTHOUSE SUITE, TAJ MAHAL HOTEL AND CASINO

Deep in sleep, I was abruptly driven to conscious clarity when an unexpected ringing erupted. I grabbed at the delicate Victorian telephone on the nearby nightstand, and roared into its receiver, "Why are you calling me? I blocked this phone until 8 AM!"

"Our apologies," the hotel operator replied in sugarcoated tones. "Is this Mr. Blutrich? Because I have an emergency call for him from Andrew Pearlstein. Will you accept?"

"Yes I will, sorry. Please put him through."

"Michael. It's me. Just got home."

"I take it this is not good news."

"Nope. Willie Marshall ran the place tonight. Seems two of those Albanian lunatics got drunk, pulled a gun over something stupid, and murdered two of our people."

As the information registered, I realized I was now standing, with no memory of getting out of bed. "Who was killed?"

"Jon Segal, the waiter, and a bouncer who started tonight. Their bodies were still in the club when I got there, as were tons of police. I had to step over puddles of blood . . ."

Andrew continued to describe the scene, but I was no longer listening. Jon was my friend; we'd recently shared dinner at Japonica on University Avenue. The amazingly handsome kid had just done a television commercial for Abflex, and now Andrew was stepping in his blood?

I realized there was silence in the earpiece. "Are you OK?" I asked.

"Yeah, shaken but fine. I haven't slept. I have a lot more damage control to do. The press is out in force; they were actually climbing the Fifty-Ninth Street Bridge to get pictures of the victims . . . "

I interrupted him, desperately turning my brain to business mode in the hope of calming down. "Listen Andrew. The cops are gonna want to putz around in the club forever with crime scene shit. Do whatever it takes, call who you need to call, but get them out. We have to open tonight or we may never open again."

"I'll go back to the club. The radio and cable news are continuously playing the story. They announced one dead and one in surgery, but he's not making it either."

I sat down on the bed and put a pillow in my lap. "I hear you. We need to get word out that we *will* be open tonight, and get our PR staff massaging the media."

"OK," Andrew answered. "Do we want to brief Howard Stern's people? Get them to downplay it on the air?"

"I just don't know yet, Andrew; we'll play it by ear."

"Whatever you say. Anyway, go back to bed. I'll be there for the fight. Save me some extra ringside seats."

"Yeah, you're dreaming. I just had to 'create' two seats with folding chairs for a high roller from TropWorld. Bring opera glasses."

"Go back to bed. Who is he kidding?" I said to myself after I hung up.

I drew a rattled breath. Dismayed and unraveling, I wandered from the master bedroom into the suite's massive living room. My mind was exploding in eerie contrast to the dark and silent world peeking through the hotel windows. Not a hint of breaking sunlight, I poured myself the remainder of a leftover bottle of Perrier sitting atop a piano and walked past the butler's station toward a row of bedrooms.

My two guests from Montreal were soundly asleep, one of the men snoring laboriously. I really wanted to wake them; I needed some physical comfort. But, I silently mused, my broken French probably wasn't adequate to make them understand either what had happened or what might lie ahead. I considered that it might be prudent to find them other accommodations in case the day became hairy with press or police. Leaning my head against the nearest wall, and pondering for the millionth time the endless ironies and secrets of my existence, I wearily mumbled softly, "You know what, fuck it."

I walked back to the main sitting area and struggled for something—anything—to occupy my thoughts. I needed to retreat to a comfortable place in my mind.

"Goddamn Willie," I shouted at the indifferent ceiling. "You swore there'd be no more crazy mafiosos allowed in the club. So much for mob protection."

I plopped myself onto a large sectional couch and sank deeply into its folds. I started to feel drowsy and my thoughts turned to the very first time I was personally confronted with a potentially violent and threatening situation, at a most tender age.

It was sixth grade, at PS 209 in South Brooklyn. Our teacher was enthusiastically showing slides of her recent vacation to Italy. The few Italian kids in the class—the school had a 97 percent Jewish student body—were gloating over all the unusual attention being heaped on their ancestral land. In reaction, I unthinkingly started cracking a few jokes about the naked statues on the slides, and one of the Italian bullies, Nicholas Spano, got all bent out of shape by this perceived offense to all of Italy emanating from one small Jewish kid. In a show of Brooklyn bravado learned from the generations preceding him, Nick vowed in front of the entire class to pummel me into snot after school.

I was terrified. Nobody ever taught me how to fight. My parents thought playing the accordion was macho. I slept in a tiny room with my Aunt Edythe and my aging goldfish. Physical confrontation was the stuff of movies, not real life at PS 209. But I was in trouble. I'd been called out—even the words gave me an exhilarating chill—and not by some soft, nearsighted Hebrew scholar angered over a Torah interpretation. This was to be a fight to the death with Italian Nick, a boy who probably had pubic hair.

What to do? In an unmitigated panic, I requested a sit-down with Lora Nuzzo, indisputably the toughest girl in the world. I knew she liked me, something in her Amazon-like smiles told me so, and I shared with her the reason for my impending, pre–Bar Mitzvah doom.

I watched her ponder the situation before stridently declaring, "You know what, you and me, we leave school together today." I thought about it for a moment, solely for dramatic effect, and moved my head slowly up and down with reverent vigor. I knew my problem had just been solved; Nick Spano, on the other hand, was happily ignorant of his impending crisis.

As the day's closing bell sounded, I was absolutely prepared. If the theme to *Rocky* had yet been written, I would've insisted it be played. And with the stone faces of seasoned warriors, Lora and I descended the main school stairway. Halfway down, I spied Nick waiting below with a malevolent grin, surrounded by a crowd of blood-crazed spectators. There were shades of *Spartacus* running through my brain; only it was supposed to be a Christian fed to the lions—not the Jewish kid.

Suddenly Spano made his move to confront me and, with the grace of a gazelle, my angel stepped between us and said in full New York accent, "Hey Nick, tough guy. You wanna fight this little kid here? Maybe you wanna fight me instead, huh?"

Nick's face was transformed into a mask of horror. And even I grew queasy as we all witnessed Lora Nuzzo beating the living shit out of Nicholas Spano—around and around the school yard fence they go. Nick was bleeding and crying and begging, and I was loving every minute of it. After all, I was winning my very first fight. Finally, and with gracious mercy, we let Nick run home to mommy.

The next day, I arrived at school to find a pink note resting neatly in the middle of my desk. The pit of my stomach already knew what was in it, but I opened it anyway. It was from Lora, and the tiny hairs on the back of my neck stood up as I read her words, "I love you. How do you feel about me?"

Talk about going from the frying pan to the fire. I probably neglected to mention Lora was not one of the brightest blooms of femininity ever created. She actually had to lift her nose to stuff food into her face. But I knew what I had to do—look what she did to Nick, and *he* hadn't toyed with her tender heart—so I quickly scrawled "I love you too" on the bottom of the note before sending it back to its maker.

Not to worry though. Luck was with me and we never married, never even dated. The very next day, a sad and apologetic Lora told me her father had nixed our budding union. Her exact words, delivered without a hint of potential offense, were, "My father says I can't date no Jesus-killing fucking Jew bastard." Who says anti-Semitism is always a bad thing? In any event, Lora and I returned to our usual roles of respectful boy and female ogre, and Nick Spano continued to flinch every time I looked at him.

I never had another fight after that, and I believe it's probably a matter of projected aura. But sometimes I like to think that maybe, just maybe, it's my reputation from my first fight preceding me.

CHAPTER TWO
Taking Control and Promoting the HBO Fight

JUNE 22, 1996, 9:30 AM

For the second time that morning, a ringing telephone jolted me into the real world.

The voice of Mark Yackow, one of the Scores partners, boomed through the receiver. "Have you seen the local morning paper?"

"I don't need the paper. Andrew called me early this morning with details."

"How the fuck would Andrew know about Roberto Durán's interview?"

Realizing Yackow and I were on different pages, I took a breath. "What are you talking about?"

"What are *you* talking about?"

"We had a shooting at the club last night. Two of our guys are dead including Jon Segal. I don't know any other specifics; Andrew is trying to sort things out."

"Oh my God," Mark stammered. "I can't believe it."

"Me neither. But what are you calling about?"

"What?"

"Come on, Mark, you just said something about the morning paper."

"Oh, right. It just doesn't seem very important now. The lead story is that Durán is accusing us of breaching his contract for tonight's bout with Camacho. It's just stupidity."

I laughed. "It's beyond stupid and total bullshit. I'll go read it, and why don't you call home and find out the latest there? Please call me when you know more."

"You got it. I'll do it right now."

I hung up the phone and went straight to the suite's front door. Opening it, I recovered the morning paper from the doorstep. The headline piece was a lengthy story about Durán's claims that his contract had been breached as to rooms and food. The story actually made it sound as if Durán and his family were being starved and housed in an overcrowded slum.

Hearing it from Mark, it had been amusing; seeing it as a front-page newspaper story was less entertaining. I snapped, grabbed the nearest phone, and dialed Durán's room.

When a child answered, I asked to speak to Roberto. Several minutes went by until he finally came to the phone.

"Roberto. It's Blutrich. I just read the piece in the paper. Have you lost your mind? You've received everything you're entitled to under your contract—more. And as to food, after luckily squeaking through that official weigh-in yesterday, you ate so many hot dogs, I thought your fight strategy was now to *fart* Macho into submission! How dare you?"

"Miguel, yo no entiendo lo que dices. Por qué estas molesto?"

"Roberto. Don't start that Spanish crap with me. You understand every word I'm saying. Did someone tell you to say this nonsense? Was this a publicity stunt?"

"Espera, voy a poner alguien que habla mejor Inglés."

"No, Roberto. Stay on the phone. Roberto. Roberto."

The phone remained silent for a pregnant pause. Finally, a timid voice said, "Miguel. Roberto say he doesn't know why you are angry with him."

I pulled the receiver from my ear and shook my head. "OK. Just tell him I will come to the suite later. By the way, do you need me to bring food, blankets, and medical supplies, or are you doing all right with the unlimited room service?"

JUNE 22, 1996, 9 PM

Despite the incomprehensible events happening at Scores, I still had a fight to promote. As was the custom, I spent fight night fielding complaints about seat locations and rooms from friends and clients. I lost my own seat when I arrived to find Governor Christie Whitman of New Jersey parked on it. Trump arrived with Marla Maples plus entourage and secured his assigned front row of prime seats on the opposite side of the ring from my people.

Mike Tyson slayer, Buster Douglas, back from retirement, had beefed up public interest in a main event of aging champions past their primes, and fought an impressive match, knocking out his opponent. Camacho won a unanimous and obvious decision over Durán—probably the result of poor room conditions for Roberto's family. Plainly, the spark was gone for Durán, the former "Hands of Stone," and he was now just sadly fighting to satisfy old tax bills.

Happily, more than anticipated numbers of cable viewers bought the fight from HBO-TVKO, Trump's arena had sold out, and my boxing company's future was never brighter.

Unknown to me, as I was packing my bags the following morning for the return to the city, Jack Karst and Bill Ready, two special agents of the FBI assigned to an Organized Crime Task Force investigating the Gambino crime family, were also packing their gear, in one of the smallest—and definitely the cheapest—rooms at the Taj. The accommodation was a far cry from the opulence of the Leonardo da Vinci Suite on the penthouse floor.

"Blutrich didn't look too happy last night," Karst mused.

"True," Ready replied, "and we didn't get much."

"I know. But it's just the beginning. And we just keep fishing."

Andrew and I flew back to the city by helicopter. By the time we landed, the police had already identified the perpetrators of the double homicide, and the Albanians were reportedly on the run. Pearlstein scheduled meetings with Marshall to talk things out with the mafia contingent, and a slew of calls from investigating police detectives were awaiting responses.

In the next month, revenues at Scores spiked by an unprecedented 30 percent. After a few well-placed calls to politicians in Albany, the State Liquor Authority never contacted us.

CHAPTER THREE
Scores-Style Softball

FIVE DAYS LATER: JUNE 27, 1996—NEW YORK CITY

Central Park was nothing less than spectacular as the summer day stretched toward its close. The air was refreshingly clean and crisp, and a strong breeze contained none of the agonizing humidity that would plague New York City in July and August.

Public shock over the lurid double homicide finally began to ebb, even as the local press continued to focus on the ongoing manhunt for the accused killers. For the owners of Scores, the decision to immediately cooperate with police had kept the club out of harm's way. Employee eyewitnesses had been cajoled into furnishing investigators with details of the gruesome crime, and their cooperation had apparently satisfied police as to the club's lack of culpability.

Despite the enormity of the crime and its crushing impact on every person affiliated with the club, there was nothing to be done except grieve and offer condolences. And it was Thursday—Scores' day to compete in the city's slow-pitch softball league, a reminder that life somehow goes on.

When I arrived at the designated softball diamond in Central Park, the scene was practiced chaos. Hundreds of fans had taken their places in the stands and in an adjacent copse. Hot dog and pretzel vendors were maneuvering umbrella carts into position to accommodate sales, and players for both teams were tossing balls, stretching, and otherwise preparing themselves for combat. Scores' cheerleaders, who otherwise plied their trade as topless dancers at the club, were busy posing for pictures with admiring fans, as clusters of police mingled and laughed loudly amidst the amiable throng. An unmistakable aroma of illegal herbs permeated the outdoor arena as the contest drew closer to the opening pitch.

Today's lineup included yours truly as pitcher and Pearlstein as catcher. Scores' house mom, Camille, would be at her usual shortstop position and, as the team's leading hitter and captain, would bat cleanup. The *Penthouse* "Pet of the Quarter Century" and longtime club dancer, Tamara Seely, was assigned chores at second base.

To the team's chagrin, this week's opposing squad was composed of officers from one of the city's large commercial banks. They were supercilious assholes who had voiced pointed disdain at Scores' well-known on-field antics, which they viewed as "unbecoming" to a serious softball league. This would surely prove fun.

The lone umpire called the team's representatives to the mound for the usual boring recitation of rules. Three players answered the call from the bank, each decked out in professional uniforms with numbers and names sewn along the back of their jerseys. Our squad made quite the dashing comparison. At 5'8", 190 pounds (with about ninety of those pounds located in my breadbasket), and wearing a pair of old jeans, yellow sweatshirt, and sneakers, I looked more like a lost spectator in search of a pretzel than a player. Flanking my right was a recent *Playboy* centerfold model wearing a cutoff yellow halter top, draping her arm around an obviously contented Yackow, and to my left were two dancer-cheerleaders sporting skimpy T-shirts.

Our opponents went on immediate attack. "Listen, ump. We're not gonna put up with this team's legendary crap. If they can't be serious, let them forfeit. No bullshit, we're playing for a playoff berth. Oh yeah, and you all know what I mean, absolutely no tits!"

The umpire looked at me. "What's he talking about?"

"I don't know, but we're playing with our tits no matter what he says."

"Listen, I'm serious." The opposing captain seethed.

"I'm sure you are." I smiled back.

As we all departed the mound, I motioned to one of the opposing captains. "Hey listen, we know this is important to you guys, but we're just looking for some fun. I'm sure you've read the papers and know we've had a hellish time lately. So look, we forfeit. We wanna play for ourselves and the fans, but you win no matter what. Deal?"

The banker agreed.

On the very first pitch, the opposing batter hit a rocket over the right fielder's head.

In New York City softball, when a lone umpire officiates from behind the pitcher, the catcher calls balls fair or foul. As was his established custom, Pearlstein immediately rose and judiciously yelled, "Foul ball, strike one."

The bank team erupted and gathered on the mound en masse. "I warned you, ump. They cheat!"

The umpire stared at an obviously unconcerned Pearlstein. "I must tell you, sir, it's hard to believe you honestly thought that ball was foul."

As the Scores team waited around in suppressed laughter, Pearlstein looked up. "Well, I'm not positive. I usually just call every ball foul."

The umpire overruled the call and declared a home run. Score: 1–0.

The subdued crowd finally erupted in joyous bedlam in the third inning. The reason for the unusually large crowd was that each time Scores pushes runs across the plate, three or four cheerleaders prance around the bases flashing unobstructed views of their abundant upper region treasures. Harvey hit a massive inside-the-park homer and, as the cheerleaders fulfilled their duties, the spectators frenzied. Cameras clicked, beer was tossed in the air, and hundreds of transfixed eyes closely monitored every bob and weave of the exposed victory rewards. Indeed, only the presence of the NYPD preserved any semblance of restraint—and even some guardians of the peace appeared to be on the verge of breaking.

The game that afternoon held something for every attendee. The Scores team scored four times and that meant four trips around the bases for the enthusiastic and deeply appreciated cheerleaders. The fans were hoarse from expressing their adulation, the vendors sold out their wares, and all available marijuana was smoked.

At the end of the game, the cheerleaders mingled with their fans and, as part of a never-tiresome ritual, passed out complimentary passes to the club for that night only—a savings of the twenty-dollar door fee. Many of the recipients would, in fact, happily head to Scores that night to continue the "connection" they believed they'd forged with one of the cheerleaders. How many times has the world heard the same tired refrain, "No really, she liked me! Really, really liked me! Nothing to do with money. It was something special between just us."

Even the miserable bank team seemed happy as they triumphed by a margin of 9–4. In fact, there were those in attendance who later speculated that Scores' last two runs were the product of intentional errors by opposing players who just wanted the cheerleaders to keep on cheering.

How unusual to voluntarily receive high rates of interest *from* bankers.

CHAPTER FOUR

Hints of Future Problems Erupt

JULY 29, 1996—THREE PARK AVENUE, MANHATTAN

An unremarkable midtown commercial skyscraper, Three Park Avenue sits at the prestigious southeast corner of Park Avenue and East Thirty-Fourth Street. At the epicenter of Manhattan's business district, the building's upper floors feature impressive views of the city skyline. At night, office windows are filled with uncountable numbers of electric and neon lights burning and stretching as far as the eye can gaze in every direction, and first time viewers stand mesmerized in the wake of panoramic sensory overload. The thirty-eighth floor was home to my law firm, and the connected offices of Scores Entertainment.

At 10 AM, on Monday July 29th, I arrived to begin another workweek. I stepped out of the elevator onto the carpeted common area, taking a moment to decide which way to turn. To my left were the Scores offices and, to my right, my law practice. Since the maze of interior hallways in both entities led eventually to my private office, I could choose either entrance to reach my inner sanctum.

Each morning when presented with this choice, I was confronted with the frenetic split personalities with which I live my existence. Did I feel like being a lawyer or a businessman? Which came first that day: contracts and trials, or tits and ass?

Quickly deciding the morning's action would best lie to my right with the law firm, I turned and opened the doors to the plush reception area. Noting that Lillian Montalvo, our longtime paralegal and receptionist, was busy on the phone, I just waved and turned left to pass through a second set of security doors.

"Michael, can you wait a moment, please?" Lillian called after me.

I reactively removed my hand from the doorknob. When Lillian disconnected her call, I said, "And how was your weekend?"

"Just fine thanks, but listen, Mr. Seavey asked that you drop by and see him the moment you arrive. He sounded worried."

"Oh, OK." I hesitated. "I might as well do that now before I get swamped."

I diverted to a door directly behind Lillian's desk. She reached under the lip of the desk for an internal release switch and, when I heard the electric buzzing tone, I pushed my way through the door into the anteroom beyond.

The "Seavey" section of the firm was physically isolated. All of the desks in the space were empty this day, signaling the staff hadn't yet arrived or weren't arriving at all. In fact, the entire wing seemed dark and deserted but for the unmistakable booming voice of Robert Seavey. I poked my head into his office and, when I caught his attention, he gestured for me to sit.

As I waited for him to conclude his call, I carefully watched the elderly bespectacled gentleman who'd been so much a part of my law firm's glory days. Back in the early eighties, Bob Seavey had been firmly established as one of Manhattan's true real estate moguls, quietly owning more residential apartment buildings and commercial properties than anyone suspected or he would ever admit. In the crowning moment of his civic service, he was appointed as chairman of the massive downtown Battery Park City housing project located across from the World Trade Center.

When my law firm was created, after Lieutenant Governor Mario Cuomo lost a gubernatorial primary to New York City Mayor Ed Koch, it was planned that Cuomo would join the new firm as its senior partner. But then, in a quirk of fate, Cuomo stunned the experts and was elected governor, leaving his new firm without its "rainmaker." Some quick shuffling of partners took place and, with the governor's blessing, his son Andrew soon joined the firm in his stead.

Concerned about the firm's viability because of the disconcerting youth of its partners, Cuomo persuaded Seavey to resign from the Battery Park City appointment and become a part of the firm, or as Cuomo aptly put it, "to put some snow on the firm's roof." The arrangement had worked well for years, but now Seavey was the only remaining vestige of the Cuomo legacy.

As Seavey replaced the receiver on the phone, he stood up stiffly, grabbing his cane, and without a word, motioned for me to follow. The usually gracious and gregarious gentleman maintained silence, and I had a sinking feeling something was terribly wrong as I followed him out the front door. In all the years of our relationship, Seavey had never acted mysteriously.

Upon entering the outer hallway, he turned right for a few paces and then left into the service elevator loading area. He picked a spot and turned.

"Michael, so sorry about all this cloak-and-dagger stuff. When I arrived this morning, one of the maintenance guys pulled me over to a corner of the lobby. He told me that workmen were in our space one weekend in mid-June going into our ceilings with wires. They were very secretive and he didn't recognize them. And worse, he never got authorizing paperwork from the landlord as he usually does. He couldn't tell me before because I've been away. Do we know anything about this?"

I was, to put it mildly, stunned. Trying to appear composed and unconcerned, my mind started revolving with unhappy possibilities. Was this the FBI investigating my personal problems in Florida over an insurance fraud? Could it be the state police looking into mafia activities at Scores? Any chance it was just our own project? I made eye contact with Seavey. "This is news to me, Bob. I guess I'll call the landlord and check out what they know."

"I would. It's just the maintenance guy seemed very antsy, almost like he knew more than he was saying but was afraid to speak his mind. Also, who would be working over a weekend for double-time union rates?"

I nodded. "All right. Let me call the landlord and check with Andrew. He did mention he was going to network the computers between the law firm and Scores. Maybe that's all it was."

"Michael," Bob interrupted. "When you talk to the landlord, don't mention our inside guy. Let's keep the information flowing. I don't like the way this smells for you guys."

When I finally reached my private office, I was surprised to find the secretarial station deserted. Opening the office door, I discovered my longtime secretary, Casey Crawford, seated behind my desk, busily reorganizing multiple piles of stacked papers. Despite the appearance of mountainous desktop madness, Casey and I had spent years creating an organizational flow that blended my legal, business, and personal matters into a filing system only the two of us understood. It was ugly, but it worked.

"What's up, kid?"

"Just the usual. Working on mail."

"Anybody call yet?"

"Let's see," Casey feigned mulling for an answer. "Are you kidding? Everyone called. And of course, Mike Sergio called screaming about Andrew bouncing another Scores check to his son. He's driving down for dinner to straighten it out." Picking up a thick stack of telephone message slips, she added, "Here's the whole pile."

I frowned and, as was my wont at such times, gazed at the ceiling in an impotent cry for heavenly assistance. "Case, just leave it all; it's gonna take me all day. Is Andrew here yet?"

"Haven't seen him or heard any noises from the other side. Want me to check?"

"Nah. What you can do for me is call the landlord's office. Ask them if they authorized or know anything about any construction or wiring work in our suites on a weekend in mid-June."

Casey nodded and looked back quizzically as if expecting more information about the odd question. Receiving none, she simply retreated.

Engrossed in reviewing the incoming mail and phone messages, I jumped when an unwrapped Cuban cigar landed in the middle of my desk. When I looked up, Andrew was sitting in one of the red leather chairs facing me. We each wore our customary variation in dress: I was in a Brioni suit, Brooks Brothers shirt, Hermès tie, and black wing-tipped shoes; Pearlstein in a striped button-down Polo shirt, tan Dockers, and suede penny loafers.

"I hear you bounced another check to Steve Sergio."

"Not true," Andrew countered laughingly. "I stopped his last check to drive him crazy. There's plenty of cash in the account."

"Why do you do this, Andrew? The guy's father is the senior Gambino mobster assigned to Scores and now we'll have him here for hours going nuts. Do we really need more aggravation?"

"It's not aggravation, Michael, it's fun. Just watch what I do. Someday you'll come to understand there's pleasure in sly, meaningful revenge. Also, if you bounce checks every once in a while, people are so happy when their checks clear, they never ask for a raise. In the meantime, let me enjoy myself."

I stood up. "Whatever. You have fun and I have Mike Sergio in my face relishing the thought of ripping out your entrails. Deep down you must know you're completely nuts. Take a walk with me."

"Something wrong?"

"Maybe."

We silently walked through the small private bathroom that connected our offices, through Andrew's office, and out the Scores reception area into the hallway. We made an immediate right turn and then a left through a metal fire door into a cavernous stairwell.

We assumed our normal positions: Andrew seated on an upward-bound stair, me pacing on the landing. Adopting attorney mode, I meticulously recounted my conversation with Seavey. Andrew responded that he knew absolutely nothing about wiring work in our ceiling over the past month.

"I think it's a problem," he quickly added. "Seavey's right, it doesn't pass the 'smell test.' But we need to find out."

"I thought we could hire one of those spy stores on Lexington Avenue to check the offices for bugs."

"I know someone in the business."

"Great!"

We lumbered back to Andrew's office, and he dialed the number of his "debugger." He placed the call on speakerphone and recounted the day's disturbing surprises.

After listening to the tale, his friend, identified only as Daniel, commented, "I can't believe there could be a legal wiretap of a law firm. Do you understand how rare that would be? How much proof it would take?"

"We agree with you, Daniel," I quickly answered. "But it could also be an illegal intrusion."

"Or it could be nothing," Andrew added.

Nodding my head in hopeful agreement, I stood and picked up a phone in the corner of the office and dialed Casey's extension. "Case, did you get through to the landlord?"

After listening to her reply, I hung up the phone, nervously placing my hands in my pockets. "Casey says the landlord claims to know nothing about any recent work in our space." I looked up and stared at Andrew. "So much for nothing."

Daniel jumped back into the conversation. "I'll get over there as soon as possible."

"Not as soon as possible," Andrew shot back. "Today."

By three in the afternoon, I'd plodded my way through the day's barrage of phone emergencies and mail. I was about to place another call when my door opened and Andrew came bounding through followed by a man in a brown suit who was sweating profusely.

"Mike. Meet my buddy Daniel."

As I extended my hand, Andrew continued as he took a seat, "I explained to Daniel what else we've learned and what we suspect. He was on another job but he came over without equipment just to take a look around for us."

Daniel cleared his throat. "Andrew tells me the law firm space begins here in your private office, and the Scores space starts on the other side of the far wall. So let's start here, in the direct middle. I'll go up into the drop ceiling. Now I won't find anything really small or well hidden, but if there's something up there that obviously shouldn't be, I'll spot it. And if I find something, we'll follow where it leads. And if I don't, I'll be back tomorrow with my men and electronics."

"Sounds perfect," Andrew said.

"OK, if you guys will leave, I'll start poking into the ceiling and see what we got."

Less than fifteen minutes later, the conference room intercom speaker chirped with Casey's voice. "Are you in there, Michael?"

"I am."

"Well, I think you two better come here now."

Reaching my office, I found Daniel standing on a desk in the middle of the room, his head hidden in the ceiling. Andrew and I gingerly walked around a black object, covered in tape, ominously dangling from a hole directly above the door.

As we formed a semicircle around the hanging package, Daniel jumped down from the chair. He was covered in sweat and dust.

"What is this?" I asked.

Daniel took a deep breath. "It's a surveillance camera, the only one in the ceiling. I've also found at least three microphones up there. I can't be 100 percent sure, but it looks like more microphones are running into the office on the other side of the wall."

"This is unbelievable," Andrew muttered in obvious shock. "How does it work?"

"Actually, it's an old piece-of-shit camera nobody uses anymore. It needs electricity and, as far as I can tell, they're tapping into the telephone system for power." As he was speaking, Daniel stepped out of my office. "The camera wire and the telephone wires are running together down this hallway toward the firm's front door. Probably running to the central telephone box. Where is that?"

"Follow me," Andrew said as he set off down the blue-carpeted road.

All the telephone wiring for the floor was gathered in a closet in the common area directly outside the law firm's front door. As our group arrived at the closet, I stopped short. "Wait a second. The closet is always locked and only the landlord's people have keys."

"Not today," Daniel said as he pulled the closet door fully open. Peering into the closet, he took on the air of a teacher on a field trip. "You guys see these wires here?" he asked, pointing to a group of batched wires entering the closet from the right side of the ceiling. "Those are the law office's normal telephone connections. Now you see the thick blue wire coming along with the group? That's the wire running from the camera in your ceiling."

"Are they tapping the phones?" I asked.

"Nope. It seems like they just followed along the phone cables as a guide for power."

Pearlstein stepped into the closet. "Daniel, where do the wires go from here?"

"Don't know yet," he answered. "Let's look." He studied the wires for a minute. "OK, they split off here and go into the wall there." Daniel stepped out of the closet and pointed to a thick blue wire jutting out of a hole above the door. The wire snaked up the wall to where it intersected with the ceiling, and then headed around the corner toward the elevators. "We have to find out where that goes."

The chase was on. With the air of a desperate scavenger hunt, the group followed the blue cable. It went past the elevators, around another corner to the fire stairwell, and disappeared through a hole above the stairwell door.

Andrew opened the door to the stairs and stepped onto the landing. "It tracks this way."

Following Andrew through the door, we stood in silence staring at where the thick blue cable reappeared through the wall and tracked up the staircase toward the upper reaches of the building. Every twenty feet or so, the wire was tacked to the wall with plastic ties and nails.

I turned to Andrew. "Can you believe we were sitting in here this morning and didn't notice any of this?"

"I noticed it. I just didn't think about it."

Several floors later, panting and running on pure adrenaline, our group reached the end of the stairs at the apparent top floor of the building. The blue wire whisked through a punched hole at the top of the wall and Daniel opened the door to continue the hunt.

When I stepped through, I was awed by the unexpected sight before me. The top floor was as large and expansive as an airplane hangar. Heavy equipment was everywhere, machines I'd never seen before, but not a soul to whom we could pose a question.

Our shoes echoed through the space, and we squinted to follow the wire as it reached high up into the indoor sky. After traveling at least seventy feet straight in the air, the suspended cable traveled to the center of the hangar, where it turned left and traversed the space on its way to an outer wall.

Sprinting to the end of the space, struggling to keep an eye on the blue cable dangling overhead, we ended up at the building wall, where the cable made a sharp downward spiral and disappeared through a hole above a munchkin-sized door.

"This is the final destination," Daniel said, as he twisted the doorknob to reveal the truth. But the door didn't budge and we all stared at a large padlock barring our entry.

"Let's just break the door down," I reacted.

"Not yet," Andrew countered. "Daniel and I will go see the landlord. Michael, please wait here."

CHAPTER FIVE
How Did I Wind Up Here?

Once I was alone, I realized I'd become disoriented and desperately tried to digest the day's extraordinary events. My mind was spinning, and I hugged a wall to steady myself. I glanced at the locked door one last time and pulled a wooden crate over to sit down. The gravity of my situation had started to sink in. No matter who had covertly slipped into my life to spy, no matter the motive or the gambit, any sane man would have recognized life was never going to be the same; it had tilted beyond the skill of any healer. As I sat down on that filthy crate, a part of me had to have known control was slipping away. I was being carried against my will into unwelcome waters, waters that would bludgeon and dismantle my world. The obvious rush of reality dictated that the puppeteer had become the puppet, although it would take some time to discover who was now pulling the strings.

My remaining rational self wanted to begin focusing on crucial issues: Who's doing this? What's the best counter-strategy? Are we in a fight or is it time to turn and run? Can the mafia help us or are they responsible?

But I couldn't bring a single one of these questions into focus. I was neither prepared to acknowledge the patent depths of my problems nor accept there would be no wiggle room to preserve the status quo. So instead of charging into the reasonable, my thoughts slipped into the comfortable, in this instance, how I'd ended up sitting there, waiting for someone to break down a locked miniature door so I could uncover our spy.

My first law-related job was as a summer intern in the office of the Manhattan district attorney, but my dream of being a criminal lawyer and a part of our system of justice quickly died on the vine. I hated the work, hated the system more. Hundreds of cases each day on the calendars of dozens of courtrooms; thousands of faces; no time, no justice, no humanity. After a while, everyone seemed like a victim—even me. The thrill of personally knowing every arrested prostitute in Manhattan quickly began to lose novelty.

After graduation from Georgetown University Law Center the next year, I quickly changed direction and accepted employment with a small midtown law firm specializing in textiles and arbitration. To be honest, if someone had whispered to me I would be spending my life fighting over yarns and fabrics instead of changing the world, I probably would have applied to journalism school.

One of the more exciting cases assigned to me was on behalf of hundreds of passengers of a well-known cruise ship who'd been food poisoned when the kitchen crew defrosted shrimp using bacteria-filled water from the ship's fire system. The Centers for Disease Control out of Atlanta boarded the ship while still at sea, fearing plague or worse, and documented the factual cause for the vomiting, diarrhea, and dizziness suffered by every passenger who'd enjoyed a shrimp cocktail as a dinner appetizer.

The "big" question in the lawsuit was whether the district court would certify our case as a class action. Working alone, I drafted motion papers and was thrilled when the judge announced his decision allowing class status. It meant an impressively large payday for the firm.

Class certification resulted in a remarkably speedy settlement with the cruise line on the issue of liability. After all, the federal government had unintentionally acted as our private investigation team. All I was left to do was prepare for mini-trials before a special master to assess damages for each individual plaintiff in the class. This turned into endless meetings and telephone calls with clients, each anxious for their piece of the settlement.

One sunny day, a member of the class dropped by the firm without an appointment. Deciding to spend a few minutes, I asked my secretary to usher the tiny, elderly woman into my office. She declined my offer of coffee or tea, and stared at me with a discerning eye. With an air of conspiracy, she leaned forward and whispered, "I have the evidence to win the case!"

"Well," I returned with a benign smile, "we've already won. The cruise line has agreed it's guilty. All that's left to do is award damages depending on how long and seriously each passenger suffered."

Seeming not to hear me, she reached into her large carryall bag, drew out a plastic baggie containing what appeared to me to be dirt, and tossed it on my desk. "Here's your evidence!" she roared.

I picked up the bag gingerly and asked, "What's this?"

"It's my diarrhea from the cruise. I've saved it all this time and now it's yours."

I dutifully thanked the proud woman and my secretary showed her the door at my request. I remember sitting and staring at the dried-out bag of shit atop my desk. I desperately needed to compose myself from a combination of dread, disgust, and sheer amusement, taking a few moments to again try to remember why I'd gone to law school in the first place.

When the wave passed, I hit the intercom and cheerily called to my secretary, "Would you mind helping me with a little something in here?"

By late 1981, I had risen to partner, but was unhappy and unfulfilled. I already knew in my heart I needed a change when I unexpectedly received a call from the most important textile client assigned to my care, Bill Levin of Gold Mills. A secret luncheon invitation was extended, and I accepted without hesitation.

At lunch, Bill informed me that he was personally close with Mario Cuomo and intended to support him in becoming the next governor of New York. I knew precious little about Cuomo, other than the fact that he was the sitting lieutenant governor, had a well-publicized strained relationship with Governor Hugh Carey, and had earned minor legal celebrity as a lawyer from Queens who'd handled a housing dispute that garnered tons of media attention.

My reaction was confusion. I told Bill it was common political wisdom that New York City Mayor Ed Koch wanted to be the successor to Carey, and Cuomo stood very little chance of defeating the popular mayor in a Democratic primary.

"Exactly," he retorted. "I said I was supporting Cuomo, not that I expected him to win." He then explained he was bankrolling the formation of a new law firm in which Cuomo would become the senior partner after losing the primary. The firm would consolidate all Levin's legal needs under one roof, and he'd already arranged for rental of luxury offices.

Suppressing my normal inability to remain silent, I sat very still, waiting for him to continue. After several pronounced bites of his lunch, and fully aware I was being held spellbound by every crumb, Levin relished in my discomfort during the break in his storytelling.

Finally, after milking things as far as they could go, he leaned forward. "Here's the rub. Mario's chief counsel, Jerry Weiss, has already resigned from government and is at the new firm setting things up. When I gave the order at Gold Mills to fire your firm and move our files to Weiss, I had a fucking mutiny. My people want you to continue as their lawyer and, without the income from Gold Mills, I can't guarantee the new firm will support itself waiting for Mario. So, I need you to become a partner in the new firm."

My mind silently raced. *Did I have the balls to just resign and become partners with a group of strangers? Was Cuomo enough of a rainmaker to support a new firm? Would I get a raise?*

As I sputtered to form a reply, Levin seized on my momentarily stunned state. "Listen, Michael, just take one baby step at a time until you get your mind around all of this. Just tell me you're willing to go to the new place, meet the folks, and share with me what you think."

I nodded in assent. As we parted outside the restaurant, I shook Bill's hand and asked, "What happens to the firm if Cuomo wins?"

Levin roared with laughter and threw his head back while continuing to grasp my hand. "Michael, we should only be so lucky!"

After meeting with the partners of the newly created law firm, I accepted their offer to join. To my delight, I immediately bonded with Jerry Weiss, a short, heavyset strawberry blond with an infectious sense of humor. He taught me everything I needed to know about insider politics and thoroughbred racing; we dined together regularly; we gambled together in Atlantic City; and we attended meetings with famous and infamous politicos and political reporters. It was a blast.

I was happily able to bring many of my clients from the old firm along with me to the new firm, and my practice proved busy and profitable. But our collective eyes were all targeted on the upcoming primary election that we anticipated would herald the coming of Mario Cuomo.

On an otherwise uneventful day, Jerry called me into his office, where he was sitting with a young man unknown to me. Both men rose as I entered the room and Jerry said, "Michael, say hello to Andrew Cuomo, Mario's son. I just hired him as our law clerk."

Andrew was tall, curly haired, handsome, athletic, and, above all else, charismatic. As I came to recognize, Andrew is one who disarms others by showing compelling interest in them. Before I knew it, over the next few weeks, I'd told Andrew almost everything there was to know about me, and he seemed impressed and fascinated by it all. In retrospect, I found myself clinging to Andrew because he made me feel that I was "special." He began regularly referring to me as "brother."

So, could life be any sweeter? My new best friend was my partner, Jerry Weiss. My new self-proclaimed "brother" was Andrew Cuomo, and Andrew was in love with our partner Lucille Falcone, my legal confidante at the firm. For me, the sun was shining and I could hardly wait for the arrival of our esteemed senior partner. The polls uniformly predicted Cuomo as a sure loser and, to me, that meant everything was right on track.

It was finally primary eve. The headline on the *New York Post*'s front page that morning predicted a Koch landslide by double-digit percentages. It appeared the world would begin writing its newest chapter for me in about twenty-four hours.

After locking up the firm, I made my way downtown to Cuomo head-quarters. Everyone had spent the day on campaign business while I held down the fort. When I arrived, the headquarters was empty except for a couple of volunteers, and I asked if Andrew or Jerry had arrived. Told they would be along shortly, I wandered to the back to find a place to wait.

Leafing through a discarded magazine, I looked up and, through a half-opened door, saw a small office with a man pacing inside. Upon closer scrutiny, I recognized the man to be candidate Cuomo. I walked through the door and found him now leaning against a corner file cabinet. I was always taken aback at how much larger-than-life he appeared in person compared to television, with chiseled features and the hands and feet of a virtual giant. His presence dominated every room he entered. But on this night, he looked tired and drawn, projecting loneliness. I quietly said, "Good evening, Lieutenant Governor."

He slowly looked up and, without changing his expression, responded with a simple nod.

For me, this was a special moment. In looking at my new partner, my eyes saw a tired, intense, spent, and dispirited man. But in my heart, I somehow knew, and I mean really knew, he was going to beat the odds and win. Believe me, I'm neither psychic nor given to visions of the future, but I was somehow certain that this virtual stranger was never going to be part of the firm.

I inched closer to him, and he looked at me as if he'd forgotten I was there. I hesitated and quietly said, "Mario, you're going to win tomorrow. I feel it in all my bones."

He answered with a tired smile, "I hope you're right, Michael. I really do."

I could feel he wanted to be alone so I just turned and silently walked away. And I kept walking, forgetting about dinner with Jerry and Andrew. I didn't want to discuss the vibrations overwhelming me.

As soon as the polls closed on primary night, all the major networks unanimously revealed their startling projection that Cuomo had defeated Koch and would be the Democratic Party's nominee for governor. Press poured in like rain, with all the politicians fleeing Koch headquarters and climbing the dais for Cuomo.

The joy for everyone in the firm was indescribable, but I wasn't really part of it. Don't get me wrong, I was happy for Mario and I wasn't that concerned about my future, which had probably manifestly brightened. It was just that I had no one to party with. Everyone I knew—Jerry, Andrew, Lucille, even the office secretary—was gathered in a private suite on an upper floor of the hotel with the candidate and his family. I was the only "insider" who'd been inadvertently left off the guest list, and nobody was answering their phones to correct the oversight.

After a while, I just got bored. I left and drove home to enjoy the enormity of the unfolding political triumph on television. Ironically, my phone rang all night with congratulatory calls from friends.

When I arrived at the firm the next morning, Jerry was giddy. He was fielding calls from around the world and being interviewed by every reporter who'd ignored Cuomo until the upset victory. I received a hug and a kiss and was directed to a seat. Jerry asked where I'd been last night, and I just shrugged.

He locked his door, held all calls, and told me the success of the firm was now immeasurable. "Our relationship with the new governor will place us in a unique position of influence and power in the state, even more so than if Mario was here as a partner. We're going to be New York's newest legal and political powerhouse."

I almost passed out.

The general election arrived quickly and Mario won in a squeaker. For reasons never explained to me, he decided he'd rather be governor than my law partner. I never saw that coming!

During that time, two other events dominated my life. First, we moved our offices from modest quarters on Lexington Avenue to spacious, luxurious footage at Two Park Avenue. We now all had large and impressive offices and furniture befitting political dynamos. Second, we all started playing an exciting new game called "Will Andrew Cuomo join our firm?"

Quite unexpectedly, Andrew had chosen not to continue working for our firm after his graduation from law school but, rather, became an assistant district attorney in Manhattan. After the election, Jerry kicked off the "Andrew" game by telling me the "governor's son" was now considering becoming our partner. This began a bizarre process of wooing Andrew. Meetings. Dinners. Movies. More meetings. It bordered on the ridiculous. Andrew was dating Lucille and was still calling me "brother." It became wearing as he seemingly couldn't reach a decision. I didn't fathom the problem.

One night, Andrew asked me to join him and Lucille for dinner at a local Italian bistro. I thought it was to be one more night of Andrew trying to decide what to do, but I was wrong. Over a toast, he announced he'd love to become a partner of the firm if we would have him, and an immeasurable joy filled my heart. I think I cried.

Events moved quickly after that. Jerry left the firm for personal reasons and Andrew moved into his office. Mario and Andrew agreed the name of the firm should be changed to Blutrich, Falcone & Miller, as adding Cuomo would "overly politicize the works." At the governor's suggestion, Robert Seavey resigned from the Battery Park City chairmanship and became "of counsel" to the firm.

So here I was, the first named partner in, as it would soon become known, the "Cuomo firm."

My first job with my lofty new status came on the day Andrew physically moved into Jerry's office. We all knew Jerry had the habit of compulsively clipping his fingernails. What we didn't know was he had religiously saved all those clippings. When Andrew tried to transfer his personal possessions into Weiss's desk, he found two drawers filled to their brims with nails.

Horrified, he called for my help, and the senior partner of New York's newly anointed political powerhouse firm was entrusted with the task of removing his dear friend's nails to the garbage.

As the transition into the Cuomo administration labored along, it became apparent that Andrew was acting as the new governor's unofficial (but universally recognized) chief of staff. Virtually every prospective state appointee of importance made the dutiful visit to our office to meet and confer with Andrew. Every political face in New York stopped by for consultations, requests, and to utilize the only surefire message delivery center to the Albany mansion.

Those days were quite a hoot for me. As a partner in the firm, I was introduced to everyone. I quickly learned to return a knowing smile and project a wry demeanor in response to questions and innuendos. I hid the reality that I was a hapless and uninformed eunuch in the midst of a hotbed of activity and power. Everyone assumed I was an intimate of the new governor, and I never disabused that assumption, as it was good for business and for my own ego.

The partnership was deluged with publicity. The "Cuomo firm," as well as Andrew and Lucille's love affair, were the subject of endless gossip pieces in the local papers, television news, and tabloids. Even the *New York Times* ran an extensive article entitled "At Andrew Cuomo's Firm, Politics and the Law Intersect," exploring the potential ramifications of a governor's son representing clients before judges appointed by his father. Andrew and I, and Lucille and I, coauthored articles in the prestigious *New York Law Journal*, a daily publication read by every lawyer in the state.

There were, of course, some personal perks. I shared a wonderful night with the Cuomos at Andrew's sister Maria's engagement party to fashion mogul

Kenneth Cole. The party was at Cole's apartment in Manhattan and was attended by all the faithful. Mario was quite sloshed that night and was an absolute barrel of fun. I spent the night listening to his war stories and he was affectionate and warm toward me to a degree I'd never before experienced.

The best part of the night was when Robert Morgenthau, the esteemed long-term district attorney of New York County, readied to leave. Mario and I were standing by the door when Morgenthau stopped to pay homage to the governor. With that accomplished, the DA turned to me and said, "Thank you, Mr. Cole, for having me as a guest this evening. Your bride-to-be is stunning and you're a lucky man."

I was about to confess my true identity when Cuomo waved me off. He was silently laughing, leaning onto the wall, and he held his index finger across his lips to silence me. I believe he just didn't want to embarrass Morgenthau.

I simply smiled back and said, "Well, thanks for coming."

As the door shut, I thought Mario was going to hyperventilate from laughing. He put his arm around me, kissed me on the cheek, and whispered, "Don't try to sleep with my daughter."

As Mario made his way back to his entourage, I called after him, "Can I at least get some free shoes?"

There is a postscript to this tale. For the months and years to come, every time I passed Morgenthau in the courthouse or elsewhere, he would stop and introduce me to those accompanying him as Kenneth Cole. After a while, I just hid from him at all costs.

One afternoon, Andrew popped his head into my office and said, "Michael, I need you for dinner tomorrow night. Make reservations for three people at a really upscale place."

"Sure," I responded, "and who's our third?"

Andrew smiled. "John F. Kennedy, Jr."

I have to admit, that answer seized my attention and, after some thought, I booked dinner at Nanni's on East Sixty-First Street. It was Italian cuisine in a very formal setting and I made the reservation in Andrew's name.

The next night, Andrew and I arrived at the appointed time wearing our "Sunday best." Andrew took immediate command, inquiring as to whether our guest had arrived. With an amused grin, the maître d' confirmed he'd been seated and was awaiting us.

We strolled to the table, and took a moment to just stare. There was JFK Jr., as advertised, wearing a white T-shirt, jeans, and sneakers. He was sucking down a beer out of the bottle, and made no effort to acknowledge our stunned presence.

Ignoring our guest's dress and demeanor, Andrew did all the necessaries: made introductions and initiated small talk. Kennedy motioned to the waiter for another beer, and the waiter asked, "May I put this one in a glass for you?"

"No," came the response. "I like it straight from the bottle."

At one point when Andrew excused himself, the waiter approached our table and addressed me as "Mr. Cuomo." Grateful that Andrew was out of earshot, I corrected him and added, "By the way, my name is Kenneth Cole."

Kennedy looked at me quizzically. "Michael, why did you just say that about being Kenneth Cole?"

"It's an inside joke at our firm," I said, and went on to tell him the whole Robert Morgenthau story. He laughed mightily and that broke the ice between us forever.

It was now 1989, seven years after the firm first opened its doors. Shortly after Andrew and Lucille mutually decided to end their engagement, they both announced their intentions to withdraw from the firm.

In short order, Andrew took the helm at a nonprofit organization, and Lucille joined the firm of an old friend whom she would eventually marry. I moved from my office to Andrew's office and, to my relief, there were no body parts left behind in his desk.

It had been a long road from the day I'd been wooed into the Cuomo fold. I really couldn't complain; it'd been an amazing run and I still had my very own Park Avenue law firm to show for my efforts. We'd amassed an impressive clientele including banks, entertainment personalities, and real estate moguls.

But I would be lying if I didn't admit that, late some nights, when I'm alone and introspective, I wonder what would've happened if Andrew and Lucille had married or if Andrew had remained as my partner. I honestly believe my life would have been very different. But some matters are just out of our personal control, and such thoughts are mere meaningless flights of fantasy.

CHAPTER SIX

The Madness Continues to Grow

JULY 8, 1996—THREE PARK AVENUE

Footsteps interrupted my wistful musings. Andrew and Daniel were returning, accompanied by a young man who obviously represented the landlord. The stranger walked directly to the miniature door in question and vigorously shook the lock. "I've never seen this lock before, and I have no idea why it's there now."

"Well, let's just break it off. We'll pay for the expense," I promised.

The representative took a moment. "No. Let's all come back at eight-thirty tomorrow morning and I'll have my boss and a locksmith here."

"And what if there's some funny business overnight?" Andrew chimed in.

"Impossible. I'll lock the door to the entire floor and leave instructions for it be left undisturbed until morning."

The air of imminent revolt in our group melted and, as the stranger led the way, we all sheepishly followed.

The next morning, I arrived to find Pearlstein, Daniel, and two other men sitting in Andrew's office. I recognized the duo as two of the police detectives who'd investigated the Scores double homicide.

"Like I was saying," one of the detectives said, "we checked with state law enforcement and with the US Attorney's Office log. You weren't bugged by the government; we think it's private."

I was immensely relieved at his words. After spending the night convincing myself it could only be the government, it was the best news I could possibly have received. With renewed hope for a less disastrous future, I felt newly empowered and suggested the entire gathering adjourn to the top floor.

"Let's go, the landlord said he'd meet us in five minutes," Andrew broke in.

After arriving, we all stared at the Alice-in-Wonderland door. There was neither lock, nor hinge, as both had been miraculously removed.

Andrew turned to the landlord. "Your man gave us his personal guarantee no one would be allowed near this door overnight."

"And I have no idea who put a lock on that door or who removed it," the landlord returned.

Frustrated into a near rage, I turned the doorknob and walked through the now-accessible portal. The door led to a small outdoor terrace that was completely empty except for two wooden crates piled one atop the other.

"Look at this," I called out, and we gathered around the remains of a Sony box that once contained a dish suitable for transmitting images.

Daniel looked around and eventually posited, "They ran the wire out onto the terrace and into this transmitting dish. No way to trace the culprits, and the images could have been sent anywhere, to the next building or to Russia."

"We were fools not to bust down the door last night, and I don't believe for one minute you don't know what's going on," I replied angrily.

The landlord looked back and sighed. "You're wrong. I have no idea what all this is about. Are you sure *you* don't know?"

In the days and weeks that followed, Pearlstein and I participated in numerous meetings about our mysterious vanishing spy. The one uniform conclusion to emerge from these meetings was that no one could agree on anything. Eventually, I accepted that we might never discover who'd bugged us, and I began to face each day with less trepidation. And then one morning, sitting at my desk, I noticed what appeared to be a layer of thin, crushed white debris atop one of the many piles of paper. I brushed the substance away and, as I followed its path to the carpet, noticed even more of the same substance on the floor.

Gulping down my anxiety, I walked to the suspicious spot and peered directly above the small pile of unknown origin. After a few squinting moments, I spied a small hole drilled in the ceiling above.

"Casey!" I screamed at the top of my lungs.

When she appeared, I said, "Call Daniel, the spy guy. Tell him to get up here right now."

I sat down and prayed I was mistaken. In about an hour, Andrew and Daniel arrived within moments of each other. I showed them the piles of white residue on the desk and carpet, and the tiny hole in the ceiling.

Daniel popped his head into the ceiling and yelled to us below, "They've been back."

He jumped off the desk supporting him and walked to the corner of the office where he'd discovered the first video camera. He again accessed the ceiling and his head disappeared. Within moments, he jumped down.

"The equipment this time is much more sophisticated, no wires to the top floor. The camera itself is transmitting."

Andrew and I just stared at each other.

In his Westchester office in a small building rented by the federal government, FBI Special Agent Paul Roman stared at the computer screen atop his desk and watched in mounting horror as Daniel's face loomed into view.

Roman stood up and threw his empty soda can against the wall.

"Shit!" the agent shouted. Then he reached for his phone.

CHAPTER SEVEN

No More Secrets

FOUR MONTHS LATER: NOVEMBER 27, 1996, 7:45 ᴀᴍ—NEW YORK CITY

The bedroom was dark and silent, drapes drawn purposely to ensure exclusion of the beckoning sunlight. It was the day before Thanksgiving, and having anticipated an unusually slow time at the office, I'd spent a late night with my friend Mark Pastore, exploring sexual haunts in Manhattan's underbelly, searching for newly arrived talent from Montreal and beyond.

Morning sleep and dreams were always deepest and most satisfying for me, and this particular morning gave no hint it would be otherwise. At eight thirty, the alarm would ring out and by nine thirty, I would be at my desk, a six-block drive from my condominium. Friends scolded me for refusing to walk the short trek from East Thirty-Seventh Street to work and back for badly-needed exercise, but I'd ignored their well-meaning reprimands in deference to convenience.

In violation of the patterned norm, I suddenly found myself sitting up in bed, arrow straight, amid an inexplicable rush of panic. Fighting to clear the cobwebs and hone in upon the source of my distress, I slowly discerned a hard, unfriendly banging at the front door. There was a pause. Seconds later, the rhythmic pounding repeated with increased persistence.

Still feeling the effects of adrenaline battering my system, I slowly wad-dled down the hallway, from bedroom to front door, and cautiously peered through the security peephole. I was already formulating a smart-ass remark to hurl at the inconsiderate, noisy intruder. Looking out to the common area, I was stunned stupid. I actually recoiled my head in disbelief and looked through the tiny hole again hoping to change the landscape. But to no avail—there were still at least ten men poised outside my door wearing blue plastic windbreakers and holding a black metal battering ram between them. FBI. Trying to get my mind around the incomprehensible assembly perched on the doorstep, I stepped back and tried to regain my slipping equilibrium.

Concluding I was about to be arrested, wearing only an oversized T-shirt and boxer briefs, I quietly retreated from the door and ran to the den. Seizing the phone, I dialed Andrew's home number and, after several rings, an obvi-ously groggy Keri, Andrew's live-in fiancée and a Scores employee, answered.

"Who the fuck is calling so early?"

"Keri, it's Blutrich. I have a major problem, put Andrew on."

"He's sleeping, call back later."

"I can't call back later. I need him now!"

I heard a few choice words muttered under her breath, but Andrew quickly came on the line. "What's wrong?"

"Andrew, I've only got a few seconds. There are a shitload of FBI in my hall with a battering ram and I'm about to be arrested. I don't know if they're on their way to you, but call the lawyers."

The noise at the front door was now fully demanding. Not knowing what else to do, I disconnected from Andrew and walked back to the front entrance. I took a deep breath, cursed myself for not being better prepared, and opened the door.

"Are you Michael Blutrich?"

"I am."

"Good morning. I'm Special Agent Dan Butchko with the FBI and I have a search warrant for these premises. Please stand aside and let us do what we have to do."

As I acceded to the terse instructions, a wave of pure relief poured over me. *Just a search warrant*, I cheered to myself.

"Do you mind if I get dressed?" I asked Butchko.

"Not right now. Just sit down in the living room, allow us to secure the premises, and then you can get dressed and place calls to anyone you want."

The agents quickly divided into groups. Carrying three or four cash counting machines, the first group set up shop in my home office for Scores, to the left of the kitchen. A second small group entered the bedroom, and the final group joined Butchko in the living room.

"Do you have any weapons in the apartment?" Butchko asked.

"I do. A shotgun in my bedroom closet."

The agent looked almost gleeful. He turned to one of his confederates and barked, "Get me a shotgun out of the bedroom closet."

Moments later, the dispatched agent returned and handed a long brown leather-and-fabric case containing my weapon to his superior. "Mr. Blutrich, New York City requires permits for legal possession of shotguns; I don't suppose you happen to have one?"

"I surely do. It's in my wallet. Shall I get it?"

The disappointment on Butchko's face was undeniable.

In short order, I was permitted to dress and make a handful of phone calls. I called my Florida lawyer, Sandy Weinberg, and secured a promise that an attorney from his firm's New York office would be right over. Finally, I left a message for Andrew advising that the FBI had only served a search warrant.

Waiting for the attorney to arrive, I sat down in the living room next to two middle-aged agents. The older one looked at me and smiled sheepishly. "This apartment has the most fantastic view of Manhattan I've ever seen."

"Thanks. I'm told it's the highest residence in the city; that's really the reason I took the place."

Before I could respond further, Butchko interrupted, and I noticed with some disconcertion he was holding a detailed, hand-drawn schematic of the apartment. "Mr. Blutrich, we know about your safe in the bedroom and I'm requesting you open it. We can do it ourselves, but it would probably destroy the lock."

"There's absolutely nothing in my safe."

Butchko and his underlings all smirked in reaction. "Well, we have reliable information to the contrary."

Although my visage remained stoic, my mind was silently churning. *Who drew that fucking map? And what information is this guy talking about? Who the hell has been talking to the FBI? Dammit, we have a mole!*

I agreed to open the safe. I walked into the bedroom, opened the closet door, and turned to the four agents crowding behind me. "You think I have cash in here? That's why you brought the counting machines? Oh that's rich, you guys really need better informants."

"Please just open the safe," Butchko spit back, but he wasn't looking quite as cocky as he had moments before.

I kneeled down, turned the tumbler several times, and pulled the safe door open. A completely empty chamber was revealed.

"Shit," escaped from the mouth of one of the agents, followed by a sharp rebuking stare from Butchko.

Within what seemed like seconds, more than half the agents departed, taking the counting machines and battering ram with them. As the group was passing through the front door, Yolanda, my housekeeper of long family tenure, and a well-dressed gentleman in his thirties appeared in the foyer. As I tried desperately to calm the near-hysterical Yolanda, the man introduced himself as Larry Noyer, an attorney with Weinberg's firm in New York. My newly arrived counsel and I quickly conferred in a vacant corner of the living room.

At Noyer's recommendation, I left and headed to my law office. Knowing there were no drugs, cash, or other illegal items to be discovered, I was anxious to get away, clear my head, and learn what other government mischief was underway.

Keri paced nervously outside their bathroom, waiting for Andrew to finish a shower. "They're arresting Michael," he shouted as he turned on the water. The phone immediately rang again and renewed Keri's anxiety as she picked up the receiver.

"Michael?"

"No, Keri, it's Gary at Scores. Is Andrew there?"

"He's here but he's washing his ass. Any message?"

"Just tell him the FBI is all over the club. He needs to get us a lawyer right away."

Waiting as long as her nerves permitted, Keri ran into the bathroom and relayed Gary's message. Andrew quickly dried himself, dressed, and headed to the front door.

"Where are you going?" Keri screamed after him, finally surrendering to the pressure and beginning to cry.

"Probably to jail," he answered.

———————

When Andrew arrived at the club, there were several blue-and-white NYPD police cars parked in front. Yellow crime scene sticker tape blocked the sidewalk and uniformed officers were moving pedestrian traffic along. As he approached the front door, one of the uniforms tried to halt his progress. Andrew shouted, "I'm the owner," and the officer shrugged and let him pass. Finding the club's entrance bolted, he started knocking. From within, a tall, muscular man in his thirties, wearing a blue FBI windbreaker, approached and cracked the door. Andrew tried to walk past him, but the agent barred the way.

The man looked tense. "Sir, my name is William Ready, a special agent with the FBI. We're here on official business." Although Ready knew the answer from months of surveillance, he added, "Who are you, sir?"

"I'm Andrew Pearlstein, one of the owners."

"Mr. Pearlstein, our paperwork indicates you are not one of the owners."

"Well, your paperwork is wrong, but let's say I'm the manager and I demand to come in."

"I'm sorry, my orders are to only admit the owner once our search has begun. You can come back after we leave." Ready, without another word, firmly closed the door and turned the dead bolt. He walked back into the heart of the club and out of Pearlstein's field of view.

As he was deciding what to do next, Gary Goldman, the club's manager, appeared out of the darkened interior. "What do you want me to do, Andrew?"

"What are they up to in there?"

"They came running in with cash counting machines like we had a million dollars in here. They got fucked up when it turned out we only had a few thousand bucks. Now they're going through the desks and the file cabinets, but there's nothing in there except employment records."

"Just stay and watch them. They'll figure out soon enough they're just wasting time."

I arrived at the law firm to FBI agents rifling through the place. Our book-keeper met me in the hall looking hopelessly frazzled. "They were here when I got here, Michael. There's some guy, Phil Arengo, or something like that, he's the one giving orders."

After offering words of encouragement to the frightened staff, I located Arengo, noticing he was holding and referring to another hand-drawn map containing extraordinary details of my office. I demanded and quickly received a copy of their search warrant and, with nothing else to do, I sat down in the library to read the document.

At first, the list of targeted items made absolutely no sense to me. The warrant, limited to the law firm, allowed seizure of evidence of loan-sharking or gambling, legal documents relating to Scores, cash, and check records. Toward the end of the warrant, almost as an afterthought, was a list of documents related to what I recognized as a whole other set of potential legal problems.

I sat back. There was apparently more than one investigation going on, but one thing was now undeniable—the endgame was finally afoot.

Pearlstein arrived about fifteen minutes later. He entered the library and sat down. "I thought you were in jail."

"Nope. Just a search warrant. Did they come to your place?"

"Not that I know of, but they hit the club too."

"Wait a minute," I stuttered. "If you thought I was in jail, why aren't you working on getting me out?"

"I referred it to the lawyers."

I frowned, shaking my head. "Nice to know. I'll remember that if you're ever in custody. By the way, what's happening on your side of the office?"

"They're seizing every single box in storage marked as Scores property."

"What's in those boxes?"

Pearlstein laughed. "American Express charge receipts for the past four years. They can have them all, all hundred boxes. These people have no fuck-ing idea what they're doing."

"What's all this shit about cash, and loans, and gambling?" I mused.

"Beats the hell out of me, but we need the lawyers and I've already alerted them."

"And Andrew, no more arguments over who's been spying on us."

We both laughed nervously.

The search of New York City's most famous strip club was the lead story on local television and radio news, playing all day and night. The story also appeared on the front pages of the city's newspapers. Endless streams of calls from every form of media were referred to counsel, and counsel uniformly offered "no comment."

Watching television reports that night, I found myself helplessly entertained. The club's food supervisor, an older gentleman, had been virtually molested by the press as he arrived for work. With dozens of questions being shouted at him and microphones pushed into his contorted face, he stopped in the middle of the street and yelled at the cameras: "Leave me alone! I just work here. Three Jews own the club, ask them!"

CHAPTER EIGHT

The Government Extends an Invitation

DECEMBER 1996–NEW YORK CITY

The following week was quiet, eerily so. There were calls between the United States Attorney's Office and our attorneys, but no substantive information had been exchanged, beyond the warrants, as both sides began the inevitable game of jockeying for position. Although all of our defense lawyers had earlier in their careers served as assistant federal prosecutors in the district, none of their contacts would admit to knowing anything about the investigation. Either it was "small potatoes" or the biggest secret in the world.

Even more inexplicable was the fact that, despite Scores' notoriety and its location in Manhattan, as well as its key players both living and working in the city, the case was being handled out of a small satellite office in Westchester County. None of this was adding up.

Toward the end of the week, the first breach in the dam appeared and information trickled through. I was paged to Andrew's office and found him alone. He stood up and walked around the desk. "I just spoke to my lawyer. He was contacted by a prosecutor named Carol Sipperly, who is in charge of our case. She requested a confidential meeting."

"About what?"

"She wouldn't say anything except we would be discussing the mafia at Scores and an offer for us to cooperate."

I entered an immediate panic state. "Cooperate against the mafia? Are you crazy? We'll get ourselves killed."

"I think that could happen, or cooperation could save us. I've had a number of discussions with our Florida lawyers. We've talked about cooperating against the mob if we really start having a hard time in Florida over the insurance mess, and they believe cooperation could work wonders for us in both districts."

"What does 'work wonders' mean?" I coughed out. "We get prime plots in the cemetery? Don't you know what mobsters do to people who testify against them?"

"I do know, Michael, but I still want to hear what's on the table. Maybe we can't make a deal, but just maybe we can. They want to set it up for next Wednesday afternoon at their offices in White Plains. And the meeting must be kept secret. We'll both be dead before we get there if you blab."

I just sat back, lost in contemplation of these totally unforeseen bends in the road. Andrew interrupted my reverie. "Did you hear me? Tell nobody about the meeting!"

On Wednesday, December 4, Andrew and I, with our lawyers, Peter Ginsberg and Larry Noyer, trekked to the prosecutor's office in the White Plains Federal Courthouse. After identifying ourselves at reception, our somber group was quickly ushered through a security door and seated in a small anteroom. As we waited, I noticed two men staring at us sternly from a small office. They both appeared to be in their early thirties: one was tall, trim, and muscular, wearing thick black sunglasses; the other was shorter and stocky.

I nudged Andrew. "Geez, take a look at those happy campers. If looks could kill . . ."

"One was the agent at Scores during the search. I don't recall his name," Andrew remarked, "but I never saw the other one before."

"Me neither. But doesn't he look exactly like Clark Kent?"

The meeting began in a small conference room. Our group sat on one side of a wood-veneered table. Facing us were two women: Carol Sipperly, the prosecutor in charge, and her first chair, Marjorie Miller. Three FBI agents were also present, including the two we'd observed staring at us earlier.

The women were short, attractive, in their middle to late thirties, and dressed in conservative suits. They adopted very businesslike and direct demeanors and, after Sipperly made introductions, Andrew looked at Miller. "Are you the Marjorie Miller I think you are?"

"How've you been, Andrew?"

We were all confused. "Andrew and I went to grade school together," Miller explained.

I instantly turned to Noyer and whispered, "Oh shit. If they actually know Andrew, we're really up shit creek."

Sipperly opened by confirming it had been the FBI that installed the bugging devices in the offices. "We also have hundreds of hours of wiretaps of members of the Gambino crime family, and those tapes have convinced us that you both are actively participating in money laundering and loan-sharking with them. All the Gambinos regularly claim that they—and not you two—are the real owners of Scores."

Andrew and I laughed simultaneously. Our reaction seemed to anger Sipperly, who blurted back, "You think all this is funny?"

"It *is* funny," I said. "For you to accuse us of money laundering for the mob means you don't understand our business. Over ninety percent of our income reaches us through credit cards. If anything, Scores is a cash-deprived business. It would be absolutely impossible for us to money launder anything, even for ourselves. Just look at the boxes of credit card receipts you seized. And as for anyone owning Scores but us . . ."

"Hold on," Ginsberg loudly interrupted. "Carol, you know I can't let this discussion go on, not without protections for my clients. Let me just say both gentlemen deny any criminal activity with organized crime. And without admitting anything, if they have any involvement with the Gambinos, it's only as extortion victims."

Sipperly's ire seemed to drastically ebb at Ginsberg's retort. Apparently his emotional protestation contained information she was fishing for, and she paused to gather her thoughts. "Let's say for the purposes of this meeting, I'm prepared to accept your statement, although I'll need much more convincing.

But let's leave it there for a moment. I want you to meet alone with the FBI for a few minutes. Marjorie and I will rejoin you when you're done."

Now comes the stick, to be followed by the carrot, I silently counseled myself.

The older FBI agent, who never actually identified himself, took a moment to introduce the two other agents. "Superman" was Jack Karst; his partner was Bill Ready. Both men continued to act as unfriendly as was possible given the circumstances.

The senior agent continued. "I'm not familiar with the investigation being conducted into your activities. I was asked to come here today because telephone wiretaps of organized crime members have convinced us Mr. Pearlstein's life may be in grave danger. We're under an ethical obligation to advise him of that fact."

The room drew a collective breath as Andrew turned very pale.

I broke the uncomfortable silence. "Oh, come on. Those guys have been talking about ripping Andrew's guts out for years. It's all talk."

"No. It's more than that," the senior agent answered. "We've been monitoring conversations for quite some time about how the mafia wants a bigger percentage of Scores' profits. Let me play one recent recording."

The agent grabbed the tape recorder sitting on a small table behind him and placed it on the conference table. He pressed the "Play" button.

First Voice: Did you do what youse was told to do on Pearlstein?

Second Voice: Yeah. We done it, we followed the prick to his garage. His apartment has one of dem parking places underneath the building. It has two different entrances from two different streets.

First Voice: How would you take him out?

Second Voice: We'd follow him and drive down into the garage behind him. Here's the thing, he has to turn left to get out of his car. So we don't turn, see what I mean? When he gets out of his car, we get out and blow him away. Then we jump back in our car and drive straight out the other entrance. We're outta the place in five seconds.

First Voice: And you're positive that does the trick with the other one?

Second Voice: Trust me. With Pearlstein dead, our boys say Blutrich will be scared shitless and he'll come to us for protection. Funny, right? We can buy Pearlstein's piece for a song.

The agent turned off the tape and looked at Andrew. "I don't know what we can do for you if you're not cooperating, but we could probably offer some advice."

"Could you let us have a few moments alone?" Ginsberg asked.

"Surely," the agent grunted, and the three men left the room, closing the door behind them.

"We're cooperating," were the first words out of Pearlstein's mouth.

"Andrew, not so fast," Ginsberg countered. "Are you aware just how dangerous it can be to testify against the mob? They have a long history of killing cooperators and you'd probably have to spend the rest of your life in witness protection."

"I don't know," I chimed in. "Maybe it's easy for me to say because they're talking about Andrew, but I think we're being played. If the government believed this was a real death threat, wouldn't they arrest the guys on the tape for murder conspiracy? They know it's all talk and they're trying to scare us."

"I hear you and I agree," Andrew raised his voice, "but if they're trying to scare me, they did. I can't believe they followed me home. And they described my garage perfectly."

"Did you recognize the voices?" Noyer asked Andrew.

"Nope, neither one. They weren't our guys."

"Me neither," I concurred. "But consider this, if we cooperate just because we're scared, there's nothing in it for us. We haven't committed any crimes with the mafia. I don't want to go into witness protection and still have to worry about some unrelated problem in Florida."

The group waited uneasily until Sipperly and Miller returned. Sipperly looked at Pearlstein and said, "You heard what your friends have planned for you?"

Before Andrew could answer, Ginsberg spoke up. "Carol, if we continue to operate under the premise that our clients are merely victims of the mafia . . ."

"Wait a second, Peter," Sipperly interrupted, "don't go there. It's a federal crime to pay extortion money to the mob. I can give you the statute . . ."

"Carol, I was a prosecutor too, and no jury is going to convict anyone for being victims of extortion. We both know that, as of now, you have no case and want our clients to cooperate because you suspect they're being extorted. We also both know you want the mafia guys, not our clients. We're willing to listen, but so far, you haven't talked about what we get from any deal."

"We can protect your clients," Sipperly began, but then she stopped and smiled. "I knew we would get to this point, but I didn't think we'd be here so fast. Speaking of what we all know, there's a serious insurance fraud investigation underway involving your clients in Florida. If they demonstrate their willingness to fully cooperate with this office, we can work out a deal—and this is not a promise yet—to move any Florida case here."

"You mean they plead guilty in Orlando and are sentenced in White Plains?" Ginsberg said.

"Exactly. But we're a long way from there."

"Carol. We need some time to think about all of this and review the risks and rewards with our clients," Noyer interjected.

"That's reasonable," Sipperly replied. "You have one week. After that, we're coming after your clients and their nightclub. Peter and Larry, why don't we end this meeting, but stay a minute with me."

———————

As I walked out of the meeting room, I tried to digest the enormity of all that had just transpired. Andrew and I were suddenly being officially recruited as cooperators in a Scores mafia investigation by New York federal prosecutors. We'd been previously aware that the Delaware Insurance Department had initiated a civil lawsuit against us in New York in an attempt to recover money they had asserted had been drained from a Delaware incorporated and licensed insurance company based in Orlando. But the New York prosecutors had just revealed, for the first time, that Florida had formally opened a criminal investigation against us as well. It seemed walls were suddenly closing in on us in a frightening way from all angles.

Andrew and I paced outside the courthouse, lost in our individual thoughts. I had no intention of cooperating against the mafia, but Sipperly certainly drew my attention with talk of a criminal case in Orlando. It seemed we might be able to kill two problem birds with one stone by cooperating, but what a threatening choice it was.

"New York is bluffing, Andrew. They can't come after us."

"I don't agree. They can bring the IRS into Scores and find some way to close us. And you're just delusional about Florida. There's no way out of that mess except by cooperating."

"You're not worried about getting killed? Concerned about being hunted for the rest of your life?"

As he started to reply, Ginsberg and Noyer walked out of the courthouse. They paused next to a parking meter and Ginsberg shook his head. "They really, really want you two to cooperate and they feel they can handle your Florida mess for you. But they don't want you guys to just debrief and testify."

"What else is there?" I asked in confusion.

"They want to put the cameras back in the offices. They also want you to go undercover and wear body wires."

My mind froze. "Are they mistaking me for someone with balls? Mobsters kill people caught with wires on the spot. We're not trained, not capable of pulling this off. I'm not doing that—no way, no how."

Over the next week, there were myriad meetings on the subject. Andrew was absolutely committed to cooperating. I continued to resist.

Andrew's arguments were simple: The New York offer was the only way to be fully protected from the mob and the only way out of the Florida debacle. The government could close Scores if they put their minds to it, and the mafia deserved no loyalty from us at all.

I remained desperately torn. I wanted a way out of Orlando, but the prosecutor's allusions on that subject had been too iffy and conditional to placate me. I also had serious doubts as to whether two untrained and inexperienced businessmen could successfully wear hidden microphones and avoid getting killed. These mafia guys weren't book smart, but they had amazing street radar. I was also worried about possible danger to my family and friends. Did I have the right to put others at risk to save myself?

As the one-week deadline approached, I felt myself being worn down, my resistance eroding. Andrew and the lawyers unanimously agreed it was best to "tentatively" proceed with initial cooperation rather than fight the government on two fronts. My lawyers explained that tentative cooperation would mean giving proffers—debriefing sessions where you tell all you know, but the information can't later be used against you if you cooperate. It's called "queen for a day" in legalese, named so after a 1950s television quiz show.

On December 11, the lawyers called the prosecutors and agreed we'd begin the process toward "possible" cooperation, and proffers were scheduled. It was also confirmed that, after a couple of debriefings, the government would decide if they still wanted us to cooperate, and we would decide if the benefits offered were "sweet" enough to induce life-threatening risks.

Weinberg called me from Tampa. "We're set up for next Wednesday. For your protection, they're going to hold the interview in a hotel in upstate New York. From now on, you're never to go anywhere near their office in White Plains. And by the way, at the first session, they want to know everything there is to know about Scores."

A single thought floated into my mind. *If that's what they want, it'll take all day. It's a long, long story.*

PART TWO

Scores: Where Sports and Pleasure Come Together

CHAPTER NINE
The Birth of Scores

To fully understand the creation of Scores, it's necessary to allow several diverse and seemingly unconnected story lines to converge. Each disparate element immeasurably impacted the shaping of Scores and, absent the remarkable convergence, the club that has become a household name (or a dirty little secret) would probably have died on the delivery room table of ideas. So, to understand the truth about Scores—its history, its life, and its players—travel with me back to its accidental birth.

Mike Sergio from Yonkers was the first true mafioso to be my close friend. Sixtyish, medium height and weight, black hair, with a demeanor meandering between worried and forlorn, Sergio was streetwise, engaging, articulate, and knowledgeable.

Although I've long pondered, I cannot recall my first encounter with Mike. Many have claimed credit for the introduction, but the definitive truth has somehow been forever obscured. All I am sure of is we first met in his Italian restaurant in Greenwich Village, Grampa's, named for veteran actor Al Lewis, best known for his role as Grampa (Lewis's spelling) on *The Munsters*.

Sergio somehow knew all about me at that first meeting. He knew about my Cuomo connections, my law firm, my comedy clubs, my discos, and my sporting goods stores. He fashioned himself an entrepreneur and viewed me as a fertile potential source of investment and advice for his inexhaustible inventory of get-rich-quick ideas.

Sergio was gregarious to a fault. He enjoyed telling me about his family, business, life experiences, and mafia affiliations. I became a regular customer at Grampa's, even though the food was less than gourmet, because I liked Sergio and my friends got a kick out of Grampa—who was a fixture at the place. Sergio was complex, enigmatic, and contradictory. He portrayed himself as very tough and demanding, but he constantly showed a soft and understanding side; he was quick to anger, but even quicker to make amends; he touted his mafia connections, but expressed resigned regret at having them; he spoke about "making his bones" (a mafia phrase meaning formal initiation into La Cosa Nostra), but always claimed to never have killed another soul (a prerequisite to such initiation). The character of Lefty in the film *Donnie Brasco* could have been tailored from the real-life Mike Sergio.

I learned from others that Sergio was not a family "soldier" (also called a "made man"). Rather, he was a respected "senior associate" of the largest of the five crime families. According to rumor, he'd achieved his place at the table by taking the rap on some money-laundering charges in Vegas to protect a soldier with a long criminal record from a lifelong prison sentence.

Sergio was certainly not a wannabe; he was definitely "connected," and not a man to be disrespected. In that arena of his life, he was known by another name: Mikey Hop, owing to a pronounced limp. He never acknowledged that name to me personally, but out of his presence, it was the moniker universally utilized by his cohorts. To me, Sergio was simply a mixed-up jumble of friend, partner, and father figure.

The first business project put on the table by Sergio was "Grampa Pasta," to feature Lewis's *Munster* character in a cartoon logo, selling various pastas by mail order through television advertising. Both Sergio and Lewis were unbridled in their enthusiasm for the endeavor and invited my participation to raise start-up cash.

I knew nothing about mail-order businesses, and I knew even less about pasta, but I wanted to somehow be involved with Sergio and Grampa so, as a first step, I sought out the advice of a friend who specialized in such matters. After undertaking some investigation, my friend called back and could scarcely contain his amused disdain for the undertaking.

"This is how I see it," the expert began, "you have a pound of pasta which, if it's premium, sells in the grocery store for about a buck. The shipping and handling to deliver that pasta would run about four bucks. Michael, would you buy a buck's worth of pasta for five bucks because Grampa Munster's picture is on the bag?"

I agreed I wouldn't bite on that deal. When I delivered these sad facts to Sergio, he agreed: mail-order pasta was a surefire loser.

Then I hit upon an idea with my friend Ron Bard, which we presented for Sergio's consideration. Both Ron and his mom, Yolana, were practicing psychics. At that time, Yolana had distinguished herself in New York and Japanese ESP circles with a long and impressive list of celebrity clients, television appearances, and by assisting with assorted high-profile criminal cases.

Our idea was a simple one: use 800-number lines to offer psychic readings by phone, charged to a credit card. Ron could recruit psychics to work on commission and calls could be filtered from a main switchboard to each psychic at home. Other than the cost of the phone lines, there was no overhead to the venture. While it was well-known that the mafia was entrenched in the 800-number market selling phone sex, no one had yet utilized those same phone lines to offer psychic readings.

Since the mob controlled all the 800-number factories, it seemed natural to bring the idea to our only mob connection. Sergio had an aversion to all things psychic, but after talking to someone up the chain in the family, a meeting was scheduled for us with the main Gambino operative in the phone-sex aspect of the underworld.

Ron and I were scared silly at the prospect of having a sit-down with an actual mafia capo. Sergio laughingly insisted we were being "babies," and brought us to an Italian restaurant in Westchester for the meeting. We all sat down at a table with a young man, wearing a suit out of *Saturday Night Fever*, who looked and acted like a classic "thug." At Sergio's prompting, I described our idea for a "psychic hotline," mentioning the rising popularity of psychics across the nation and our belief that the availability of psychic readings by phone, in the privacy of one's own home, was a financial winner with unlimited potential.

The mafia "expert" disagreed. He stared straight at me and pointedly said, "I heard you was smart, but youse a moron. Anyone in the 800-phone game knows only sex sells. Only sex, you hear me? Anything else is small potatoes." He then turned to Sergio and dismissed us. "Sorry, Mike. It's a stupid idea, pitiful."

We walked out of the restaurant feeling as low as could be; our dreams of "wheelbarrows of cash" destroyed in one fell swoop. Sergio put his hand on my shoulder and said, "Don't feel bad. I liked the idea too, but believe me, this guy knows. He runs all our 800 numbers."

A few years later, Dionne Warwick introduced the first psychic hotline on 800-phone lines. The business grossed more than a billion in its first year. Those should have been our wheelbarrows.

The next episode in what would become the Scores drama began when a club I owned in Los Angeles was in the process of reconfiguring itself into Alzado's, in association with NFL superstar Lyle Alzado from the Oakland Raiders. I was searching for new investors and additional capital to finance the transformation when a friend suggested a meeting with a private banker, Jay Bildstein. With nothing to lose, I agreed to meet Bildstein for dinner at Grampa's.

When he arrived, I looked around for a back-door exit. He was tall, thick, muscular, and mean-looking. He was dressed like a pig, sporting jeans, rumpled sweatshirt, and baseball cap. He seemed completely unhappy and disinterested to be meeting me.

But, never one to judge a book by its cover, I launched into my pitch for Alzado's. I told Bildstein about the in-progress makeover of my original LA restaurant failure, and about my concept of a celebrity-named bar where the celebrity is always present to meet and greet patron fans. It was for this very reason I'd chosen Grampa's for dinner; it was a prime example of a restaurant that succeeded on the pure power of the presence of celebrity. I ended my remarks and asked him if he would consider raising capital in exchange for a piece of the Alzado's venture.

Bildstein, who'd been silent during my entire spiel, looked back at me and asked sarcastically, "And what did I do to deserve this generous offer?"

I looked back at him and quipped, "It sure isn't your personality and fashion sense."

He thought about it for a moment and then burst out laughing. That seemed to break the ice between us and he went on to tell me of his passionate dream to open an upscale topless bar in Manhattan.

You must understand: Bildstein's concept was truly radical. Until then, Manhattan's topless joints were blacked-out holes catering to the lowest form of nightlife—over-the-hill hookers dancing on poles for drug addicts in dangerous neighborhoods. It was simply bad form in the Big Apple to patronize strip clubs; they were viewed as dangerous haunts to be avoided.

When I shared my reaction to his dream, Bildstein launched into a lecture on how New York was behind the times; how upscale gentlemen's clubs featuring topless lap dancing were the wave of the future, flourishing everywhere. I was embarrassed to tell Bildstein I didn't know for sure what a lap dance was.

What I really wanted to say to him was, *Look, I'm a closeted gay man in financial trouble with a California restaurant, a defrauded insurance company in Florida, a failed pasta concept, a law firm devoid of Cuomos, and a "missed boat" on psychic hotlines. The last thing I want in my life is to own a club filled with naked women, catering to a homophobic straight crowd. All my friends would be eyeing the girls, begging to bed them, and I'd be sneaking peeks at the rear ends of the bar backs.* But I bit back my frustration.

After some more small talk, we mutually agreed that our interests were on divergent paths. I would continue on the "celebrity sports bar" road, and he would continue seeking out investors for an upscale Manhattan strip bar. Good luck to us both!

I ran into Bildstein again months later, after the birth of Alzado's in Los Angeles to overwhelming success. As Bildstein had found no investors for his strip-bar concept, he was now more amenable to working with me in raising capital to expand a celebrity sports-bar chain. He visited the LA club, became fast friends with Alzado, and worked closely with me on a private placement presentation for initial funding of our new joint venture.

We also embarked upon a meaningful friendship. The only negative was his inability to stop talking about his "pet project." On and on, day after day: tits and ass, ass and tits. The man was relentless, but I still just couldn't see it; it would be like opening a tanning salon in a black neighborhood. Rich, professional New Yorkers would not patronize a strip club!

To shut Bildstein up, I told him I'd think about it.

David Davies, born and raised in Great Britain, and now the chief financial officer of National Heritage Life Insurance Company, the Florida enterprise that would one day be at the heart of my problematic fraud investigation, had been "missing-in-action" since lunch. Heritage was one of my law clients and I needed Davies's approval on a real estate matter. It was now four in the afternoon, and according to his secretary, "He'll come back eventually, he went to Rachel's," as if that was supposed to mean something to me. I figured he had a new girlfriend.

Davies never made it back to his office that day. It wasn't until the following morning that he returned my urgent messages. After quickly clearing up the matter on my menu, Davies's tone became conspiratorial.

"Michael, we need to seriously talk about something."

I stood up in my office, fearing new negative developments in Florida.

"Problems?"

Davies laughed roundly. "Not at all, chum," he began in his very British accent. "We have a club here in Orlando called Rachel's. It's a very high-end titty bar with magnificent women who perform lap dances for a fee. I was talking to the girls yesterday and they tell me there is no comparable establishment in New York City. I am of the considered opinion New York needs a classy lap dance club and we should be the ones to open it."

I was stunned. Was there a conspiracy to lock me into a room with naked women? Did Davies know Bildstein? Was this to be my karmic punishment for sins of another life?

"Michael, are you there?"

"I'm here. I just can't believe what you said."

I explained that one of my business associates had been pushing that very concept endlessly and I'd rejected it because strip bars in New York City are disdained, scum-like businesses.

Davies, however, would hear none of my negativity. "I am telling you, Michael, if we are the first in New York to parade magnificent naked women in a luxury-club environment, it will be very, very big."

Talking to Davies was like talking to Bildstein. As a compromise, we agreed I would fly to Orlando with Jay to talk the matter through. Everyone in the world goes to Orlando for Mickey Mouse. I was on my way for bare breasts.

I couldn't bring myself to tell Bildstein I might be able to make his dream come true. After all, I'd been the naysayer since his first attempt to sell me on the idea.

When our working day ended and after sharing dinner, I drove him home. When we pulled up in front of his apartment building, I stopped him from exiting the car and casually said, "I almost forgot, I think I may have a way to open your strip club."

Bildstein's eyes widened and his mouth dropped open. He looked at me as if he was mentally confirming it wasn't April Fools' Day. For the first and only time during our friendship, he had nothing to say.

When the silence became embarrassing, I just laughed. "Get out of my car, and pack a bag on Sunday night. We're flying to Orlando on Monday to see if we can make a deal."

When I got home, my phone was ringing off the hook. Unfortunately, Bildstein had regained his ability to speak. He wanted to know everything about the possible deal.

I sadly explained I had very few details; I could only tell him that a wealthy client in Orlando, who was addicted to breasts for profit as badly as he was, thought the club was a fantastic idea. I told him about Davies, about our conversation, and about the invitation for exploratory talks.

"I won't be able to sleep till Monday. I've got some phone calls to make and some notes to dig up. Good night, Michael."

I retired to bed still believing the whole matter to be an unachievable lark. But I'd made up my mind to stop being the "deal-killing" lawyer, and to open myself to the possibility that I was wrong. After all, I didn't want to be remembered as the strip-club equivalent of the guy who said psychic readings would never sell by phone.

When Jay and I landed in the Orlando airport, Davies met us at the gate. Like two greedy comic-book collectors, the two breast addicts were all over each other extolling the virtues and profitability of lap dance enterprises. I felt like a dress salesman at a nudist colony.

We went straight to Rachel's for lunch and, I must admit, I was unexpectedly impressed as we passed through the portal of my first upscale gentlemen's club. It had the ambiance of a fine restaurant and the energy of a Vegas casino. The crowd consisted of suited businessmen who busied themselves with eating, drinking, eyeing topless dancers on stages, and enjoying lap dances at their tables. It was an atmosphere charged with sex and money—and totally alien to any of my prior club experiences.

After walking us around, David led the way to a private section upstairs. He was clearly a "regular," receiving handshakes from fellow customers and staff, as well as kisses and smiles from entertainers. The private area was quieter and more dignified. Davies secured a table for us and motioned one of the girls over to me. As she made her way, I noticed a further distinction in the upstairs—the dancers were totally nude.

It was a setup. Davies and Bildstein were giggling together like two little girls as my hand-chosen entertainer began her dance. As my face was being covered by long, silky hair, Davies sidled to me and whispered, "No touching, chum. House rules."

As this was my first experience of this nature, I found myself feeling somewhat "off." Uncomfortable. This beautiful and athletic stranger was finding ways to expose every inch of her body to me. Not even her gynecologist had more intimate views. It was undeniably titillating and yet, the luxury of the physical surroundings and the maturity of my fellow patrons precluded any sense of juvenile naughtiness or embarrassment. For the first time, I truly grasped that this form of intimate entertainment could work successfully in New York—if properly introduced.

Davies and Bildstein were watching my lap dance as if it were a pornographic movie. They were whispering to each other and seemed to enjoy my mixture of discomfort, exhilaration, and realization. When the dance ended, Davies slipped a bill to my entertainer. She kissed me on the cheek and went her own way. Davies looked at me, with Bildstein over his shoulder. "Tell the truth, wasn't it exotic, mesmerizing, exciting? Tell me exactly what you're thinking."

For the sake of our future, I refused to share what I was really thinking.

Back at Davies's office, we started to explore in earnest the realities confronting us in re-creating a "Rachel's-type" club in New York. Despite my more positive reactions at lunch, I remained deeply dubious that we could overcome ingrained Big Apple resistance to strip bars.

Bildstein broke in. "You know, David, Michael is right. I always discounted his arguments, but I've been trying without success to open a table dance club in New York for years. Every investor I approached had the same anti-strip-bar mentality."

"So what do we do?" Davies asked.

"Here's my idea," Bildstein continued. "We avoid the issue. We don't open a strip club, we open a sports bar featuring topless shows and lap dances. We won't sell it as sexual pleasuring; we'll put television screens everywhere and show every sports contest in the country, as well as pay-per-view boxing. We'll decorate with sports memorabilia, invite sports celebrities, and put in basketball courts and golf machines. Customers will first visit the club for the sports; they'll come back for the lap dances. What are the two things men like most? Sports and sex. We're gonna offer both."

Davies heartily and immediately agreed. I think he would have agreed to eat vomit if it meant he could own New York's first luxury titty bar.

This was the moment I accepted my fate. Bildstein's vision was brilliant and I was certain it could work. He combined the best elements of our celebrity sports-bar concept with his own lap dance mania, and envisioned a formula to overcome New York's strip-bar aversion. Certainly we could attract New York's elite to an upscale sports bar; and the fact touchdowns came along with hard-ons could be an amazing plus. I can't say I was happy, as my interests in life flowed in other directions, but I could envision this concept as potentially the hottest ticket in town.

We adjourned with plans: Bildstein to come up with a location and a budget; Davies to arrange finances; and me to investigate what legal obstacles, if any, we might encounter.

We also needed a name.

CHAPTER TEN
An Unexpectedly Difficult Creation

1991—NEW YORK CITY

As multiple dramas were playing out in early 1991 on different screens of my life's multiplex existence, my attention now turned to researching potential legal pitfalls lurking around our lap dance parlor. For advice, I went straight to Charlie Carreras, an attorney specializing in New York liquor law. It was always a pleasure to meet with Carreras, who was in his mid to late sixties, white-haired, plump, and jovial. He possessed extraordinary knowledge in the practical workings of the State Liquor Authority and, after listening to the plan, he threw up a brick wall.

According to Charlie, there were two major legal obstacles to our envisioned venture. First, in any premises serving alcohol in New York, female dancers were required to have their nipples covered by an "opaque" substance. This was most often accomplished through fabric pasties. Even worse, topless dancers wearing pasties were required to perform on platforms at least eighteen inches high and six feet away from the nearest patron. After an extensive discussion, it seemed New York's laws had been specifically enacted to preclude just the sort of entertainment we were contemplating. In short, we could only offer lap dances if we didn't sell alcohol, and that wasn't an option.

Feeling defeated, I returned to my office and met with Bildstein. I recounted Carreras's gloomy assessment, holding back my amazement that Bildstein hadn't previously discovered all of this information himself. In tackling the question of "opaque" nipple covers, his immediate reaction was that we could overcome the statutory prohibition by requiring the dancers to paint their nipples with theatrical latex paint. According to Bildstein, when properly tinted to match a dancer's actual skin tone, latex paint becomes virtually undetectable, giving the illusion of uncovered nipples. He went on to say strip clubs in many other states had reverted to this solution when faced with similar legal restrictions.

I honestly thought we might be on to something. It was the word "opaque" that kept grabbing my attention. I pulled out the dictionary to look it up, finding the definition as, "impervious to rays of visible light." After mulling over this information, I turned to Bildstein. "Do you think theatrical latex is impervious to light?"

"Beats the hell out of me," was his honest response.

He agreed to obtain a sample bottle of the paint from a cosmetology store in New Jersey that worked closely with Broadway producers on nudity issues. I phoned one of my expert textile witnesses at the University of North Carolina and found him most encouraging, advising that "opaque" had a definite scientific definition, replete with published standards and testing procedures. He saw no impediment to testing our paint to determine whether it met accepted tests to be labeled opaque.

A sample of the latex was immediately shipped off to North Carolina for testing and, in a few days, the expert called with his initial results. According to tests conducted on a spectrograph, the theatrical latex paint was *more* opaque than a Brooks Brothers cotton dress shirt. Since there could be no possible legal objection to a dancer performing in a dress shirt, there was no reason why that same entertainer couldn't satisfactorily cover her nipples with opaque latex. I was convinced we'd found ourselves a loophole to defeat governmental prohibitions—basing our defense on the same scientific standards invoked in the government's own law.

The second legal requirement was more formidable. If an entertainer was required to dance at least eighteen inches in the air and more than six feet away from a patron, lap dancing was a physical impossibility. The issue was: Would the club still work with stage dancing, but no lap dancing?

"Absolutely not!" was Davies's immediate unconditional response. "It is the lap dancing which is key, the ingredient which simulates intimacy."

Bildstein was in total agreement; we needed to offer lap dancing to succeed.

What followed were a series of rapid-fire questions aimed at me, New York's newest expert in the growing field of "tit law." Could the government sanction us for offering lap dances? Would the latex satisfy the law? Could we be closed immediately? Was the law enforceable, or even constitutional?

I refused to supply impromptu, knee-jerk responses. I needed time for research and told them so. We agreed to reconvene in one week's time to continue the debate.

During that week, I met again with Carreras, as well as with Warren Pesetsky, another celebrated liquor attorney. Of course, there turned out to be no clear-cut, easy answers to our concerns, but I reached my conclusions based on the best available advice and addressed the crew as promised on a conference call.

"This is what I believe," I began. "The State Liquor Authority will be immediately coming after us for no pasties and for lap dancing. Count on it, and count on the fact my political connections will provide no zone of comfort. The commissioners are extremely sensitive to charges of favoritism and, think about it, they have no choice. If they allow us to have lap dancing, it will become a citywide epidemic of flouting the statute.

"With that said, I'm just as sure we couldn't be immediately closed. There's a long-standing policy that once violations are served, closure procedures are stayed until completion of both administrative hearings and court challenges. That means it would take more than a year, perhaps two or three, to close our doors for latex-covered nipples or lap dancing.

"I also believe we'll win on the latex issue in court so long as the experts continue to confirm that latex is 'opaque' based on accepted scientific standards. As far as I'm concerned, our nipples will be legal. But, we'll certainly lose on the 'six foot' rule, nothing we can do about it. You can't sit on a lap if you're six feet away. But you know what, I believe there are 'freedom of speech' problems with that law and I'd actually enjoy giving it a good run. And again, we're looking at three years or so before we could be closed.

"So you wanted to know what I think," I concluded rhetorically, "I say we go for it. If we find a location we love, we open, we expect a fight with the liquor folks, and we prepare to battle them all the way. If our invested money isn't back in our pockets in three years, we'll already have closed and been long forgotten."

Davies led the enthusiastic responses. He was completely in favor of going forward with the club, latex, and lap dancing at full speed. With a sly laugh, he added, "Mark my words, we won't even be served with a violation. The liquor people are not going to want to fuck with you. You underestimate yourself, Michael."

Bildstein, who'd been a nervous wreck all week, was now excited in the extreme, his dream still amazingly on track. After hearing we were a "go," he chirped in, "Guys, I think I've found the perfect spot for our club."

Bildstein had gotten wind of the rumored availability of space at 333 East Sixtieth Street, between First and Second Avenues. This was, in fact, quite an impressive address in the heart of the stylish and snobbish Upper East Side. According to Bildstein, the place had been rented, but the tenant ran out of construction funds and was about to default on his lease. The place would soon be back on the market.

When Bildstein went on to say the space had once been home to Club A, I realized I was quite familiar with the location. Indeed, Club A had been a long-term success as a watering hole for the wealthy, the elite, and the mafia. I'd been to Club A numerous times and, if we could actually secure that lease, we would've truly struck gold.

We jumped into a taxi to reconnoiter the location and its surrounding neighborhood. It was exactly as I recalled: the club was in the direct center of the block, in the shadow of the Fifty-Ninth Street Bridge; Rodney Dangerfield's comedy club, Dangerfield's, and the world-famous male strip club, Chippendales, were around the corner on First Avenue; and both surrounding avenues were filled with exclusive and famous restaurant haunts.

The only disturbing aspect of the existing landscape was Sixtieth Street itself. Unlike the days when Club A catered to a tuxedoed and bejeweled clientele, it'd fallen into frightening disrepair. The city had apparently taken to using the sparsely traveled block as a dumping ground for bridge repair equipment; garbage was strewn everywhere; homeless coteries had constructed a small village out of paper cartons; and rats the size of dogs roamed brazenly. It was as if a ghetto block had been miraculously transported into the middle of one of the nation's richest neighborhoods and, here we were, hoping to convert that ghetto into a dazzling new home.

Several days later, Bildstein appeared at my desk looking sullen, reporting he'd reached out to the landlord's lawyer and confirmed the space might be available soon. Unfortunately, the landlord's representative hadn't been enthusiastic about considering our application. "In fact," Bildstein tersely muttered with a strained face, "he said a friend of the landlord will probably be getting the lease. Just my damn luck."

I let the mood of disappointment deepen until I could stand the gloom no longer. I walked over to him, put my hand on his shoulder, and said, "Don't worry, I'm that landlord's friend."

Abraham Hirschfeld, an Eastern European immigrant, was one of Manhattan's true real estate moguls. With a halting foreign accent and the aura of a jovial grandfather, he owned some of the city's most spectacular parcels of commercial property. His fame and recognizability had grown exponentially as he began to dabble in politics, becoming a perennial candidate in Senate campaigns featuring bizarre and unconventional advertisements. Everyone in New York knew "Abe," although few ever voted for him.

I'd come to know Abe well through politics. He'd discovered the best way to secure Andrew Cuomo's attention, and thereby the governor's attention, was through me. I happily ran messages between them for years and had grown very fond of the man with his unique style and personality. When a little research revealed to me that the leasehold we so coveted was in one of Abe's properties, I knew what I had to do.

The space at 333 East Sixtieth Street is really the basement of a premises with a main entrance on Sixty-First Street. The main tenant of the building was the Vertical Club, one of the city's premier gyms and spas. The Sixtieth Street side, with separate entrance, was treated by the main tenant as a sublet. Although any lease for the premises was technically a relationship between the Vertical Club and the subtenant, the landlord had veto power over any subtenancy.

I quietly reached out to Abe and begged my first and only favor from him. I wanted to be the new subtenant in the former Club A space. I told him honestly of my plans and he immediately agreed to grant me the tenancy. I was put in touch with Tex Seeger, Abe's lawyer for the property, and he drew up a lease. The only glitch was a lease provision that prohibited any "nude" or "seminude" entertainment. I objected to the clause and, after consulting with Abe, it was agreed "seminude" would be deleted. This left us wide open for topless, lap dance entertainment.

Before any lease signing could proceed, I insisted Davies fly to New York to personally inspect the club. While he remained gushingly enthusiastic about the venture, he'd yet to fund our first penny and there was no way I was going to allow a lease to be executed until I was satisfied with the arrangements for finances.

My first visit to the basement that would eventually be leased to us was in the company of Davies and Bildstein. The place was in shambles, having been partially demolished by the defaulting prior tenant. Nothing except an extensive kitchen was salvageable and we would need to undertake a complete interior reconstruction.

From inception of our tour, we were in unanimous agreement; the place was simply fantastic, a slam dunk. It was enormous and sprawling, and could be molded into anything we desired. Acting very much the conquering hero, Davies rapidly barked out orders: sign the lease, hire an architect, and commence construction. He was also unsettlingly insistent on learning when auditions for dancers could be scheduled.

As we were exiting the club, Bildstein held us back, ushering us to a dust covered beat-up wooden table. "I have come up with a name and a slogan for our club."

"No flag and fight song?" I remarked.

Ignoring my meager attempt at dry wit, Bildstein leaned back and said one word: "Scores."

There was a short silence and Davies cried out, "I love it!"

"I knew you would," Bildstein returned. "It's so perfect; get the score of the game, try to score with a dancer."

"And the slogan?"

"Where Sports and Pleasure Come Together."

"Another double meaning." Davies smiled. "Perfect."

Truth be known, it *was* the perfect name and the perfect slogan. In all the years ahead, I'd never hear ones I liked as much or better. So now we had a place and we had a name. I went back to the firm and ordered the incorporation of "Scores Entertainment, Inc." and "333 Entertainment, Inc."

Note that 333, the address of our new club, is half the devil's number. In the years that followed, many would claim the name and slogan were products of their uncredited creativity. But no matter who was responsible, I owned the trademark; whether it would prove valuable was yet to be seen.

Once the promised funds arrived from Florida, I finalized the terms of the lease. Extremely helpful and honest, Seeger shared with me his concern that the local community leaders would oppose our club with all their collective might. "The last thing in the world these rich old biddies want," he warned, "is a titty bar in their hotsy-totsy neighborhood. Once they discover your plans, they'll be on a mission to prevent you from opening."

Taking the warning to heart, I reached out to my expert in such matters, Warren Pesetsky. From Warren, and his partner Bob Bookman, I learned to my horror that local community boards can veto the issuance of new liquor licenses for any one of a host of reasons. But community boards are only empowered to block "new" licenses and have no power over renewals. Once you're in, you're in.

Realizing the potential for brewing trouble, I quietly obtained a list of the community board members in our district, pieced together who knew who and how, figured out who were our potential friends and allies on the board, and went politically fishing. As a result of this investigation and a slew of meetings, I came to understand the internal procedures of our board in reviewing and passing upon new license applications.

When I'd uncovered all there was to know, I settled back with an irrepressibly devious smile. I actually knew how to pull off getting our liquor license in spite of a hostile board. It was a masterful plan, requiring the same kind of intricate and precise planning I'd utilized at PS 209 to topple Nick Spano. And just like Spano, the board members would never know what hit them.

And then the mafia arrived.

CHAPTER ELEVEN

Mafia for Dummies

EARLY 1991

Mike Sergio invited me to dinner at his restaurant. I was tickled when I arrived because "Grampa" Al Lewis was dining with us that night, and he'd invited Fred Gwynne, the famous Herman Munster himself, for the meal. Just pleased to be a fly on the wall, I listened with interest to these veteran actors discussing their memories from and their roles in the 50s television hit *Car 54 Where Are You?*—along with Lewis's plans for a *Munster*-esque Halloween reunion bash that would include Butch Patrick (Eddie Munster), but not Yvonne De Carlo (Lily Munster) because her ballooning weight was causing her to avoid public appearances.

For my benefit, Sergio goaded Gwynne into voicing his disdain and regret over his *Munster* role. I was unaware that "pre-*Munster*," Fred had also been considered a serious dramatic actor with an impressive resume in Shakespeare. For Gwynne, Herman had forever typecast him, limited his future opportunities to obtain parts his talents merited, and reduced his professional legacy to that of a "green-skinned joke." Who would have thought? And he sure as shit wasn't going to attend any Halloween reunion party dressed as Herman.

Gwynne, who lived nearby in Greenwich Village, quickly departed after the meal. As Grampa returned to patron-shmoozing, Sergio guided me over to a table in a quiet elevated section to the right of the pizza ovens where, I'd learned, private business was regularly conducted. Unusually, Sergio postured himself with a serious air.

"Tell me about the new club you're planning uptown," Sergio said.

"Nothing much to tell," I answered, hiding my shock. "I put some people together and we're working on a club venture up in the East Sixties."

"I hear it's in the old Club A space. Right?"

I nodded my head.

Sergio pulled his face very close to mine and whispered, "Michael, do you know who owned Club A? Do you know who controls that space?"

I drew back from him in confusion. "I haven't the slightest idea who owned Club A, but I know the building is owned by my friend."

"I'm not talking about the fucking landlord," he barked. "I'm talking about who owns the neighborhood; who controls the street, the garbage collection, the linen supply, and the liquor wholesalers!"

I just stared back. This was a very different Mike Sergio from the friend and partner I'd come to know so well. He was normally even-tempered and approachable, but tonight he was confronting me with a veritable stew of anger, disdain, and menace.

He shook his head. "You telling me you really don't know?"

"I really don't know," I meekly admitted in halting monotone.

"Well, time to learn. The space you've somehow involved yourself in has always been and will always be personally controlled by John Gotti, Sr. and his crew. A capo from another family owns the pizza place around the corner, and if you and your pals think you're gonna open a place in that spot without making proper accommodations, you're asking for trouble, potentially permanent trouble. You just don't go and disrespect the head of the Gambinos."

My head was swimming and my heart started racing. None of my prior commercial ventures had been in Manhattan, and they had never seriously captured the attention of organized crime. Although the mafia was well-known for "shaking down" clubs and restaurants in "protection" rackets, I'd failed to consider we would draw their interest. Did they know something I didn't know? I bit back a remark about having seen nothing in the lease about paying tribute to the mob, sensing this was a time to suppress my instinct to use humor as a defense mechanism in stressful situations.

"I'm lost," I confessed.

Sergio looked back at me as if trying to decide if I was playing with him. Concluding that I really was as naïve as I was projecting, he drew a deep breath. "Look, Michael, your space belongs to the Gambinos. Plain and simple, and the only way you're gonna open is to have me register you with the family."

"I can't believe all this," were the only words I managed to croak back. Here I was, stepping into a scene from *Goodfellas* having just left an episode of *The Munsters*. Bring back Herman!

"What does it mean to be 'registered?'" I continued, although I was sure I knew where this was heading.

"That means I go where I gotta go and speak with the people I gotta speak to, and tell them you and your club are with us. You're registered and everybody who needs to know will know. And then we protect you and we protect your businesses. Or, on the other hand, we can do nothing together and you can take your chances on your own."

"And taking my chances means?"

"In my opinion, that means someone may burn down your place before it opens. That means gunplay in your club on opening night to scare away customers. That means no liquor deliveries, no linen or laundry service, no meats for your kitchen, no garbage pickup. That means any other family, Italian, Albanian, or Russian, has an open invitation to shake you down. Who you gonna call, the cops? We own them too. That means your customers and their cars are fair game. That means you better watch your cash on the way to the bank. That means you're considered a disrespectful piece of shit and nobody gives a damn what happens to you or your little Jewish ass. Any questions?"

I was now sweating through my shirt, my only comfort coming from the fact that he'd called my ass "little." I thought of a million stupid things to say, but I remained speechless.

He next tried to console me. "Hey, Michael, you look like someone died. I didn't mean to upset you; I was just trying to help, to keep you from having problems you wouldn't see coming."

I slowly collected myself. "Look, we haven't even begun construction, or applied for our first license, and I have no idea if the place will even open. How am I supposed to make an accommodation when the club may turn out to be a complete bust, like nine out of ten new businesses in Manhattan always do?"

"I'm not asking for you to agree to nothing . . . now. After all, we can't make money if you don't make money. I just wanna know if you want me to register you with the family, with John Gotti, Sr. If you say yes, I'll go do the right thing. If you say no, forget about this here little talk." He then added with a laugh, "And I'll just wait for you to come running for my help later on—when it will be much more expensive."

I promised to talk to my partners and get back to him quickly. He then called over a waiter, ordered me a club soda, and a glass of red wine for himself.

"Let me ask you something," Sergio said. "You know I can't get no liquor license here; some stupid law about the church down the street being too close. You think you could help me get one?"

As the waiter brought over our order, I said, "You mean you sell all this wine and beer every night without a license?"

He looked back at me with a mocking grin. "And who's gonna tell me not to? But think about a way to get me a license. I'd like one."

I'm surprised I didn't kill myself driving uptown, my mind was racing so fast. On the one hand, I couldn't decide if Sergio was telling the truth or just pulling a low-level shakedown scheme for himself. I decided it was probably a little of both. If he held himself out as a Gambino representative and wasn't, or if he claimed to have "registered" us and didn't, he'd be a dead man. So, all the stuff about Gotti was probably true, but Sergio wanted to be the man to bring the new potential "golden goose" to his family.

On the other hand, there was a definite degree of comfort knowing we would be protected, even at a price—so long as the price was reasonable. City history was rife with violent and murderous shakedown tales, and we weren't exactly a group of tough guys.

On the *other* other hand, I was concerned I might be opening the door and letting the wolf walk right into my little flock. And who would control the mob once they were granted a foothold? They were making a smart approach, through a friend, but there was no doubt that things would turn nasty if I declined their kind offer. And the devil you know is better than the one you don't know, or so they say. Right?

On yet another hand, did I really want to deal with threats of arson, disruption, and urban terror? We were already into the club for a half million dollars, and that money wasn't coming back if the mafia scared us off the deal.

Realizing I had no other hands, I decided to relax and bounce the issue around with Davies. When I called him, he cut me off immediately. "Michael,

I'm from England and I know absolutely nothing of your New York mafia. This is your decision, all the way. If we need them, we need them; if we don't, we don't."

Faced with deciding, I did what I always seem to do. I chose the path of least resistance and, at a subsequent meeting with Sergio at Bill Hong's Chinese restaurant in Manhattan, I told him the club wanted to be registered.

"Wait a second, Michael," he interrupted. "I'm registering you, Michael Blutrich, no one else. From now on, you are the only one who counts at your club, or in anything else you open. *Capisci?*"

I really did understand. And that understanding simultaneously filled me with feelings of self-importance and with dread. For better or for worse, I was to be the mafia's man at Scores.

Sergio beamed back at me, saying he would now do all the necessaries. He ended our dinner, leaving me as always with the tab, and a bear hug. "Don't worry 'bout nothing. Trust me."

In May 1991, due to personal issues, including legal woes over child support with his ex-wife, Davies announced he could no longer continue to fund the club. The burden of financing now shifted to me, so I started looking for creative ways of completing construction and getting the doors opened. I turned to my banker and friend Mark Yackow for help.

The "Yackow Inducement Plan" required a strategic mixture of subtlety and outright deceit. I invited Mark to visit the construction site, and we spoke as we walked though the leasehold together. I described the work-in-progress as a "high-tech sports bar," knowing he would be enticed and enthralled with that kind of establishment. He was immediately enthusiastic. A former patron of Club A, Mark recognized the location as premium. We had his complete attention with talk of big-screen televisions, computer sports games, and memorabilia on the walls. He flipped when we showed him our designs for a half-court basketball court for patron use. But when I added as a feigned afterthought that we might also be featuring "adult entertainment," I noticed a frown cross his face.

I walked Mark over to a corner for the "kill," telling him how much we'd sunk into the venture, with another two hundred grand deferred until post-opening, and confessing we were still short to finish. He anticipated my next volley and shot it down in midair. "Michael, there's no way, no how the bank will make a loan on a new club. It's against lending policy."

As I was now in a severe panic, with my best hope for additional money slipping away, Mark put his hand to his chin and mused, "But you know what, I'd love to be involved in this place. I think I can put together a group of private investors and raise the missing cash as a loan. My investors get interest for the loan; I get a piece of ownership."

We spoke at length and he agreed to contact some of his "money" people and make a genuine effort to lead a new group into the Scores family. As we wandered back to the others, he stopped short. "You know, it's really a bad idea to brand the place with 'adult entertainment.' People will get the wrong idea, thinking it's like a strip bar or something." With a smile, he added, "You meant, like a Hooters, waitresses in bikini tops and stuff like that? Right?"

I'd never been to Hooters, but I immediately looked back and responded, "Yeah, that's exactly what we have in mind."

"Perfect," Mark said happily. "Just perfect."

CHAPTER TWELVE

Landing the Liquor License

JULY 1991

Construction continued. We hit a glitch with the brass subcontractor when his price for our stairway and bar railings seemed way out of line. Sergio stepped up to the plate and recommended a subcontractor, friendly with the Gambinos, who could definitely do better. And in fact, the "family" guy came in with a price more than 40 percent less than the original estimate. Our mafia relationship had already begun to pay dividends.

It was also time to apply for our liquor license. All of the necessary paperwork—stating that my friend and undisclosed nominee, Irving "Blitz" Bilzinsky, was the sole owner of the business—arrived in good order at the processing center of the State Liquor Authority. I brought all the influence I could muster to have our documents reviewed and investigated during August.

While supremely confident I'd devised a strategy to defeat the "enemy" community board, I was now distracted and uneasy during the investigation period. If my plan failed and it turned out I was wrong about "beating the system," the entire venture would be in the garbage.

It was truly a simple plan. When a liquor license application is filed in New York, the applicant must send notice of the filing to its local community board. Under state law, a board has only thirty days to object to an application. Failure to object within that period forever waives all objections.

Now, I'd learned through political "friends" that our board traditionally closed operations for vacation on August first, and didn't reopen (or even read their mail) until after Labor Day in September. If we could deliver our notice in early August, after the board's vacation began, the board would have consented by inaction to our application thirty days later—even before opening the envelope containing our notice.

Of course, there were major potential pitfalls: the board might get wind of our scheme and kill it; it might not take its "usual" vacation; maybe someone would open the mail in August and take action; perhaps even a late objection might be somehow entertained by the licensing agency. But "falling through the cracks" was our only reasonable hope of getting licensed.

By the grace of Mammitu, the Babylonian Goddess of Mammary, the plan worked! Our application was reviewed and approved by the state and, because the community board failed to make a timely objection, we were issued our three-year license.

When the board returned and got around to opening its mail, all hell broke loose. Emergency community meetings were called and the local squadron of ancient biddies marshaled themselves for war. The cry went forth that the new "porn club from hell" must never be allowed to open its immoral doors. At a formal meeting, the board voted to deny our license, but it received the same reception everywhere it went—administratively and judicially. The refrain was, "As you failed to object in time, your objection is barred. Blame yourselves, who ever heard of not opening mail for a month?"

Our opponents gave it their best shot. They set up picket lines outside the front door, but the media quickly lost interest in the silly story. After all, this was Manhattan, home to all that is diverse and sophisticated. Outrage over topless lap dancing just couldn't win the day. I've been told the community board has since closed the loophole; they now open their mail year-round.

Once our liquor license was granted, Mark Yackow and his group of "silent" lenders came aboard. Mark had raised the cash we desperately needed to open, and the ownership oars would be shared between Davies, Bildstein, Yackow, and myself. At last, we settled upon an opening night.

Scores—a sports bar and lap dance parlor, the first upscale gentlemen's club to grace Manhattan's nightlife, would open its doors to the world on October 31, 1991.

Halloween.

Once the opening was announced, I was summoned to Grampa's. After some small talk, Sergio announced the bounty his family was demanding in exchange for its "participation" in our new venture. I held my breath, and it boiled down to three items: one thousand dollars in cash every week, control of the valet parking operations, and ownership of the club's coatroom.

Sergio went on to explain his rationale. "The grand a week goes directly to John Gotti, Sr. I'm gonna arrange to deliver the cash directly to his house. The valet parking goes to the capo who owns the pizza joint around the corner. That's all he wants. And the coatroom is to help support my family. Steve, my son you met at the restaurant, he'll run the coatroom and keep all the money from that spot. He'll also be at the club most nights dealing with any problems that come up on the floor. I'm too old to do that anymore."

As to the cash, I countered that it obviously depended on whether the club could afford it. He sneered and stared back at me. "It's a thousand every week until you close the place, and don't fuck with that payment. I swear I'll come down and take it out of the register."

I couldn't have cared less about the valet parking as I was planning to contract out that service anyway. Between insurance, claims, and personnel, I wanted no part of the valet business.

The coatroom was the hardest pill to swallow, even though it represented only seasonal income. Like the door charge, the coatroom was an easy nightly source of cash and expense money. I'd been counting on a goodly sum each week in the winter, but that income had just been permanently diverted from my grasp.

All in all, I could live with the deal. It was not dependent on gross revenue, it left the door income alone, and kept the mob out of dancers' fees and liquor sales. Looking back, I was just an idiot who was yet unversed in the ways of mafia infiltration.

I would come to be severely educated.

As Halloween approached, the club started looking more and more spectacular each day. The former bomb shelter took on the appearance of a true first-class establishment.

Days before the opening, an article appeared in *Crain's*, a major respected business magazine, which noted with interest the upcoming arrival to the city of its first upscale topless lap dancing parlor. The piece brought waves of interest but, unfortunately, Mark Yackow reads *Crain's*.

"Michael, what is this stuff in *Crain's* about a lap dancing strip club? Where did they get that? We should call the editor and make it clear we're a sports bar with 'Hooters-style' entertainment."

What could I do? I'd amazingly kept the truth from my friend long enough. Faced with the reality now publicly revealed, I gathered up my courage and lied to Mark some more.

"You know what, we decided we *may* experiment with lap dancing. No big deal, right? We're still first and foremost a sports entertainment center. Bildstein swears it's the wave of the future sweeping the country and, if it doesn't work, we'll just cut it out. But maybe it'll catch on and we'd be the first in town."

After a pregnant pause, he answered, "I guess it's OK. I don't really care, let's see how it goes."

Whew!

The day before the opening, Mark Yackow and his investors toured the bustling premises. Like everyone else, they expressed their satisfaction and excitement. What went unexpressed was the overwhelming pressure and nervousness pounding inside each of us, especially me, because if New York wouldn't buy what we were selling, I'd be financially buried.

As the group was departing, one of the investors, a construction man himself, stopped by to wish us luck. "Michael, you've done a great job; the place is wildly impressive. New York has nothing like it. But just one thing, with all we've poured into the effort at luxury, why install faux brass on the railings? It looks so cheap and cheesy."

I almost swallowed my tongue. "What are you talking about? We paid top dollar for real brass from a highly recommended contractor!"

"Well, I don't care what you paid or who you paid it to—that's not brass. It's not even good brass-like metal; it's pure garbage, the kind of shit the mafia forces on helpless people. We'll need to replace it in six months."

Holding my temper and smiling as the group passed through the outer vestibule, I turned to the receptionist and screamed, "Get me Mike Sergio on the phone!"

October 31, 1991. Opening day. My answering machine at home was loaded with reminders from friends and clients expecting to be on the guest list. Other messages inquired as to dress code or whether dinner reservations were necessary. I ignored everyone, figuring it would work itself out.

As I was departing, I heard my sister Carole's voice leaving a message. She sounded irritated, so I walked back into the apartment and picked up the receiver.

"What's wrong?"

"Your nieces are planning to go to your new club tonight and I'm not sure that's such a good idea."

"Why not? Sheri and Kim are adults, and it's gonna be a very professional and classy crowd."

"They say women will be topless. I don't want my daughters walking around topless in a club full of strangers. What kind of club is this anyway?"

I shook my head in disbelief and realized she wasn't kidding. "Carole, it's a sports bar with topless dancing. Customers aren't topless, only the professional dancers."

"Oh, well I guess that's all right then. I'll tell them they can go."

"And Carole, our family's women aren't exactly built for topless dancing anyway."

"That's okay. Our family's men wouldn't qualify for *Playgirl* centerfolds."

Touché.

When I arrived at the club, Bildstein had gathered the staff together and was laying down the ground rules one final time:

- Every customer is to be treated as royalty.
- Customers are to be charged a twenty-dollar minimum for every four-minute lap dance.
- No free drinks except with authorization of a manager or owner.
- No touching entertainers during lap dances. Call a manager for control.
- No sexual activity of any kind with customers, no talking about it either; expect undercover vice cops to be in constant circulation.
- And the most important rule, there is to be no sexual activity among staff: no dating, no kissing, and no playing around. No boyfriends or girlfriends in the club. Violation will be cause for immediate and permanent firing.

Interestingly, the first person to violate the "most important rule" was its author: Bildstein.

CHAPTER THIRTEEN

Welcome to Scores

OCTOBER 31, 1991

Opening night, and two giant Hollywood-style sky lanterns shoot broad beams of light into the heavens from trucks parked in front of Scores. The block between First and Second Avenues is immaculate, bearing no resemblance to its appearance on the first afternoon we came a-looking. The city's bridge machinery is gone, the homeless have moved, and there's no evidence of giant roaming rats.

Faithful to our promise to an ungrateful community board, the entrance is low-key in the extreme. A simple black-and-white canopy printed with our logo and motto breaks the uniform building line, and a red carpet extends from the glass entrance doors to the sidewalk. A doorman, in full braided uniform with matching hat, opens the doors of arriving vehicles, and a string of tuxedoed managers stands primed to answer questions and escort guests into the club. No posters or pictures of any kind grace the exterior, and no uninformed passerby could possibly glean any clue as to the nature of the entertainment offered within. Even the front doors are filled with mosaic stained glass to prevent peeking.

Upon entering through the front doors, the patron finds himself in a small, unspectacular rectangular anteroom. Along the right wall is a wood-and-glass case containing objects of Scores memorabilia and souvenirs for sale: hats, towels, T-shirts, and the like. Behind a waist-high counter, in a strapless and sparkling evening gown, stands a remarkably stunning hostess. Payment of a twenty-dollar entrance fee results in a manager opening the next portal into the awaiting inner sanctum.

Passing out of the spartan anteroom and through a second set of doors, the patron steps onto a beige marble floor and faces a circular wooden counter offering an impressive array of cigars and tobacco products from yet another model-quality hostess. Stepping to the left, and for a fee of five dollars per item, coats, hats, or briefcases are exchanged for retrieval stubs; each fee, an unwitting donation to the mafia.

The customer now retraces his steps and travels counterclockwise around the sales kiosk to a semicircular series of twelve ascending marble steps. On the way, the patron passes a set of 100 humidors resembling a wall of a bank vault's safe deposit boxes. For a mere $1,000 per year, a customer may purchase the rights to a locked box containing a small cigar humidor and room for other personal items, and can request a name prominently engraved on the face of the box. As it's opening night, no humidors had yet been offered for sale and, obviously, no names engraved. But, in the coming years, some of the world's most celebrated and recognizable names will appear on the vestibule humidors, and a long waiting list established.

As customers climb the marble steps, their senses are bombarded with a scene out of Vegas and Monte Carlo combined. To the right is the main theatre, where a quick set of carpeted stairs lead to a sunken floor. A long, standing bar sits on the left with large television sets adorning it; and on the right, a sprawling area is filled with tables and chairs, booths, a large central stage, and multiple solo dance pedestals. Additional television screens featuring professional and college sporting events are everywhere.

The main theatre room and bar area are filled with rainbows of bouncing colors. Neon signs blaze, offering direction arrows and identifying areas of interest; red, blue, and green spotlights affixed in the ceiling provide alternating showers of tinted glow. The general aura of lighting is muted, providing a sense of privacy—yet more than ample to prevent blind stumbling.

Topless dancers move sensually on the solo pedestals; others dance on the central stage. Rhythmic music pours out of a battery of enormous speakers and pervades the club, while the DJ, in overly emphasized and dramatic tones, introduces each of the ever-alternating performers. Not a single customer appears to be watching the sporting contests; other pursuits have captivated them.

Except at the bar, all of the customers are seated. A few are sampling complimentary finger foods, most are transfixed by the occupied stages, and many are draped by topless female forms, and are enjoying lap dances. The entertainers who aren't on stage circulate in evening gowns, in search of guests willing to engage their services for erotic fantasy.

Few New Yorkers have ever previously experienced a lap dance, and after the initial introductions and explanations of the charges to be incurred, the dancer turns away from the patron, removes her dress, and turns back covered only by a thong. Of course every dancer has, before entering the room, had her nipples coated with latex paint matched to her natural skin tone by our professional cosmetologist; the practice seems to go unnoticed by our patrons.

As most of the dancers sport long, straight hairdos, the rite uniformly begins with a showering of hair. The entertainer next moves ever closer and simulates the gesture of an intimate kiss. By this time, the customer, who has been alerted to the "no-touching" rule, is gripping his chair arms as if in a dental treatment chair, enjoying the exotic moment but fearing a breach of the rules.

When the first dance ends, the entertainer inquires whether the patron wishes her to continue. If not, twenty dollars is exchanged; if so, the dance goes on. With each new retainer, the atmosphere grows in allure. Life stories are exchanged and, as amazing as it may seem, the entertainer finds every word out of the patron's mouth both amusing and insightful. As the dances flow, and the customer grows more confident and self-assured, he reaches out and gently brushes the dancer's legs. The touch is so light he can always claim it was an honest mistake if admonished. When she permits this intimacy, there's a genuine thrill resulting from a combination of naughtiness and adolescent rule-breaking.

Once past five dances, and a hundred dollars owed, even greater heights of familiarity evolve. The dancer may rest a moment in her new friend's lap, or massage his neck, or hold his hand. By this time, customer and dancer are old buddies, and he is proud that the sheer force of his personality and sexual "scent" have engaged and amused this beautiful young stranger. She feels his mystique and wants to know him better, learn his inner self.

When the customer declares the session over, he inquires as to when his new intimate will be dancing again at the club, and he debates whether to send flowers to her as a reminder of their new "connection." By the time he reaches his car, there is momentary worry whether his wife or girlfriend will detect the aroma of a hot twenty-year-old blonde, blue-eyed cowgirl from Dallas. "But I didn't do anything," he assures himself. "I didn't even really touch her." Then he smiles that smile he hasn't engaged for many a year and adds, "Not yet, anyway."

To the right of the stage in the main theatre sits the "Champagne Lounge," identified as such in scripted neon. The lounge provides more comfortable seating and a better view of the main stage; it also offers a sense of greater privacy as it extends to the club's back walls where there are shadowy nooks and crannies. For a modest tip to one of the accommodating managers, a customer can climb a magical staircase into the first level of Scores prestige.

To the right of the Champagne Lounge sits the half-court basketball court. Since the doors opened, patrons have rolled up their sleeves, climbed into the netted pit, and challenged one another to contests. There have been two injuries in the first hours of operation and we are obviously going to need better wall and floor padding, or a bigger insurance policy. The basketball court was plainly a mistake to be rectified.

To the left of the main stage is an area filled with sports and sports-computer games: basketball foul shooting, golf putting and driving, baseball and hockey games. Few if any customers are curious enough to spend any time or dollars in this section; other available activities seem to have overwhelmed any desire for arcade entertainment. The viability of this area will need to be reevaluated as well.

After ascending the initial semicircular stairway, had the customer chosen a left turn, away from the main room, he would have encountered the bejeweled doors to the club's restaurant, offering a full range of continental cuisine. The dining area is separate, completely walled off from the balance of the club, but music is pumped in from the main theatre. A full-service bar stands available, and multiple solo pedestals are in use by gyrating topless entertainers. Table dancing is certainly permitted in the dining area, although most patrons seem to prefer eating without naked women in their laps.

On this opening night we see, for the first time, a fetish-like desire in some patrons to have bare-breasted companions share their tables for meals, the price being negotiable. Scantily clad massage girls also circulate, offering immediate relief from tense and overtired muscles at lap dance prices.

And finally, at the rear of the restaurant lies the locked entrance to the height of Scores' preferential status treatment, "The President's Club"—the exclusive area reserved for the rich, the famous, and the gullible. The Club is for "members only," with memberships offered on a yearly or nightly basis. For approximately $100 per person per night, or $1,500 per year, the doors swing open. While the club inside is intimate, lined with champagne magnums, and serviced by a higher ratio of staff persons to patrons, there is no appreciable difference between a night at Scores or a night in its President's Club. Membership is a matter of ego and status, of bragging rights, although since the wealthy gather to hunt there, and the space is defined and confined, there is a true sense of increased and stylish privacy.

There is also a secret area of note offered to a valued few within the President's Club's walls. A spiral staircase leads up to the "Crow's Nest," the only truly unmonitored and impenetrable section of the entire space. It holds no more than ten people and requires a fat "bribe" to a manager to gain access. Forgive me for saying this, but what happens in the Crow's Nest stays in the Crow's Nest; and no undercover government spy ever breached its holy barrier.

Opening night was a stellar success, with wall-to-wall approving and impressed patrons. Our ownership group was thrilled by the line around the block waiting for the privilege of entering, by the drinks poured without relent, and by the favorable comparisons made by our entertainers to established haunts throughout the country.

One must recall that Scores on opening night was not the Scores of its own future, not yet the favorite night spot for celebrities, movie stars, television personalities, and professional athletes. Such lofty status was not even a dream on my radar and, in fact, the only "stars" on opening night were Regis Philbin and Jackie Mason—not exactly the stuff of watercooler gossip. No, our opening-night crowd was made up of our targeted base: lawyers, stockbrokers, businessmen, and a smattering of politicians; all in suits, carrying briefcases and platinum American Express cards.

As the night began to slow, an older gentleman in an unimpressive polyester suit ambled over to me, inquiring if I was the club's owner. I responded warily, identifying myself as corporate counsel and owner's representative.

"You'll do just fine, then," he retorted, adding, "I'm an investigator with the SLA, the Liquor Authority, and I'm serving the club with a summons for activities I observed here tonight which violate our rules."

Keeping my face stoic, I accepted the paper from the investigator's hand and walked slowly into the office. There wasn't much to read, but I was surprised by the mixed bag of news it contained. We had been cited for permitting our entertainers to perform without their nipples properly covered with an opaque substance—which was completely untrue—but there was no mention of violations of the "eighteen inch in the air/six feet away from a customer" rule. Interesting.

It was thus on our grand opening night, before the glue on the phony brass had yet fully dried, that New York State unveiled its legal objections to our continued existence as Manhattan's first table-dance establishment. It appeared the initial battle was to be waged over the opaque properties of theatrical latex paint, and perhaps the legal impediments to lap dancing were to be held in the wings as a secondary assault weapon.

In the morning, I formally retained my scientific expert from the University of North Carolina and ordered a full spectrum of tests performed on the latex paint. I also called the legal arm of the SLA and worked out a stipulation that no further summonses would be served for the same violation until full administrative hearings and court appeals had determined our guilt or innocence on the charge.

There was no doubt in my mind—the slow wheels of justice would grind this matter out for years, yet I was startled at how quickly the summons had come. But so what: the fight was now officially on, the gauntlet thrown, and the anticipated challenge to our nipples defined. There was no way under heaven my exuberance over the walloping success of our first night could be, even mildly, dulled.

CHAPTER FOURTEEN
How to Own a Strip Club

TWO MONTHS LATER, DECEMBER 1991

As the Christmas holiday season arrived, I'd discovered that, at least for me, there'd been "Four Stages of Strip Bar Ownership," and I'd ripped through each stage in astoundingly quick succession. It was only much later that I came to recognize and identify the subtle processes playing within my closeted gay psyche.

Discomfort: My first stage of ownership was the most sharply and acutely felt. When I arrived at the club before the doors first opened, our 100 nervous and excited entertainers were crammed into an undersized dressing room preparing their minds, but mostly their bodies, for their performances. There I was, in the midst of wall-to-wall nakedness: gowns being tried on and tailored, pubic hair being shaved to fit thongs, make-up being applied, and countless breasts of every size and shape being colored, powdered, blushed, and latexed. It was all seriously intense—all business and very professional.

Believe you me, there were more bare breasts in that one room than most healthy and sexually active men could reasonably expect to see in a lifetime. And what was my reaction? Honestly, I was uncomfortable; perhaps embarrassed would be the better description. And it was not a gay thing! It was the sort of discomfort one feels as a child stumbling into a sister's bedroom at an inopportune moment. My first instinct was to abandon the area, to flee as if I were a wrongful invader of privacy.

Titillation: But discomfort simply cannot last when you are the only person in a crowd feeling uncomfortable. Almost immediately, word spread that the "lawyer-owner" was in the house. Dancers ambled over to me in the altogether seeking answers to mundane questions of work schedules, tax reporting requirements, and pay periods. The women were wholly at home with their state of undress, and it quickly became impossible for me to retain any continuing feelings of stress.

Suddenly I found myself titillated to the core. My expert opinion was being sought by naked dancers on the amount of latex I thought necessary to comply with law and, upon request, I started examining breasts for color, tint, and hue. There followed discussions about augmentations, implants, and the prices for those procedures in different locales. I wanted to remark I'd never taken any "breast law" courses at Georgetown, but I was having too much fun to turn snide.

It was all so matter-of-fact, but within me, there was the undeniable rush of having forever breached a lifelong barrier—a barrier of guilt and shame connected with casual nudity. Before long, I was totally at home, one of the insiders, and I was inebriated in a flood of mammary overload. It was nothing less than lovely.

Power: The titillation stage also cannot be long maintained because it finds no physical release; there can be no touching, no passion, no climax. Failure to adjust one's emotional reactions would surely turn titillation into the constant pain of "blue balls."

Faced with this unavoidable reality, the strip bar owner seamlessly moves from feelings of stimulation to feelings of power. Now I don't mean to imply any sense of power as in "life or death," or "property rights." Quite the contrary, it's more a feeling of empowerment—a right to stand clothed among the naked, a right to have others completely exposed in normal discourse. While all of these nuances of feeling are, of course, illusory and more than a little silly, the sensations of power are real, emotional feelings that truly replace initial titillations.

Boredom: Unfortunately, it is this final of the four stages that winds up lasting forever. On the first night of ownership, you get to see 200 breasts; after one week, you've borne witness to 1,400 breasts; after one year almost 73,000 breasts; after five years, a whopping 365,000 naked breasts!

Understand this: there's only so long one can feel embarrassed, titillated, or empowered by dancing glands. After a while, they have all the emotional pull of furniture. To be honest, in my first hours of Scores ownership, my eyes were glued to every passing pair of bouncing orbs. Within a month, I actually preferred to interact with clothed dancers. I do concede that my arrival at this stage may have been accelerated by the "gay thing."

Sadly, the presence of constant nudity became so run-of-the-mill that when I was introduced to newly-arrived naked entertainers, my mind wandered to guessing whether their breasts contained double or triple implants, or to which surgeon performed the procedure by eyeing the hidden surgical scars.

Maybe you *can* have too much of a good thing.

Starting with the first morning after the first night, expensive bouquets of fresh-cut colorful flowers arrived at Scores with daily regularity. Each arrangement was invariably adorned with a card addressed to a dancer and contained heartfelt words in appreciation for a wonderful night and a hopeful future.

Here's the rub: The girls come and go constantly, use different names on different nights (or with different customers on the same night), and certainly don't want to be bothered with flowers. So what were we to do with the never-ceasing crush of deliveries?

I made an immediate and selfish decision that continued throughout my ownership years. We placed one bouquet on the club's reception kiosk, and the rest were delivered to my law firm and home. I was consistently flooded with compliments from friends and clients in admiration of the time, concern, and care I undertook in filling my environs with sweet flora.

I'm sure the senders will find solace in knowing their offerings went to good and meaningful use, even if not as intended.

Our first brush with the power of celebrity took place early on. I arrived one night to find a young black man dancing on our bar as the center of the club's collective attention. As he lacked even the most minimal anatomical requirements of a Scores entertainer, I sensed something was awry.

I cornered Mark Yackow who excitedly told me the dancing man was Mike Davis, All-Pro cornerback for football's Oakland Raiders. According to Mark, when the DJ identified the well-known athlete for the crowd, the place went buggy. At staff's urging, Davis became a guest bartender, graciously signing autographs, and just lately had taken to bartop dancing.

I thought all of this was just terrific; after all, we were supposed to be a sports bar too. As I happily observed the unfolding scene with Davis's exuberance growing by the second, Yackow handed me an oversized manila envelope, remarking it contained X-rays he had agreed to hold for Davis.

I took the films for safekeeping to the office. I have to admit curiosity got the better of me and I removed the X-rays from the envelope and held them to the light for a peek. Bemused, I found Mark and asked him to step into the office. With him standing beside me, I again held the film to the light and asked, "Well, what do you think?"

"What is that?" he gasped, pointing to a square object in the middle of the chest cavity on the film.

"Well Markie, that's a pacemaker, and it sure as shit doesn't belong to an NFL All-Pro cornerback."

We looked at each other and burst out laughing. "We've been had," Mark roared, "me, you, and all the customers. We should throw his ass out of here."

"You know what," I disagreed, "this guy is good for business. Let him get tired and then quietly let him know we're on to him."

I was standing with Bildstein at the front door one evening when a small, slight black woman walked through the anteroom entrance. As we were not particularly crowded, I eyed her progress through the main theatre and into a public bathroom. About ten minutes later, I noticed the same woman emerging from the bathroom wearing an evening gown. She strolled into the lounge area and mounted one of the solo dance pedestals.

As it would be unthinkable for a club dancer to dress in the customers' restroom where latex application could not be supervised, I shared with Bildstein all I'd witnessed. He became instantly agitated, saying we'd been experiencing a few women sneaking into the club and secretly dancing for cash. I followed him as he set out to confront our uninvited guest entertainer.

Yackow joined me at the pedestal as Jay pulled the dancer down and confirmed she was not an employee. As Jay threatened our trespasser with prosecution if she repeated her transgression, Mark interjected, "Maybe we should offer her a job. She's cute and it took balls to do what she did."

I looked back at Mark in patent disbelief. "Mark, it didn't take balls, she *has* balls!"

When Yackow's eyes wandered to her crotch, he went wide-eyed to find our dancer was as well-endowed as your average mule in heat. "Still think she's cute?" I shouted after him as he fled the scene.

Contrary to public perception, Saturday nights proved a misery for Scores, and bachelor parties were money-losing nightmares. On Saturdays, our usual clientele of wealthy businessmen, dressed in suits, ties, and credit cards, are home with the wife and kids. In their stead arrive an onslaught of blue-collar men in droves. These fellows complain about the parking and door charges, and especially bitch about the coatroom fee. To top it off, they have no money, try to convince all the women to have sex with them on the spot, and nurse a beer or two for the whole night. Entertainers earn significantly less on weekends and resist working, the club earns smaller revenues from minimal sales, and we have to employ an extra cleaning crew to rake up the vomit and steam clean the carpets to remove the acidic stench left behind.

Here's how bachelor parties invariably work. To save money, the stag gang usually loads up on booze at home or at local bars with cheaper drinks. By the time they get to us, they're completely polluted, out of control, and usually looking for a fight. If I had my way, I would have abandoned the servicing of bachelor parties, but that just isn't an option. By four in the morning, half the bachelor party guests are passed out on the floor and the dancers can't wait to escape the premises.

I remember one particular Saturday when I arrived at the club fairly late to find a young man sitting on the curb next to a deep pile of his own vomit. I sat with him because he seemed very familiar and I thought he might be a friend of a friend. The man was incoherent, put his head in my lap, and started to sadly moan. I called over one of the managers and admonished that "no customer should ever be allowed to get this drunk."

"I know, boss," he replied with obvious exasperation, "but it's hard to say no to a celebrity."

"To a celebrity?" I whispered in confusion. I then looked again at the young man driveling in my lap and realized it was Joey McIntyre from the boy band New Kids on the Block.

I roared into action, directed the bouncers to take Joey back to his party in the club, and made arrangements for a limo back to his hotel. As we had no hoses to wash his gore from the sidewalk, I supervised its collection and removal into a plastic garbage bag.

When I handed the bag to the doorman in disgust, he grimaced. "What should I do with this, boss?"

Frustrated and not thinking, I sarcastically responded, "You could take it inside and put it on display with a sign, 'New Puke on the Block.'"

I went directly to the staff washroom and attempted to rid myself of the smell. When I returned to the club, I discovered to my amazement that the doorman had followed my instructions to the letter—the bag of barf was atop the anteroom's display case, with identification sign proudly attached.

"No one could possibly be this stupid," I declared laughingly. My next thought was, *I could take it to the law firm and store it with the dried bag of shit from the cruise line case*, but I rejected the notion of starting a collection of unusual body wastes.

Picking up the stinking bag from the kiosk, I walked outside and tossed it in a large dumpster, reminding myself to watch what I said to staff in the future.

In our opening months, one of the biggest challenges we encountered was the fact customers were constantly running out of cash to purchase lap dances. We began publishing a list of local ATM machines, but patrons were either too annoyed or too drunk to go off into the night in search of cash dispensers.

While regulars knew it was necessary to bring sufficient currency to satisfy their nightly needs, first-time patrons were often frustrated and angered. When I turned to Bildstein and the rest of our staff for answers as to how other successful clubs handled this problem, blank stares were returned.

We were going to have to find a solution to our customers' cash needs, especially since our entertainers were, in their minds, being denied their basic right to pick the clientele's bank accounts clean.

CHAPTER FIFTEEN
Valuable Lessons for Strip Club Owners

APRIL 1992

As we reached our six-month milestone, I'd learned many lessons about the skin trade, and had become disabused of some urban legends about strippers and strip clubs. Despite the projected heterosexual ambiance of a strip bar, the majority of dancers are lesbian or bisexual, which actually makes perfect sense. Entertainers are expected to earn their nightly livelihood through constant projected sexual interest in any man—fat, skinny, bald, scraggy, lean, or smelly—holding a twenty-dollar bill. It's far easier to successfully accomplish this equality of attention when the entertainer is already "acting," and not truly aroused. Certainly there's no anti-male attitude pervading the industry; quite the contrary, as no dancer wants to bite the hand that feeds her, but when an entertainer takes to her own sexual pleasuring, it's likely she'll be doing so with one of her own.

Entertainers are not druggies, stupid, or sex addicts; that description applies more aptly to their customers. They are not scared little girls seeking to overcome sad or bitter relationships with their fathers. To my experience, most upscale strippers are, first and foremost, dedicated businesswomen. They support families, educate themselves, create luxurious and nurturing homes, study the *Wall Street Journal* for investment guidance, and own small businesses. With a small percentage of exceptions, the typical Scores girl was bright, savvy, motivated, and passionately involved in planning for her future. Entertainers are women who have chosen a short-term career, knowingly using their extraordinary looks to earn obscene amounts of money in ways not in conflict with their personal perceptions of morality. I know I received more good stock tips from dancers than brokers during my time at Scores.

Upscale strip club dancers aren't prostitutes either. Putting aside the matter of sexual preference, why would a young woman earning several thousand dollars each night risk her health and her job to grab a few hundred—or even thousand—dollars for sex? Now I'm not saying that a movie star, a professional athlete, an Arab sheik, or a true and generous millionaire couldn't woo a Scores girl into the sack, but for the average Joe—forget it, pal! Not happening.

Most Scores customers were not looking for sex anyway. Most regular patrons are middle-aged, married, and raising teenage children. They're not seeking a tumble in the hay to assist their egos through a midlife crisis; they simply wish to experience the pleasure of female attention.

Scores customers were more than satisfied with the acrobatics of a magnificent, lithe "Lolita," so long as the duration and content of the encounter were limited and defined. Our men were pleased with the imposed limitations; they don't want commitments, an end to their marriages, or disgrace. Most were smart enough to understand the dancer was in love with the money in their wallets and not their flabby, arthritic-bound bodies. Scores provided relief from life's tensions and, more than anything else, a night of true fantasy—a chance to finally experience, without any guilt, the adoration of that cheerleader in college who thought you were a nerd! Well, you were a nerd, most rich guys were; so go for it, Dad, you're not doing anything wrong. Your marriage vows will not be broken.

As with every general conclusion, there are sad exceptions. There are misguided patrons who sadly buy into the fantasies of adoration and love purposely projected by ruthless entertainers who ought to know better. Such men are perfectly willing to forfeit their marriages, their friends, and all their worldly possessions to "feed" the fantasy of stripper devotion. Believe me, there is nothing sadder than a man ruined by the mocking love of a lesbian dancer on the day he discovers he's been a fool.

Let me tell you about one of my friends. He was a happily married businessman earning millions annually. To his credit, my balding, paunchy pal had a beautiful, charming, intelligent, caring spouse. I used to think he was the luckiest fat bald guy in the world. My buddy fell in love with a dancer, who also happened to be a lesbian with a life partner. Of course, my friend knew nothing of the dancer's private life; he only knew she professed a deep and abiding love for him. On his visits to Scores, she would spend the entire night with him and he'd reward her with mounds of cash, thrilled to be the object of such ardor.

I first became concerned when my friend bought the dancer a Mercedes and arranged for her to live in a luxury apartment in Manhattan. Weekend trips, jewels, and designer clothes followed in bundles. When word around the club suggested a new living arrangement was in the works for my friend and the dancer, I knew I needed to intervene.

I called the dancer and threatened to end her career unless she and her girlfriend were willing to confess what they'd been concealing, and scheduled a meeting with all parties at my office. I will always remember the contorted face of my friend as the dancer admitted her sexual orientation, introduced her permanent partner, and confessed their relationship to be only a matter of money.

After the ladies departed, my friend cried in shame and disappointment. But in the end, his anger turned against me. "Why did you put your nose in my business? Do I bother you? I would have won her away and you've ruined my happiness."

He never spoke to me again.

Entertainers are ultimately protective of their positions at the club. There is a pecking order. Dancers know they can earn two or three times the cash working Tuesday, Wednesday, and Thursday nights, when the rich businessmen party, rather than Friday, Saturday, and Sunday, when the blue collars attack. As a consequence, many dancers—straight, lesbian, or bisexual—will offer their bodies to managers or owners in exchange for a better work schedule. They will also seek friendship with staff in order to sabotage rivals on the roster. More than most businesses, the strip business is only about the "holy dollar"—there are no degrees to obtain, promotions to earn, bonus perks, or vacations. There is only money—and don't get in the way of a hot and earning entertainer if you can help it.

The marriage of virtually every owner or manager of Scores was destroyed, or at least significantly damaged, by the sexually-charged reputation of the club. Wives do not recognize or believe in the final "Boredom" phase of ownership-management, and jealousy and insecurity are natural, unavoidable by-products of involvement. If you are the male manager of a strip club, ask yourself: if your wife was working in a place featuring 100 handsome, sculpted, and well-endowed naked men, wouldn't your ego find itself under subtle, and constant, attack? Would you be persuaded by your spouse's protestations that hundreds of penises and tight buns have no effect upon her?

While I sat on the sidelines and observed the formerly happy union of one colleague after another go down the tubes, I came to realize I was happily immune from all such intrigue. As a gay owner of a female strip club, I lived in a relatively safe harbor while maintaining an extraordinary advantage in my position. If a dancer was looking for a favor, or someone to bend a rule, I was the last to be approached. I was impervious to the dancer's most potent weapon—sexual attraction. Stripped of her ability to bribe me with pleasure, the otherwise confident and manipulative entertainer was required to plead her case on its merits—a desperate proposition. My exclusive concern was the well-being of the enterprise.

I don't raise this issue in judgment or condemnation of my fallen compatriots. To the contrary, I empathized greatly with their plight, knowing I could never act fairly or impartially with entertainers if I were the owner of a gay strip club. It just became radically clear that strip bar management and marriage are uncomfortable bedfellows, and the happily married should be wary of having their "dream job" morph into reality.

It was a Tuesday night and the club had just begun filling. I'd seated a group of friends in the Champagne Lounge and was headed back through the main theatre to the office. It had been one of those days when everyone and everything annoyed me, and I was joyously looking forward to heading home to the arms of a waiting Calvin Klein model. Nearing the office, my eye was caught by some unusual bustle in one of the high-backed booths. As I came closer, a vigorous ongoing lap dance drew my attention. I was frozen by the playing scene, actually blinking several times to ensure my mind wasn't playing tricks.

One of our entertainers was completely naked and indelicately gyrating herself around a casually dressed patron; and that was the "good" part. As the dancer plunged her tongue as deeply as it could possibly go into the customer's mouth, his fingers were weaving their ways into and out of her vaginal canal. Both were sweating, moaning, and plainly close to climax. I choked back my reflex to forcibly rip the two apart.

I hastily grabbed the closest floor manager and marched him over to the continuing pornographic improvisation. I harshly whispered through clenched teeth, "Doesn't anybody watch what goes on in this place? Do you know how many laws those two are breaking? For God's sake she's naked, and we could all go to jail. I want you to break them up, fire her on the spot, and throw both of them out!" Then I stormed off.

Looking a bit dazed and confused, the manager soon found me at the bar. "Boss, I can't fire her."

"What are you saying? You want me to fire her?"

"It's not that. I can't fire her because she doesn't work here."

I'd heard enough and brushed past the manager, sprinting over to the couple. Before I could utter a single word, the offending customer extended his hand and said, "We're really, really sorry."

I ignored his offer of a handshake. "Are you two insane? Do you even understand the consequences of your actions?" Turning to the woman, I added, "And I hear you don't even work here. Are you here hustling for cash?"

The man pleaded, "Please sit down for one minute and let us explain. Please."

Not knowing what else to do, I sat down as the red-faced fellow continued, "My name is Terry and this is my wife Karen—"

"Your wife?" I interrupted. "What the hell?"

"Listen, this is all my fault. Tonight is our third wedding anniversary and I've always had this fantasy of Karen dancing for me nude in a big, crowded strip club. I talk about it all the time."

"So tonight," she interjected, "my anniversary present was to fulfill Terry's fantasy. It was dumb."

I really couldn't think of a single appropriate response. I just looked at the two as they continued to mumble apologies. "Let me tell you guys something, 'dumb' isn't the right word. Do you know I'm required by state law to call the police and have you arrested? You've not only violated criminal statutes, you've broken about ten different liquor laws that could cost me my license."

The woman started to cry and her husband asserted in desperate tones, "It can't be that serious. Maybe we're guilty of being idiots, but the club didn't do anything wrong."

I made them wait several moments as I cradled my head in my hands. I finally looked up and said, "I want three things. One, you two are never to come back here. Two, you are never to tell anyone what you did here tonight." After a long pause, I concluded, "And third, happy anniversary. Next time, please pick on some other club owner; I have quite enough on my plate."

CHAPTER SIXTEEN

Can Scores Be Rescued from Financial Ruin?

1993

As Scores moved into its second year of business, we were in deep financial trouble and I couldn't put my finger on why. The club was always crowded, the entertainers were pleased with their earnings, and the bar was in constant high gear. Yet at the end of each month, there was barely enough to pay the bills. I was now the proud father of New York's hottest new form of entertainment, the club was demanding an ever-growing amount of my time and effort, and I wasn't making a thin dime. At least John Gotti was making his thousand each week.

At the same time, Bildstein was going through a difficult period of personal disillusionment. He was pocketing only a small weekly salary, but his power over dancers' earning abilities made him a target of their attention, which had gone to his head and compromised his otherwise good judgment. He'd violated his own rules of conduct and fallen in love with one of our entertainers. He was searching for some way to exit—with his new lady on his arm and a large wad of cash in his pocket.

As a result, aggressive management of the club had begun to seriously slip, and no one seemed capable of or interested in taking charge of operations. And now, long-postponed architectural and construction bills could no longer be avoided; new carpeting, repainting, and replacement glass and tableware were badly needed; the air conditioning system slid into the crapper; and we weren't doing the kind of advertising required for growth. Even Yackow's ever-patient investor group was grumbling for at least "some return" on their loans. No doubt about it, Scores was teetering on the brink of collapse.

Just when the bottom was poised to fall out, Andrew Pearlstein, who'd become my partner in other matters related to the insurance mess in Florida, began an urgent personal campaign to become one of Scores' principals. Once I agreed to allow him into Scores as my partner, we feverishly began investigating steps to rescue the venture.

Since Bildstein was seeking a personal exit strategy anyway, he feigned instant dislike for Pearlstein and demanded to be bought out. After a round of difficult negotiations, we reached an arrangement for the purchase of his minority interest.

At the same time, Davies declared he was on the brink of being sent off to jail for nonpayment of child support, and demanded his share of the venture be bought out as well. A lump-sum down payment and an extended monthly schedule of additional payments was successfully negotiated.

With the buyouts finalized, Jay and David were instantly gone from the scene; the corporate shares and licenses remained in my nominee's name, and underlying control was shared between Andrew and myself, with Yackow's interests piggybacking along.

After all was signed and sealed, Andrew and I sat down in the law firm's library, rolled up our sleeves, and created a new agenda. Our first step was to take a quick tour of strip clubs to observe and learn from the competition. According to common wisdom, Scores was operating in the most profitable business imaginable, and yet, with an incomparable location, magnificent premises, an unmatchable available clientele of wealthy businessmen and professionals, and gorgeous entertainers, it was headed to the poorhouse via the express lane. We were obviously doing something inherently out of step with the rest of the industry.

Success can sometimes be a strange and inexplicable stepchild. It seems certain undertakings are ordained to succeed, against all odds and despite common sense. Consider Scores. A gay lawyer, specializing in commercial arbitration and politics, with less than zero interest in operating a lap dance club, finds himself inheriting the dreams of others who later abandon the venture. Moving forward with his banker (who thinks the club will be a sports bar) and his collaborator in an insurance fraud as fellow owners, he sets himself on an utterly foreign path for which experience has ill equipped him. What odds for success would you assign to this mish-mash? One hundred to one? Ten thousand to one?

And what was the result of this untenable collection of miscreants? Magic: pure, unadulterated, and unstoppable. From the moment we assumed total control, we could do no wrong. Every move was the "right" move, every decision retrospectively correct and perfectly timed. It was as if the powers that control lives and fortunes insisted without reason upon having Manhattan serve as home to an environment "where sports and pleasure come together" and nothing we could do, no stumbling over one another, could in any way derail the oncoming train of unprecedented achievement. The "wheelbarrows of cash" were finally about to arrive and no amount of inexperience or negligence could slow the train's momentum.

Drawing upon our collective knowledge, investigations, and instincts, Scores was subjected to a series of transformations that forever changed its character and standing.

First, we quickly closed the troublesome basketball court. "What the fuck was in your minds?" one of our consultants scoffed. "If customers are playing basketball, they're not drinking or buying dances, and that means you're not making money!" The court was dismantled and the area replaced with a second and profitable service bar for waitresses.

In the same week, we removed the sports arcade, as it had continued to be nothing more than wasted space. "You're running New York's hottest adult sports bar with table dancing, not a Chuck E. Cheese for pimply teens," was the remark that won the day. And once the golf, free-throw shooting, and arcade game machines were unceremoniously hauled out, we were able to vastly enlarge the main stage, giving it greater prominence in the showroom. The new stage permitted presentation of popular simulated lesbian dance exhibitions, and accommodated "beauty pageant-style" parades, providing customers with repeated nightly views of every available entertainer for lap dance selections.

The restaurant was originally constructed as a closed-in section of the club, standing wholly separate and apart. It was suggested this had been a major design flaw and we ordered removal of the separating wall behind the main bar. The result was overwhelming to the senses, a "new" club emerging from the change. The club's glitter and light shows were magnified and now permeated everywhere, and what had been two standing bars—one in the showroom and one in the restaurant—were joined as one massive and impressive oval structure. With the wall torn down, the club evolved into a breathtaking spectacle of movement and light, creating new vantage points for viewing everywhere.

We next trashed every table and chair in the place. Out went the luxurious and spacious furniture, replaced by tiny tables and small, constricting chairs. No doubt about it, much of our rich ambiance was forever lost, but we could seat almost twice as many customers and the resultant feeling of being "crowded in" only served to enhance the already hypercharged mood—not to mention the vastly increased number of lap dances sold.

In order to set our initial drink prices, Bildstein toured local watering holes for comparison pricing. Our charges had ended up mirroring the neighborhood bars and restaurants. "Wrong, wrong," was the reaction from our experts. "Your prices are insanely low. You're catering to the richest and most status-conscious men in the biggest city in the world. Do you think they give a shit what they pay for a beer? Do you think they even look? Your bar needs to make much more moolah."

Effective immediately, the price of a bottle of water or glass of soda escalated from $2.00 to $12.00, beer from $3.50 to $15.00, and bottles of champagne from $80 to $500. We also introduced specialty drinks such as Louis XIII cognac at $150 per shot (a favorite of NBA players).

We received nary a complaint about the new prices, and those patrons who expressed outrage were the ones we didn't want anyway. Bottom line, it became a whole lot more expensive to nurse a couple of beers for an entire night while watching free stage shows.

There was uniform agreement that we'd also been failing to take full advantage of our most important resource—the dancers. According to our house mom and staff, "Strippers travel from city to city in packs like mongrel dogs, and we're not tapped into the best packs. That needs to change."

It soon became evident that dancers did indeed travel together for safety and support, touring all the major cities. Before Scores, New York hadn't been on the travel roster, but after a few carefully placed phone calls with invitations to the Big Apple, several units were deployed in our direction. Suddenly, fifteen girls were arriving from the South, and we needed to reserve twenty spots the next week for a group from the Southwest. Not only were the new dancers more captivating and savvy than our original troop, who tended to be slightly older and definitely local, but the constant turnover of blonde, blue-eyed new talent kept our customers both contented and constantly returning for more. For some, it became an addiction with an accompanying fear of missing that "special one." To my glee, my condo and law firm were now filled to overflowing with increased daily deliveries of floral arrangements.

We also imposed an industry-standard "house fee" on the dancers who, for tax purposes, were treated as independent contractors—not employees. As we were supplying our "contractors" with a safe workplace and a means of making extraordinary incomes, word went forth we would henceforth require a lease payment of $100 per dancer per night. In other words, the house would be collecting an average of $10,000 each night in house fees alone—before the first nickel of customer money hit our registers. Anybody still wondering why we hadn't been making money? Anybody wondering how this major income stream had been missed by our original partners?

Scores also dove headfirst into the souvenir business. Until that time, we'd been haphazardly selling T-shirts and other memorabilia at the front door. The result had been no pressure, no reward, no sales. Now, our dancers were recruited to become a nightly sales force for shirts, hats, and sweat-soaked towels. Here's how it worked: Three times each night, every dancer was required to offer "Two for One" Specials—the customer received two lap dances and a souvenir item for twenty dollars—the usual cost of one dance alone. The only difference was the income from the specials went to the house, not the dancer; and if the lady failed to sell her specials, she was required to buy the souvenirs herself.

Using towels as our example, instead of selling a handful of towels during an entire week, we started systematically selling 300 towels each night (100 dancers x 3 specials per night). That's approximately 2,100 towels sold each week, 8,400 a month, and over 100,000 a year. With each towel selling for $20, and supplied at no cost by Budweiser, you do the math. There are seven figures a year at the end of that particular rainbow—a business within a business, a cottage industry.

While these sweeping changes clearly aided in the transformation of Scores from a dying albatross into a frantic profit machine, they collectively paled in comparison to the concept that forever solved our customers' nightly cash-shortage squeeze. The answer came in two glorious, gold-leafed words: Diamond Dollars.

Scores retained a private mint and began printing its own currency in twenty-dollar denominations, featuring the picture of an attractive dancer in lieu of an American president. The private currency became informally known as "funny money."

Funny money worked simply: A customer presents a credit card and charges, for example, $1,200. After the charge is processed, the patron receives $1,000 in Diamond Dollars, which could only be used for lap dance payments. Having just made $200 from the customer's side of the transaction, when the dancer presents her Diamond Dollars at the end of each night for exchange into cash, the club pays her $800 in greenbacks for every $1,000 in Diamondbacks. Cha-ching! The club just made $200 from the dancer's side of the very same transaction. So let's review: on the customer charge of $1,200, the club grabbed $400, or 33 percent, and all from a previously untapped income source.

And it gets better, as each funny money bill expired in thirty days. Some customers would inadvertently take a few bills home and then destroy them to avoid marital detection, and still others would take a bill or two back to Kansas as souvenirs to brag about. In our experience, the club would rack up another 10 to 15 percent in profits from never-cashed expired bills.

It was funny money that finally ensured Scores' success forever. Not only could customers now dip into their corporate entertainment accounts via credit card, no night would ever again be spoiled by a lack of cash ammunition to keep the dancers dancing. Thinking funny money transactions through, we brainstormed and decided to bill the funny money charges to a separate corporation without "Scores" in its name. That way, when the credit card statement arrived at home or office, the night at the club was indistinguishable from a charge at any expensive restaurant or executive retreat.

We began earning upwards of forty cents on every dollar charged for lap dances, and it was the norm to sell hundreds of thousands of Diamond Dollars or more each week. When certain Middle Eastern or Japanese clients arrived, we could sell more than six figures in funny money in an hour.

This simple solution was the key to the golden door. The club's income soared, the income for entertainers exploded—with some dancers bringing down $5,000 per night—and we made the eventual decision to allow Diamond Dollars to be redeemable for all gratuities in the club, including the newly-introduced (and wildly popular) massages performed by scantily-clad entertainers, so that every employee could get rich. We found that customers treated funny money like casino chips, or Monopoly money—the bills had no value when spent; the damage was only realized when the credit card bill arrived.

Scores was now a happy place indeed. We still had problems—there was the possibility that lap dancing would be declared illegal, and the mafia's greed was perking up—but it was nothing we thought we couldn't handle. Yet, popular and profitable as it was, Scores was still only a *local* phenomenon. It would take one more piece of the puzzle to make it an urban legend.

CHAPTER SEVENTEEN

Howard Stern and Scores: A Love Affair

for the Ages

1994-1996

The rich and famous began trickling into Scores. In its early stages, celebrity nurturing was a slow and tedious task. As lap dance parlors had just entered the city's nightlife, there was an understandable reticence on the part of celebrities to publicly experience the phenomenon; an evening at Scores might serve to diminish their images and careers in the eyes of America's heartland.

All that, however, was about to radically change.

Our public relations expert had a personal relationship with one of radio shock-jock Howard Stern's posse of oddball characters. At our invitation, the entire Stern on-air cast and production group, with the exception of Howard and his cohost, Robin Quivers, began regularly patronizing the club. As we dazzled and impressed them with our entertainment and ambiance, the posse started recounting tales of their adventures to Stern—both off and on the radio.

First curious and then actively engaged, Howard ultimately became obsessed with the new Manhattan club providing a home to thousands of young and beautiful topless dancers from around the world. Seizing an opportunity for unprecedented publicity, we arranged, to Howard's glee, for Scores dancers in thongs and bikini tops (or less), to be interviewed, hawked, and coddled on his radio and TV shows several days a week.

Before long, Scores was a daily topic on the Stern programs. The cast constantly related their remarkable times at the club, and Howard interviewed fawning dancers by the dozen about their lives, their work, their problems, their sexual fantasies, and their lesbian inclinations. All of America soon came to know and to laugh along with Howard's compulsion to talk about Scores, making the club comfortably familiar to millions of fans. Hardly a night would pass without a customer arriving at the door and inquiring, "Is this the 'Scores' Howard Stern talks about all the time?" The Stern tentacles became so pervasive that strangers in airports would stop me and offer to buy my Scores T-shirt right off my back.

At first, I believed the Stern phenomenon would ebb; Howard would surely grow bored with the club and move on to other comic pursuits. But the contrary became the reality, and Stern's compulsion with strippers and our lesbians only fueled more frequent and detailed segments about the madness and glory of the club. Thanks to the self-proclaimed "King of All Media," and without purchasing a single commercial, Scores became the willing and appreciative beneficiary of profound and tantalizing public attention.

As time went on, the relationship between the club and Stern strengthened. With Howard's support, a video series titled *The Women of Scores*, featuring scenes of lesbian love performed at famous city landmarks, was produced and later offered in a joint venture as a cable pay-per-view event. When Stern wrote the sequel to his book *Private Parts*, its dedication was to the "Women of Scores."

It was a memorable afternoon when our public relations consultant strolled into the Scores executive offices and announced he had stunning news from Stern. We almost fell off our chairs when a question was posed, "What would you guys think of throwing private parties for Howard at the club? They could start after the radio show wraps for the morning, and would be over before we opened to the public at four. He's gonna invite celebrity friends and he'll talk about the parties on the air."

Now this was obviously a most difficult and tortured decision to ponder, and after mulling over the proposal for a nanosecond, I yelled, "Tell Howard we'll throw him parties whenever and as often as he'd like. Free food, free booze, free dancing girls, and no press!"

And so, yet another unanticipated Scores chapter was born. Every month or so, Scores hosted a "Stern Party Royale." Forget *Les Miserables* and *Lion King*, forget the Yankees and Knicks, forget Radio City Music Hall, a Stern-Scores party was now the hottest ticket in the Big Apple.

On party days, Howard and his guests would arrive at Scores after the radio show ended and, as we would not be opening to the public for at least four hours, they were accorded unfettered run of the place. Food, drink, and female entertainment were available in obscene quantities. Attendees were strictly limited to a guest list compiled by Howard, and absolutely no gawking strangers were allowed into the fold.

When Howard arrived for each party, he or one of his staffers would be handed a massive pile of complimentary funny money printed in a special color for use as gratuities. What Howard didn't know, and what the dancers were sworn to keep secret under pain of dismissal, was that we paid significantly less than usual value on redemption. Yet even at the reduced rate, the parties were outrageously costly, sometimes running as much as thirty thousand dollars.

On the air, Stern would spin stories in drooling detail about dancers, his guests, and their antics, all of which rapidly became woven into New York urban lore. Guests on the show would compete for invitations to the next scheduled bash, and curiosity about Stern's fetes gained inquisitive momentum.

My own curiosity about the Stern extravaganzas finally got the better of me and I arranged to be on the list at a party honoring the birthday of actor and martial arts expert Chuck Norris. While I could have attended without an invitation, I wanted to avoid being accused of gate-crashing.

When I arrived at the Stern-Norris party, festivities were already underway and a manager guided me over to Howard. The "King," dressed in a natty old gray sweatshirt and matching sweatpants, immediately pumped my hand, effusive in his expressions of gratitude for the parties already thrown and to-be-thrown. He smiled wryly at me and said, "You know, I've met no less than fifty people, now including you, who've claimed to be the owner of Scores. How can I be sure you're the real one?"

I laughed roundly in response, knowing for a fact he wasn't kidding. "You and me both, Howard. But you know what? None of those other owners ever help with bills. I always say there are scores of owners of Scores, but only a precious few have equity."

"I like that." Howard laughed. "I'll have to remember that line." And remember it he did, as I heard it repeated on the following day's show.

With my audience at an end, I walked through the crowded restaurant and President's Club areas, taking time to say hello to friends and to Stern radio cast regulars—now Scores regulars as well. When I spied the party's honoree seated on a stool at the bar, I walked over and introduced myself.

Norris was gracious and disarming. He told me it was his first visit to Scores, that he found it far more impressive than anticipated, and our reputation had blanketed the nation thanks to Howard's "curious obsession." After he mentioned the party was not one of his "average" birthday celebrations, we went on to discuss a myriad of subjects. The conversation and "mutual admiration society" ended with an invitation from Norris to visit him in Texas and be an extra on his show, *Walker, Texas Ranger*.

The pièce de résistance of every Stern party was a private lesbian stage performance in the club's main theatre. The procedure for each show was invariable: Howard would be asked to approve the selected cast members and, without a word to anyone, he'd be whisked away into the showroom at the designated time. In a darkened theatrical environment, our entertainers performed with each other in every real and simulated form of imaginable lovemaking.

I will always remember Howard turning to me at this day's very private show and whispering, "This is what I imagine heaven would be like."

In small measure, I came to know Howard and to respect his off-air personality, finding it had been honestly, even if painfully, portrayed in his film *Private Parts*. Stripped of his thunderous microphone, Howard was a shy, noble, attentive gentleman, and I have no doubt that his repeatedly expressed gratitude to Scores was heartfelt. And when I was invited on his show to accompany boxers that my company, New Contenders, was promoting in upcoming HBO-TVKO pay-per-view bouts in Atlantic City, Howard was consistently respectful and kind to me, even on the air.

CHAPTER EIGHTEEN

Celebrity Hordes Rock Our World

Once Stern started spreading awareness of the upscale gentlemen's club in Manhattan, famous and infamous visitors to our fair city eagerly made it a point to visit and discover firsthand just what all the fuss was about. Unlike Los Angeles or Las Vegas where well-known faces are common fare, stargazing in New York is far less frequent—or even possible. Scores rapidly became the city's lone nightspot where sharing party space with celebrities from movies, television, politics, and sports was a virtual guarantee. Day after day, the gossip columns in the *New York Post* and the *Daily News* reported celebrity sightings at Scores.

Dennis Rodman, NBA all-star, was one of our first celebrity lap dance addicts. Without regard to season or temperature, Rodman would arrive at the club's front door garbed in shoulder-to-floor-length fur coats, and his massive presence would invariably send shockwaves throughout the showroom. Patrons would line up to ask for autographs or a handshake. Dennis would frequently complain about his lack of privacy, but always refused to take advantage of the club's private entrances and party areas to avoid public scrutiny. After a bit, we simply concluded, "the lady doth protest too much," and ignored his hollow Greta Garbo-ish sounding protestations of "I vant to be alone."

Rodman caused headlines internationally when he took a Scores entertainer from Texas, Stacy Yarbrough, to be his bride. Although the union between Rodman and the lady was short-lived, it lasted long enough to become a tale told and repeated in every tabloid in the world.

Madonna was another of our earliest star-regulars. In the beginning, she would arrive in unspectacular clothing, a scarf covering her hair, and quietly watch NBA basketball games at the main bar. As the years went by and her comfort level grew, she would reserve party space in the President's Club with the likes of Tupac Shakur or Pamela Anderson, and happily watch Miami Heat games as dancers mingled and entertained both her and her boisterous crowd with table dances.

Certain celebrities wanted to avoid public attention at all costs. Steven Spielberg wore a large hat pulled down over his head. David Hasselhoff fled the premises in the wake of fan attention, but not before photographer James Edstrom caught a shot of him on the run and sold it worldwide for a reported six-figure reward. Charlie Sheen always called ahead to use the private entrance and hid in the Crow's Nest. Members of the New York Knicks, especially Patrick Ewing, who sucked down shots of Louis XIII cognac like it was Evian water, always took advantage of the President's Club's privacy as the team's then head coach, Pat Riley, bragged about posting a locker-room memorandum specifically banning his players from Scores.

Other stars were outgoing and welcomed exchanges with doting fellow patrons. Jon Stewart enjoyed hanging out with staff in the vestibule, as did Mark Wahlberg when he wasn't acting as escort to Madonna for the evening. Bill Maher regularly held court at the restaurant bar as did Yankee pitcher David Cone. Jim Belushi was gracious and playful with everyone. George Clooney held his birthday party in the President's Club. Mark Messier of the New York Rangers sponsored open parties in the showroom, preferring it to the private areas, never refusing a handshake with or an autograph for a fan. Regis Philbin was ever gregarious and charming, and Donald Trump preferred his parties in the Champagne Lounge. Actor Ethan Hawke, so enthusiastic about his Scores experience, willingly posed for photos with dancers. Colin Farrell, a favorite of our entertainers, usually arrived around thirty minutes before closing and stayed after-hours. One adventurous morning, he treated twenty-five dancers and staffers to breakfast. Gene Simmons, never drinking or smoking, just wagged his infamous tongue at everyone. Whenever one of her songs played, Christina Aguilera would mount the stage and start dancing.

One evening I was walking the club's main floor when I heard a voice calling urgently behind me. "Hey, Kenny Cole. Kenny Cole, wait up! How the hell have you been?"

My insides shivered as I assumed the only person who could possibly be calling after me was New York County District Attorney Robert Morgenthau. Resolving to finally straighten out this mortifying misidentification issue owed squarely to Mario Cuomo, I turned back with a smile.

To my astonishment, I found myself facing none other than a laughing John F. Kennedy, Jr., wearing a crewneck sweater, jeans, and a black beret. "I can't believe you remembered that story," I sputtered at him.

"It was a memorable aspect of an otherwise forgettable dinner."

I grabbed Kennedy, exchanged handshakes and hugs, and gave him the complete "super-duper" tour. He couldn't get enough of the history and high jinks that had preceded the club's opening, and seemed fascinated by the financial profit streams.

In 1994, when the New York Rangers won the Stanley Cup after a championship drought of fifty-four years, Mark Messier brought the Cup to Scores for a team celebration. At the team's insistence, we filled the trophy with champagne and every customer, dancer, and staff member was invited to step up and sip from the iconic symbol as if it were the Holy Grail.

When the bombastic festivities finally died down and the club began emptying, I noticed that while Messier and the other Rangers had departed, the Stanley Cup in all its majesty was sitting alone atop the bar. Not believing my eyes, I stood with the Cup and pondered the audacity of my potential morning conversation with executives at Madison Square Garden. "Hi, this is Michael Blutrich, owner of Scores, you know, the strip bar. Listen, some of your folks left the Stanley Cup here last night. We can keep it for a while, or if you prefer, you can arrange to send someone over to get it."

My imagined conversation never came to be. About thirty minutes later, Messier poked his head through the front door. "Did I leave a large cup here?" he inquired with a nervous smile.

"I'm not sure," I returned. "We can go to the lost-and-found basket and check."

Messier almost fainted and I relented and told him the truth.

For some inexplicable reason, Scores took on the role of official watering hole to troubled and broken hearted celebrities.

John Wayne Bobbitt, at the height of his infamy, was a guest at the club and found himself rip-roaring drunk. At the unforgivable urging of some of our more perverse dancers, he climbed one of the solo pedestals and whipped out his wife-damaged manhood for all to bear witness.

After finishing a book tour, David Smith, husband of Susan Smith, the mother convicted of murdering their two sons, sat for hour after hour ordering lap dances from a multitude of alternating dancers.

While the tabloids and gossip columnists hungrily devoured internationally acclaimed actor Hugh Grant for his never-to-be-forgotten episode with Divine Brown, he hid at Scores, taking cover from more career damage.

In rare visits to Scores, Jerry Seinfeld was spotted drinking sullenly following the announcement of the end of his relationship with Shoshanna Lonstein. On one of those nights, Michael "Kramer" Richards was happily partying and performing in the Champagne Lounge.

On the night before his arrest in Los Angeles for domestic battery, Christian Slater passed the hours before his red-eye flight at the club. He appeared troubled and distant, repeatedly refusing offers for complimentary entertainment.

Lindsay Lohan partied hearty in the club's inner sanctum after rehab, only to be discovered passed out in the wee hours of the morning.

Bobby Brown had to be severely reminded of the club's "no-touch" policies after an entertainer complained he'd harshly bitten her nipple.

On the day Dwight Gooden received a suspension from baseball for cocaine use, he drowned his sadness with a dose of comfort from the gals of Scores.

Russell Crowe earned a dubious reputation at the club for mistreating a waiter for trying to pour his champagne, and by wrestling with a dancer in an unsuccessful effort to rip off her thong.

Kate Moss loved the sexually charged ambiance of the club and, without warning, left her table, climbed a vacant solo pedestal, and showed off the vixen in her soul with an erotic series of gyrating pole-dance moves.

Kid Rock sought and was granted permission to conduct his first MTV interview at Scores.

Marc Anthony was so enamored with one of the club's entertainers, he grabbed a microphone and performed an impromptu rendition of "Ladies Night."

Leonardo DiCaprio began frequenting Scores with Mark Wahlberg when they were filming *The Basketball Diaries* in Brooklyn. Once introduced, Leonardo returned to the club often, with a varying posse. The first time I met Leonardo, I was taken by two physical attributes: his surprising six-foot stature and his piercing eyes.

Sylvester Stallone selected and filmed Scores, with our consent, for the opening scene of his movie, *Cop Land*. Using both the club's main showroom and exterior entrance, including the logo on our entrance awning, the decision turned out to be quite popular with patrons. Both Andrew and his mother were recruited as extras in a fleeting opening scene, although it required a frame-by-frame slowing of the disc to identify them.

Scores was contacted by Demi Moore's representatives. They informed us the actress had signed to portray a stripper in an upcoming film, *Striptease*. With no experience in the "art" of stripping or lap dancing, Moore sought and received permission to visit the club: to observe, practice, and learn the trade from our dancers.

On her first night, wearing a turtleneck sweater, a long-sleeved shirt, and black pants and shoes (hardly "stripper-in-training" attire), she simply watched, seeming to absorb the flavor of the place as she signed autographs. As time passed, and her level of comfort mushroomed, she became very chatty and friendly with a host of dancers and staff.

As her time at the club was drawing to its close, Demi started talking about actually performing on the floor to gain an authentic "feel" for striptease. After walking the floor, Demi decided what she was willing to do and where and when she was willing to do it. On the selected night, she approached a solo pedestal in the main showroom, donning a black curly wig and round black-rimmed glasses. She danced topless for about fifteen minutes and descended the stage exhilarated, her heart plainly pumping wildly.

Chuck Zito is an actor, stuntman, and a noted executive member of the Hells Angels. I first met him in Los Angeles as a customer at my restaurant-club,

Alzado's. On his visits to New York, he'd become a Scores aficionado as well. Zito was also responsible for the most famous and publicized fight that ever took place within our boundaries.

One night, Zito was enjoying Scores with a trio of friends: actors Jean-Claude Van Damme, Mickey Rourke, and journalist A. J. Benza. According to the managers on duty that night, and published accounts, the group was drinking heavily when a verbal exchange broke out. Purportedly, Van Damme, Rourke, and Benza had harsh words for Zito, obviously confusing his real-life toughness with their own brand of Hollywood screen macho.

When neither group would back down, they secured the Crow's Nest for a private parlay and, when the smoke cleared, Van Damme was out cold on the carpet.

The next morning, the front page of every New York newspaper, as well as local television news, carried the story of the knockout of the screen martial-arts expert as its lead story. The ever-sensationalized *New York Post* ran the banner headline, "Jean-Claude Van Slammed." Unlike most nightspots, where acts of violence send customers running away in fear, the Van Damme fight caused a month-long spike in our door income.

On one cold, snowy New York winter night, when few patrons had chosen to brave the weather for our entertainment, I found myself shooting the breeze with 100 temporarily idle dancers. With nothing else to do, we decided to take a poll of certain amusing and never-before-confronted questions. I'll share the results of our night's polling, and in all fairness, it should be noted our results were not scientific and represented only the opinions of women polled:

Most Pleasant Celebrity	Jim Belushi
Most Unpleasant Celebrity	Tom Arnold
Most Stoned Celebrity	Dennis Rodman
Cheapest Celebrity	Too Numerous to List
Most Generous Celebrity	Howard Stern

CHAPTER NINETEEN

Breasts on Trial in Manhattan

1993

After postponing our latex pasty trial at the liquor authority for as long as possible, Scores' day of legal reckoning arrived. We were about to find out whether our latex nipple-painting procedure was going to pass statutory "opaque" muster.

As our trial date approached, I was astounded by the tactics the state government decided to adopt. There would be no challenge to our lap dancing in violation of the "six feet away and/or eighteen inches in the air" regulation; nor was there to be a challenge to the opaqueness of our latex nipple paint. Instead, the government's charges were reduced to a claim that, on the night in question, our dancers performed bare-breasted. In other words, the case was only that our entertainers performed without their nipples painted with latex.

The administrative hearing was assigned to a large, dingy courtroom in the bowels of the New York State Liquor Authority's downtown Manhattan offices. After waiting for more than an hour in the main lobby, we were ushered into the courtroom where an elderly, grumpy, and obviously unhappy administrative law judge sat erect on the bench. In short order, the judge made it abundantly clear he was offended by the subject matter of the case and anxious to bring matters to an expeditious close.

The government's case-in-chief was presented in less than five minutes. The investigator who served the opening night summons was called to the stand. He detailed his long experience as a field agent and his recollection that, on the night in question, multiple dancers were observed performing in the premises bare-breasted.

With the court's unhappy permission, I deferred cross-examination of the government's only witness as part of our defense. It was now our turn and, as I rose to begin, I remember thinking to myself I still couldn't believe what I was about to do.

I first called one of our managers, who submitted copies of our official policy requiring every dancer to have her nipples painted with latex prior to entering public areas of the club. The government made no objections and asked no questions.

Next, our expert from the University of North Carolina took the stand and described the scientific definitions and industry-approved tests for ascertaining whether a particular substance was "opaque" as required by the law for nipple coverings. He testified that each and every test confirmed our latex surpassed standards to be deemed "opaque," and concluded that nipples painted with the tested substance would satisfy statutory dictates.

In a final flourish, the expert produced a pane of glass painted with latex and, holding up fingers behind the pane, obtained the government's stipulation that it was impossible to see through the glass to the fingers. "Just as one cannot see my fingers behind the latex-painted glass," the expert expounded, "no patron is able to view any portion of a dancer's actual nipple. The latex is the equivalent of a rubber pasty."

We next called both the club's cosmetician and house mom. Their cumulative testimony confirmed the cosmetician painted every dancer's breasts with latex every night, and the house mom monitored the dressing room exit to ensure only dancers with latex-covered nipples entered the club. Both witnesses told the court that on opening night—the night in question—security was especially heightened.

When these witnesses were excused, our sole remaining goal was to dispute, or at least create doubt, as to the investigator's alleged visual findings. To accomplish this, I re-called the investigator, and my first questions established that he didn't know, and hadn't bothered to identify, the names of the dancers who'd allegedly violated the law. I approached the bench and advised the court of my intention to re-create the club's lighting ambiance in the courtroom utilizing portable lamps, and to place five bare-breasted women at the proper distance from the witness to determine whether he was capable of determining which women had painted their nipples and which had not.

The judge rose to his feet in response. "Are you out of your mind? This is a court, not a peep show. I absolutely won't allow my courtroom to be turned into a carnival. Have you no respect?"

Straining with all my might to keep from smiling, I jumped into the fray. "Your Honor, no disrespect is intended. This isn't some frivolous or immaterial exhibition. The club's defense is straightforward: when areolas are painted with latex, which has been colorized and toned to match an individual's skin type, it is virtually impossible to visually detect the opaque covering in colored light. If we can prove the investigator is incapable of detecting the presence of a latex paint shield on a nipple, his testimony becomes worthless.

"And two more things, Judge. First, if Your Honor objects to performing this demonstration in the courtroom, I move we adjourn to the club where I can exactly duplicate conditions on the night in question. Second, we're being forced to proceed in this manner because the investigator failed to name the purported offending dancers. I have to challenge his observational skills because I can't call any particular witness to rebut specifics. I respectfully submit the court cannot deny us this very relevant simulation."

I thought the judge might be having a heart attack; his face reddened and his hands began shaking. After a few moments of reflection, he rose and quietly ruled, "I will allow your so-called simulation. But I want the courtroom cleared of spectators and I want things to move along very quickly. Set up your lights and we'll continue when you're ready."

As the judge's form disappeared through a door behind the bench, I sprinted into the hall, barking orders to our crew to set up the portable lights in the courtroom. I next headed over to a small conference room reserved for witnesses. Seated there were five Scores dancers and our drowsy-looking cosmetician. The girls had been selected for specific physical attributes: small breasts, small dark nipples, and olive skin. Our tests in preparation for trial concluded latex shields were most difficult to observe on women with these characteristics.

After confirming the latex had been applied, I inspected each dancer carefully. Lord, the things we're forced to do as a sacrifice to our profession! I was quite impressed with the results; it was hard to detect the latex paint. I also reviewed what was expected of the women: remove tops, stand erect, no smiling, no dancing, no nothing. They donned white robes and followed me into the courtroom. We emptied the gallery of guests, turned off the overhead lights, pulled the shades, turned on the portable color lamps, and called for the judge.

When the investigator was again seated in the witness chair, I asked the entertainers to stand in a row before him and remove their robes. As the women exposed themselves, I stole a glance at the judge, who was cradling his head in his hands.

I approached the witness and advised him that some of the women had covered their nipples with latex and some hadn't. Before he could answer, a shrill voice pierced the courtroom's quiet. "Young lady, do not move that thing again!" As I fiercely looked around for the source of the interruption, I realized it was the judge. He was standing and pointing to the right breast of a blonde dancer on the end of the lineup.

"Is there a problem, Your Honor?"

"Yes, there's a problem," the frothing-at-the-mouth jurist snapped. "I want that woman to stand perfectly still, no movement. Every time she shifts her weight, her privates are bouncing all around."

"I can't help it, Judge," the annoyed blonde blurted out, "they jump around on their own."

I was close to losing it, but I knew if I started laughing, the whole case would be sacrificed. I motioned to the judge and walked over to confer with the dancer. "Listen," I whispered, "the man can't handle all this. Just try to keep still."

"Piss on that little old nerd. Who does he think he's looking down on? I'll tell him I earn more in a few months than he earns all year with his big, important job."

Helpful idea, I mused to myself as I returned my attention to the judge. "In all fairness, Your Honor, the investigator observed the breasts in motion and keeping them still weighs the test heavily in the state's favor. But in deference to your wishes, the women will try to keep motion to a minimum."

When I repeated my question, the investigator remarked he believed he could pick out the painted nipples from the unpainted ones. We held our collective breaths as he proceeded to choose two dancers whom he claimed weren't painted.

Bingo! Yes! Cha-ching! The witness was wrong on both choices and, to prove it, I instructed the selected women to peel the latex shields from their nipples. I placed the rubber pasties in a plastic bag and offered them into evidence. Although refusing to look at the evidence or to even touch the bag, the judge reluctantly accepted the latex as an exhibit, acting as if I'd offered him dried shit from a cruise line case or New Kid on the Block vomit or fingernail clippings.

The judge then retired, asking us to wait in the courtroom for his decision. As we paced in anticipation, one of our managers approached me and asked what I thought our realistic chances of prevailing might be. "To be honest, slim to none. This is a kangaroo court; we were doomed before things started. These judges only have stamps that read 'Guilty.' The battle will be in civil court in a couple of years."

As scripted, the judge returned shortly and announced his finding: guilty as charged. As the gallery groaned in response, he went on to "unofficially" explain that the witness's inability to identify the unpainted nipples was immaterial. "I find that the use of latex is not a substitute for cloth covers. You may be complying with the letter of the law, but not with its spirit. Scores Entertainment is guilty and, in due course, will receive written findings."

Curiously, neither a decision nor penalty was ever issued. I called the Liquor Authority several times, fearful of missing the time limit for challenging administrative findings in court, only to be told to "stand by." Something was up.

Then came the day it was announced by the highest court in New York that it had unanimously voided the statute containing the "cover those nipples" and "dance six feet away and eighteen inches in the air" rules. As a result, I soon received notice that the case against us was dismissed and, even better, the City Council had no intention of reenacting the prohibitions. It was over. No more latex, no more opaque tests, no more SLA summonses. Our gambit had paid off, and our nipples were free.

Bare breasts, lap dancing, and Scores were here to stay. Manhattan had been yanked out of the Puritan Age and joyously joined the ranks of such liberal states as Mississippi, Alabama, and Louisiana.

CHaPTER TWENTY
Trying to Tame the Mafia Beast

1994

Throughout my tenure as the principal owner of Scores, I viewed our involvement with the mafia as a necessary evil, an unavoidable cost of doing business in New York. Despite all that's happened since, I still believe that view to be an accurate depiction of then-existing facts of life. The New York club scene was a jungle, and while the mafia adds nothing to business promotion itself, it offered a buffer that the sickest and most violent street animals feared to breach.

In looking back over the experience, I am wholly unable to discern whether the relationship between Scores and the mob was pathetic or comical or both. And recognizing that a complete history would surely make an entertaining memoir unto itself, here are some of the highlights of life at the club with the Gambino crime family along for the ride.

As discussed, the original negotiation for mob protection included a one thousand dollar weekly payment and, like clockwork, every Thursday night, Steve Sergio would amble over to the cashier and sign out the cash—no permission requested or granted. We were first told the funds went directly to the home of John Gotti, Sr. in Queens, and later to his son, Junior.

Over the years, our computers tracked our income from each source, and a reliable pattern developed based on daily, monthly, and yearly comparisons. With this pattern as our guide, I became quite concerned when, for no apparent reason, the Thursday night door income began to markedly decline. It made no sense because our tracking of bar, food, and funny money sales revealed those categories to be rising in the same period. Unless our door people were admitting more than half the customers for free, there was only one plausible explanation—someone was stealing.

At first, we simply admonished our cashiers and door managers, voicing our suspicions. But as time marched forward, the Thursday night "door dip" became larger and larger, eventually reaching almost twenty thousand dollars. We clearly needed to do something.

Our solution was to place a ceiling camera in the vestibule above the cashier. From that vantage point, we could tape and review entering patrons and incoming cash. We were already monitoring our bartenders successfully by the same method and hoped the camera would intimidate potential thieves. But, on the next Thursday night, the camera failed to record, and the door dip continued undeterred. Our technician, after examining the camera, concluded it had been intentionally sabotaged. This meant our thief was brazen, confident, and not working alone. All clues were now pointing to the mafia.

To ensure our surveillance success on the following Thursday, a second camera was temporarily affixed to a stanchion on East Sixtieth Street with a view to monitor the vestibule and keep an eye on the cashier camera. This time, both cameras were discovered wrecked the next morning. All our questioned employees professed complete ignorance, and that absolutely meant it was the work of the mob. A war was now officially "on."

Calling for covert assistance, we contacted a "spy store" on Lexington Avenue and arranged for a camera to be installed on the Fifty-Ninth Street Bridge, just above the club and directly aimed at the street camera. No one but Andrew, myself, and the spy store knew about the third camera. We now had a camera watching the camera watching the camera!

On Friday morning, our technician advised that both the cashier camera and the street camera had again been pummeled beyond repair, but the bridge camera had performed perfectly and captured one of our mafia bouncers smashing the street camera with a baseball bat. The same bouncer was later filmed departing shortly after the destruction, carrying an unidentified paper bag. After reviewing the tape, I called Mike Sergio and requested an immediate meeting with him, his son, and the bouncer in question. When he asked what it was all about, I tersely told him his bouncer was a part of a "ring of thieves."

At the meeting, it was calmly explained we had reliable information that the bouncer was responsible for destroying our surveillance cameras to cover up thefts of door cash. In response, the bouncer swore to Sergio with fervent emotion—on his life, on his mother's soul, and on his future children's eyes (my personal favorite)—that he had nothing to do with destroying any cameras or stealing any cash.

At that point, we went to the videotape and silently watched as the bouncer's exploits were revealed in living color.

Sergio rose and, darting toward the bouncer, struck him in the face, toppled him off his seat, and loosed a long series of expletives. He told us we'd never see the bouncer again and ordered him to wait in the car downstairs. Sergio apologized profusely and beat a quick retreat. Interestingly, there wasn't a single word mentioned about repayment.

We came to learn through the grapevine that the bouncer had been simply reassigned by the family to work in another club as a bouncer. And now we knew the theft was emanating on orders from the top of the crew. If a simple bouncer, acting alone, had stolen more than a hundred thousand dollars from a protected club, his punishment would have been far more severe than a slap and a transfer.

From inception, we'd happily ceded the valet parking business to the mob capo at the corner pizzeria. The valet deal was simple: arrangements were made to park patrons' cars at a nearby lot for four dollars per car, and the mafia got to keep the difference between that cost and the ten-dollar fee charged to customers.

We started receiving a small stream of letters from patrons complaining that the city was enforcing collection of past-due parking tickets for cars entrusted to Scores valets. With penalties, each thirty-five-dollar ticket had grown to more than one hundred dollars.

We soon discovered many of our valets were illegally parking cars around the corner on East Sixty-First Street and not in the arranged lot. When the customer retrieved his car, the valet would rip up any ticket issued to the vehicle, return the car to the unsuspecting patron, and pocket the four dollars.

Now each four-dollar scam was turning into a one-hundred-dollar-plus loss for the club.

The small trickle of complaints turned into a tsunami, and swarms of outraged customers demanded compensation. Who could blame them? I turned out to be one of them! We accepted collection notices from all complaining customers and paid the tickets with penalties at a cost of more than fifteen thousand dollars. At an angry meeting with the mob, the pizzeria captain's representatives apologized and gave assurances the practice had ended.

Once again though, there was no talk of repayment.

All revenues from the coatroom were pocketed by Steve Sergio. While one would think a coatroom business would be a worry-free operation, and immensely profitable at a cost-free five dollars per checked item, it was a source of unending woes.

Sergio's position was that, although he was earning every coatroom dollar, it was somehow the club's responsibility to keep the equipment in good repair. Our position was the exact opposite: you're making all the money, you fix broken equipment. This brought us to a standstill and, after a while, the electric rotating racks were permanently broken, the carpeting was ripped and filthy, and constant complaints were being lodged about items being stolen from pockets of checked coats. On some occasions, customers became irate over fur and leather coats disappearing after being checked.

We explained to customers that the coatroom was independently owned and operated. We passed all complaints to Steve Sergio, who promptly ignored them. Throughout our ownership of the club, coatroom problems went unresolved. While we were forced to settle many claims behind Steve's back—as we would never give him the satisfaction of admitting our actions in the name of customer accommodation—the issue led to a bitter hatred between Steve and Andrew. It took every ounce of Mike Sergio's imposed restraint to keep his son from ripping out Andrew's throat.

Perhaps the most significant damage caused to the club at the hands of the mafia came from the array of bouncers foisted upon us. Early on, as with virtually every club in the city, the mob insinuated its own corps of nightly bouncers, usually overgrown bodybuilders with steroid-retarded brains (and private parts). Imagine Scores on a Thursday night: customers in suits, dancers in evening gowns (when dressed), managers in tuxedos, bartenders and bar backs in uniforms, and bouncers in jeans or sweatpants, leather jackets, and black muscle T-shirts with cutoff sleeves. Our bouncers were a source of constant embarrassment—seemingly unneccesary embarrassment, as there were very few altercations except those the bouncers got into themselves.

In fact, the majority of fisticuffs at Scores were either initiated by our bouncers or grossly aggravated by them. The most frequent fights involved, of course, the coatroom. Since every bouncer was coached on the importance of the coatroom revenues to the family, bouncers would congregate at the club entrance to ensure all coats and briefcases were checked. On the rare night when a customer would refuse to check an item, probably because of a prior miserable experience at the club or fear of losing a valuable possession, a bouncer would physically insist on the item being checked.

Inevitably, some patron would stand up to the bouncer and the bouncer would attack, then run out the back entrance of the club with his small tail between his legs, leaving his mess for management to resolve.

The club was also under financial attack from thieving contractors and employees. It seems that when you are a success in this business, everyone involved feels an entitlement to profits. For example, we printed our funny money at a private mint recommended by our mafia friends, changing the color every month; once the color changed, the prior color became worthless. One month, the color change was scheduled for a specific date and, as chance would have it, I was held up at a meeting and didn't have time to bring the newly colored instruments to the club. No big deal. Right?

Yet when I arrived at the club that night, both green (the old color) and red (the new color) bills were all over the place. This was impossible: all the red bills were safely locked in the office. Noticing customers were actually arriving with red bills in hand, I retraced their steps and found a man selling red funny money out of his car trunk around the corner. There was a long line of soon-to-be Scores patrons happily paying ten dollars in American greenbacks for twenty dollars in Scores currency. When the police arrested him, we discovered it was someone who worked at the company we were paying to print the money for us.

1995

The mafia's boldest gambit was an effort to seize ownership of the club and all its assets. That plan, we later learned from federal investigators, was conceived between Steven Kaplan, the owner of a strip club in Atlanta called the Gold Club, and the then acting head of the Gambino crime family, John A. Gotti, Jr., with his senior captain, Michael "Mikey Scars" DiLeonardo.

It all began when a Scores employee, an acquaintance of Kaplan's, complained about his treatment at the club by management. Kaplan, Gotti, and Scars perceived the complaint as an opportunity to register a protest, through a different family, and to seek a formal sit-down between families based on a demand that ownership of Scores be transferred to Kaplan.

Kaplan recruited Angelo Prisco, a captain with the Genovese family, to file for and represent his interests at a sit-down; Gotti appointed Mikey Scars to preside over the proceeding; and Mike Sergio was advised by his superiors to prepare the club's defense.

Since inception, the Gambino family captain assigned to Scores had been Tori Locascio, son of powerful mobster Frank Locascio. The appointment of a representative captain is a normal process upon registration but, in our case, Mike Sergio was ineligible for the role as he was not a made guy. Sergio was required to inform Tori of the demand for a sit-down because he would be required to attend and defend. But over the years, Locascio had evolved into a very successful businessman and was no longer interested in participating in serious family matters such as sit-downs. Our captain immediately resigned, leaving us high and dry.

Sergio was able to recruit a substitute representative—an acting Gambino captain from Westchester named Craig DePalma, son of the incarcerated captain Greg DePalma. The sit-down had thus initiated a significant shift of mafia power at the club; the DePalmas were now in charge and they assigned an associate from their crew, Willie Marshall, a longtime acquaintance of mine from my disco ownership days, to oversee their operations in the club in conjunction with Sergio.

The sit-down was held and, purportedly pursuant to a plan within a plan, Mikey Scars ruled that ownership of the club would remain in our hands, but a one hundred thousand dollar fee would be required for the accommodation. We paid the demand in cash within days, and a trio of representatives delivered the funds directly to Gotti in Queens.

I always believed the entire scenario was designed from inception as a six-figure shakedown of Scores with no intent to wrestle ownership. But the eventual ramifications of these events were more significant and far-reaching than anyone ever imagined at the time.

DECEMBER 1996

In preparing for the presentation I am about to make about Scores and the mafia at the proffer with New York prosecutors, I realize that my experience at the club had been the ride of a lifetime, and that the ride is over. To me, the mafia had become an inextricably interwoven fabric of protection, intimidation, friendship, and fear. No matter how close and comfortable the mafia makes one feel, there's always that hint of violence, that knowledge that if pushed too far, these unstable folk could bite.

It may be hard to understand, but having mafia protection lands one in a comfort zone. Sure, financial concessions are constantly demanded or stolen outright, but they're rationalized away because you're made to feel safe and important. For the first time in my life, no one could fuck with me. No one could confront me, no one could hurt me, no one could say no to me, because I had an endless horde of monsters protecting my back. And that protection extended to my family, my lovers, and my friends. Who cared if, while my back was protected, the mafia was well paid and pampered?

Understand this: it's one thing to argue with mafiosos as they earn or steal millions from your business, it's quite another thing to strap on a wire, capture mobsters in the act of committing felonies, and send them to jail. If I agree to go undercover and get caught, I know I will be executed without thought, hesitation, or regret—probably a bullet to the brain.

But even worse, if I survive, after the smoke clears, this means I can never go home. I will *have* no home. It means a stint in a witness jail and then farewell to family, friends, and lovers. A new name, a new past, a new city, a price on my head, a lifetime of looking over my shoulder will be my ultimate rewards. For some that may sound bearable, but to me, it's my worst nightmare. My life is my people; they are all I am. I can't imagine going on without them, in an alternate universe where I am somebody else and everything I love is ripped away. I don't know if I have the courage to do what's being asked of me. Maybe it would be better to run, maybe it would be better to go to a real jail—at least I would eventually emerge as me.

And all of this is for what? I will lose everything and accomplish nothing. The mafia will abide and overcome—count on it.

I know what I'm doing is morally right; it will end the madness my life has become. It may be the only chance I ever have to do the right thing, to pay for my mistakes by risking my very life. But deep down, I know I will never be able to pick up the pieces; I will never be able to make things right. I am heading into unknown territory and I honestly think I'm losing my mind.

PART THREE

Dancing with the Devil

CHAPTER TWENTY-ONE
The First Proffer: Time to Start Spilling
the Beans

WEDNESDAY, DECEMBER 18, 1996

Despite freezing wintry temperatures, I was sweating profusely; there were beads of cold perspiration running down my back and into my eyes from my forehead. But for the presence of my attorney, Sandy Weinberg from Tampa, I would have flooded the car with air-conditioning. Assuming Weinberg was already in winter shock, having just left the warm comfort of northern Florida that morning, I simply decided to crack open the power window.

As we headed north on our way to the opening volley of my possible cooperation, my first "Queen for a Day" proffer, there was little conversation—just not much left to say after all the heated exchanges over the last week. I was achingly tired anyway, having spent a tortured and, for the most part, sleepless night.

The whole concept of undercover cooperation against La Cosa Nostra, the real-life mafia, still churned my stomach, retaining an aura of unreality. As an attorney with no meaningful experience in criminal matters, my only perceptions of covert stings were rooted, like everyone else's, in movies and television.

Of course, I kept reminding myself uncomfortably, *none of this is yet written in stone.* I would have to satisfactorily perform, an organ grinder's monkey doing his dance, before any promises or rewards would be finalized and reduced to enforceable writings. And so that day, having decided not to break ranks with Pearlstein, and not to disregard our attorneys' collective advice, the unfathomable journey began.

Our car pulled into the circular driveway of a picturesque hotel in Westchester County, north of Manhattan. Adding to the day's drama and my level of apprehension, the prosecutors had decided it would be too dangerous to hold the interview anywhere but a secret location. While the government was surely trying to convey concern for my safety, the expression of need for such ultimate secrecy only escalated my private visions of impending doom.

The two of us, both wearing blue suits and red ties, traversed a floral-lined walkway to the hotel's front portals. The beauty and serenity of the retreat-like location existed in sharp contrast to the excess of adrenaline coursing through my veins. To the outside viewer, and calling upon decades of experience as a trial attorney, my demeanor did not betray any of the raw fear tearing me apart. I was nothing less than an outward picture of confidence.

Seated in the hotel lobby restaurant, waiting for orders of coffee and muffins, I looked up and unexpectedly focused on the face of Marjorie Miller, the second-chair prosecutor in the investigation. She took a seat just as the small breakfast order arrived. After the usual exchanges, everyone assuring themselves everyone else was just dandy, Miller stood up. "We have plenty of coffee and food in the room. I suggest you request the check and follow me so we can get started."

The government had rented a junior suite on the hotel's ground floor. Upon entering, a narrow hallway led to a dining room area with a kitchenette on the right. Turning right at the end of the hall, we found ourselves in a large living room, with straight-backed chairs and armchairs forming a semicircle around a large couch backed to the wall.

Carol Sipperly, the lead prosecutor, again wearing a conservative business suit, stood in front of one of the straight-backed chairs. Smiling, she motioned us to the couch and the FBI agents, Jack Karst and Bill Ready, extended their hands in greeting. Karst took a seat in a nearby armchair, Ready on a small couch, and Miller assumed the chair next to Sipperly. Everyone in the room, except me, pulled out large yellow notepads and started writing.

Sipperly opened to Weinberg with an official air. "We've prepared the standard letter agreement we use covering proffer understandings and protections under Rule 11."

Handing the letter to counsel for review and reading mild confusion in my demeanor, she turned to me. "The long and short of this agreement, which our district uses for every proffer, is that you promise to tell us the truth about any and all criminal actions you have participated in or have personal knowledge about and, if you do so, we agree never to use your words directly against you. But we can use your statements if you don't agree to cooperate in the end, and wind up taking the stand in your own defense and say something inconsistent. Then we can impeach you with whatever you say here."

I looked to Sandy for his reaction. He leaned over and whispered to me, "This is all very standard stuff. Nothing to be concerned about at all."

With that said and accepted, we all signed the short, two-page agreement. The questioning began with confirmations of harmless personal data, and with each answer, to my uneasy disconcertion, five pens scribbled furiously as if I was recounting the Sermon on the Mount.

With preliminaries at an end, Sipperly leaned forward, took a deep breath, and said, "Tell us all you know about crimes committed by Mario Cuomo, Andrew Cuomo, and your law partners."

I almost fell off the couch.

"Wait a second, you told me to be ready to talk about Scores!"

Miller broke in. "We'll get to Scores, Michael. We prefer to start with the law firm."

My mind started furiously reeling; I was utterly unprepared and hadn't anticipated this line of questioning. As for the governor, I had only met him a dozen or so times and had no knowledge of any wrongdoing on his part. But as for my law partners, I decided in the span of a troubling second not to open Pandora's box. I lifted my head and stared directly into Sipperly's eyes.

"I'm not aware of any crimes committed by the governor or any of my law partners."

"Oh come on," Miller interrupted, adopting an exasperated tone of disbelief. "All those years in politics, and you never witnessed any violations of law?"

I purposely measured my breathing and silently counted to five. "I have nothing for you. I just don't. I'm sorry." I tried to look and sound pathetic.

I noticed a sidelong glance and a return nod exchanged between Miller and Sipperly.

"Well, we want you to think about it," Miller relented. "We'll come back to this topic again."

For the next three hours, I told the story of Scores and answered an onslaught of pointed questions. By the time I came up for air, the room was in awed silence. These prosecutors, from a small suburban satellite office of the Southern District of New York, had opened their empty guns against Scores with nothing more than rumor, hearsay, and gut instinct: a true "shot in the dark." They were now, to put it mildly, sitting atop a powder keg of possibilities. And even better, the crimes I was describing were ongoing and reached to the very highest tiers of organized crime's hierarchy.

Sipperly, Miller, Ready, and Karst collectively knew they'd hit a mother lode, perhaps the most significant inroad into organized crime of the decade. But they had no intention of sharing the value of this cooperation with me; I was a "diamond in the rough" needing careful polishing.

After a break for creature comforts and private talks, the groups reassumed their original positions. Sipperly once again took control of the gathering, sitting very straight in her chair. "Michael, Sandy, we're satisfied we've made an excellent beginning today. We're not yet quite convinced we've heard the whole truth about your involvement with the Gambinos, but we'll be having more proffers in the upcoming weeks and months with you. We're also going to need to know a great deal more about your problems in Florida.

"But as I said," she continued, "we all agree this was an excellent beginning. Now let me explain exactly what we're going to require from you. One, we want to go back into your law offices and reinstall cameras and recording devices in those areas where the mob privately conducts its business with you. Two, we want you to start working with Agents Karst and Ready as undercover operatives. They'll train you on the wearing of body wires and on undercover techniques of questioning. They'll protect you."

Sipperly stood up, walked over to the couch, and sat down next to me. It was the first time she seemed to consciously move out of prosecutorial mode and spoke softly, as if we were alone. "I'm not gonna soft-pedal any of this for you. What you're agreeing to do is very dangerous; life-threatening is the only honest way to describe it. You may think these mafia people are your friends, that they care about you. Believe it or not, that's quite a normal reaction. But you're dead wrong; you're nothing to them but a dollar sign, and not one of them would hesitate to end your life in a heartbeat if they learned or even seriously suspected you were working with the government to put them in jail."

Carol stopped and took a deep breath. "With that said, you also have to consider we have lots of experience protecting undercover cooperators, and if you just get it into your mind to follow our instructions to the letter, you'll be safe. There's just one rule you'll have to start following from this moment on: other than your attorneys, Andrew, and the people in this room, you're not to discuss your status with anyone. Not your family, not your best friends, not your partners. You never know what someone, even someone who loves you, might say in a moment of anger or thoughtlessness.

"It's your life on the line and we can't take the chance of having an inadvertent word result in your death. Even from our end, and this has been authorized by the highest levels in Main Justice in Washington, no one in law enforcement outside this room, even other prosecutors and FBI agents in our office, will know of your cooperation. You'll be flying under the radar because we won't risk your safety on a remark overheard in a hallway. Our highest goal—more important than the success of our investigation—will be your safety. Trust me."

I couldn't breathe, silently wishing Sipperly hadn't thrown in the word "death." This was all happening way too fast to be reasonably processed; a million thoughts were flying through my rapidly numbing mind.

"If I agree, when would all this actually start?" I weakly asked.

Sipperly stood, nodding to Karst, and the FBI agent cleared his throat. "We want to go back into your offices to plant the bugs this Saturday. We'll have to talk through the best way to get into the building without causing a stir, and we'll definitely need you and Andrew with us."

I turned back to Sipperly, but when I casually raised my hand in a gesturing move to punctuate a point, I noticed it was visibly shaking. So much for my nerves of steel, honed by decades of court battles. Lowering my hand with the hope no one had noticed, and tightly gripping my thigh, I asked, "And how long do you think this undercover work will go on?"

"There's no way to answer that," Sipperly returned. "The more successful you are, the longer it will go. In my opinion, for what it's worth as a guess, probably between a year and two years."

Her answer surprisingly settled me down a bit; at least I would have almost two years at status quo to figure things out, to plan for myself and my people. "And what about our Florida problem?"

"Listen to me, Michael," Carol responded. "If your undercover work bears meaningful fruit, I believe your Florida case will become part of a plea agreement here in New York, and that's the best news you could ever hope to hear. Cooperators receive far more lenient treatment from our judges because they understand and appreciate the dangers and risks you're undertaking."

I couldn't resist a little further probing; the issue was just too important. After all, I'd only agreed to entertain the whole concept of cooperation when I learned from my attorneys that the Orlando prosecutors were of a particularly vicious and spiteful ilk, and would undoubtedly be going for my jugular—seeking a frighteningly long sentence. "Carol, you're choosing your words very carefully, saying you 'believe' that the Florida matter will transfer here, but can you quantify for me the chances that you'll be able to deliver on these promises?"

"You mean in terms of a number, a percentage?"

"Any way you can answer it."

Sipperly smiled benignly. "I would put the chances of moving your case to our district from Florida at about 99.9 percent."

"And you've discussed this with people who can make this happen? Because, and I'm being really honest with you, without that understanding I'm not sure I have the courage or the incentive to take all this on. For God's sake, just the thought of doing all this is making me shake."

"Rest assured we've had all those necessary discussions at the highest levels."

After a brief silence, I raised my head. "And what happens if I fall into the 0.1 percent?"

The whole room laughed in reaction—except me. "I really wouldn't waste my energy thinking about something so ridiculous," Sipperly barked back.

"Can I ask one last question?"

Sipperly now laughed and tipped her head back, signaling for me to proceed.

"When this is all over, when your targets are arrested and convicted, what happens then? Is there any way I can stay in New York?"

"Not a chance." Carol spiked her voice sharply. "Get that thought forever out of your head. You will be a marked man, heading straight for the Federal Witness Security Program, WITSEC. You'll be a target of the mob, probably with a 'dead or alive' bounty on your head, and you'll need a new name, new birth certificate, and new social security number. If you stayed in New York, you'd be murdered as a warning to others not to cooperate."

Sipperly's words sent my mind reeling again. Try as I might, I simply couldn't take in the scope and gravity of this information. Cameras back in the office; videotaping armed mobsters; wearing wires; keeping everything secret from family, partners, friends; spending two years at risk; leaving the greatest city in the world for Buttfuck, Iowa. And what happens to Scores and its millions of dollars in annual profits? This was a horror show.

I forced my mind to cut off all thought, convincing myself it was pointless to break down in front of these strangers. My bottom-line analysis was short and simple. A carrot I desperately needed had just been dangled in front of me by none other than the United States of America. I decided I would snap it up.

I stood, purposely looking into the eyes of each government representative. "You're all asking me to trust you, to put my life in your hands. You're asking me to rely on a 99.9 percent promise." I stopped for a deep breath. "OK, I'm yours. But don't let me down, that's all I ask." Turning to Weinberg, I added, "And you're down with getting none of these promises in writing before we begin?"

Before Sandy could react, Sipperly interrupted. "No promises in writing ever, Michael! Join us, believe we'll do the right thing, or walk out the door right now. Ask Sandy; he was a prosecutor in our office, a very respected prosecutor. Ask him how many times cooperators had to take his promises on faith. The Southern District of New York lives and dies by its word, otherwise no one would ever agree to do what we've asked you to do. It's a matter of reputation—and ours is stellar."

Sipperly, who was walking toward the coffee urn, stopped midstep. She turned back, smiled, seemingly to herself, as she apparently made a personal decision. Then, she looked straight at me. "I never say things like this, but

I know you're not savvy in criminal law and you're worried about how the criminal justice system works. So here's reality: if your undercover work actually winds up convicting major players in the Gambino family, I'm confident you'll never see the inside of a jail cell. Take that one to the bank."

Just as I began feeling a welcomed stream of relief pour over me from the lead prosecutor's final words, she again rained on my parade. "But understand this as well. We're not interested in Mike Sergio or his son Steve, or your bouncers, or Willie Marshall. They're bit players in the real drama we're investigating, and we don't need you for them; we've already got them nailed on wiretaps. You'll have to take serious risks with dangerous people, high-level members and captains, even the head of the family if you want the kinds of rewards we've been talking about. This is no game, and we want to capture bosses in the act of admitting or committing crimes."

My sense of momentary relief vanished as quickly as it had appeared. My stomach started to hurt as I wondered what the hell I had actually gotten myself into.

CHAPTER TWENTY-TWO
Hello Cooperation, Good-bye Sanity

SATURDAY, DECEMBER 21, 1996

A biting and bitterly cold wind blew without relent toward Manhattan's East River down East Thirty-Third Street. Alone, I huddled in the alcove entrance of a commercial stationery store, underdressed in a light leather coat. My eyes shuttled back and forth between Park and Lexington Avenues, searching for the appearance of the team of FBI operatives. It was only 7:20 AM on a dreary Saturday morning, and the timetable for re-bugging the office was behind schedule.

After the first proffer, I'd participated in an FBI-initiated conference call with Karst and Pearlstein. The agent's instructions had been uncomplicated: the office's landlord was to be advised contractors would be arriving on Saturday to install wiring for networking between the law firm's and Scores' computer systems. We were to meet the installation team on East Thirty-Third Street, and were to be prepared to recommend areas for placement of cameras and recording equipment—the most likely places to capture the mafia plying its extortionate trade.

In preparation, Andrew and I conducted an impromptu walking tour of the offices and drew up a list of suggested bugging spots. We also agreed Andrew would pick me up at ten to seven and we'd travel together. But in what would turn out to be the opening volley in an unrelenting pattern, the phone rang as I was readying myself for the excursion.

"Hey, Andrew," I answered.

"I'm not coming. Keri is giving me all kinds of shit, accusing me of running out to cheat on her. If I don't go back to bed, she's just gonna follow me."

The sour taste of bile began bubbling in my throat. "She thinks you're cheating at seven in the morning? So let her follow you, all she's going to see is we're meeting workmen at the office."

"Don't sweat it. I ran the problem by Karst before I called you and he said as long as you meet them, it'd be all right. He doesn't want to get Keri involved."

Disconnecting, I thought, *This is such bullshit. He's going to use his wife as an excuse all the time, just wait and see. Keri would be even more suspicious if he cancelled going to the office because of her accusations. Bad omen.*

As I was deciding whether to page Karst, I spied a caravan consisting of two panel trucks and a nondescript, dark-colored sedan coming down the street. Following the parade as the vehicles parked across the street, I was relieved when Karst popped out of the lead car. Stepping out from the shadow of the alcove, my eyes met his and he offered a stern nod.

Taking in Karst's tall frame, muscular torso, short hair brushed to one side, chiseled facial features, and thick black glasses, I began laughing inwardly. *I have to get over this Clark Kent thing, otherwise I'm never going to take this man seriously.* We shook hands and he quickly started walking up the street, turning right at the corner toward the entrance to Three Park Avenue.

After clearing matters with lobby security, the landlord's written approval thankfully on file, we walked together through the otherwise empty and echoing lobby and boarded an elevator for the offices. "Is Andrew's wife going to be a constant headache?"

I pondered for an instant and decided to be honest. "The woman is completely without self-control and extremely emotional. If Keri somehow discovers what's going on, she'll blow our cover the first time she gets mad at Andrew, which is at least twice a day."

"Well that's certainly a disaster waiting to happen."

"We just have to be careful and work around her. Andrew manages to carry on behind her back with some of the Scores dancers and she's never caught him. Of course, she's doing the same thing behind his back and he's also in denial."

After entering the law firm, we quickly looked around. Satisfied we were alone, Karst pulled out his cell phone and dialed in a code when his call was answered. Waiting for the team, Karst turned to me. "You know we've met before, years ago."

"You're kidding."

"Not at all. Before the FBI, I was a New York state trooper assigned to the governor's detail. I remember you from your visits to the Governor's Mansion in Albany."

"You mean you were one of those state troopers who were ever-present in the Mansion, acting like human furniture? Those troopers were so spooky."

"That was me, at least part of the time. Small world, huh?"

I shook my head in agreement, pining just a bit for those days of yore in my life.

My thought processes were interrupted when a sharp knocking at the firm's front door grabbed our attention. Bouncing up from my chair, I walked to the door and opened it. What I observed took my breath away. Standing before me were five gigantic men wearing ski masks. Momentarily forgetting the day's purpose, my lungs emptied in fear, instincts telling me the mafia had discovered what was afoot and sent an assassination team.

I only started breathing again, feeling pathetically stupid, when Karst stepped to one side and motioned to the group's leader, "Follow me." With Karst leading, we entered the law firm and walked down the long central corridor to my private office. When we reached my secretary's workstation, the masked assemblage started unloading their gear.

While everyone else was busy, I motioned Jack into my office and closed the door. I stared directly into his eyes with a mixed look of amusement and disbelief. "Why are these guys wearing masks? Don't you think that's just a bit overly dramatic?"

"Not really. They don't want you to see their faces. This group is on contract to the FBI; they also work for the CIA and Army Intelligence. They guard their identities jealously to ensure anonymity."

"From me? I thought I was part of the team?"

"Not their team. To them, you're just a snitch."

Karst and I and the masked leader traversed the offices. I showed them all the spots we'd pre-selected as potential recording areas. At each stop, the leader signaled a thumb sign, up or down, never speaking aloud. If conversation proved necessary, the leader and Karst exchanged words outside earshot. The group reached final consensus on multiple areas.

The next order of business was to find a closet where VCRs and recording supplies could be safely and secretly stored. I suggested the closet behind my secretary's station. As everyone approved of the choice, the workmen emptied out the closet and secured its contents in a corner of the hall.

"Make sure you call your secretary, what's her name?" Karst asked.

"Casey."

"Well, make sure you get in touch with Casey and give her some explanation for why her closet is suddenly locked and her belongings in the hall. The last thing we need is her running around the office on Monday asking everyone for the key to her closet. And by the way, for evidentiary purposes later on, you're not gonna have a key to the closet, so come up with a reason for that too."

As I walked into my office, mulling over possible scenarios for Casey, Karst followed. "One more thing, Michael, we can't have you around today. So we need you to work up a letter explaining we're authorized to be in the space doing ceiling wiring between computers. I want to have something in my hand in case any of your people show up unexpectedly and challenge us."

After typing the requested letter, I handed it to Jack, stapling a copy of the landlord's approval notice to it.

Karst looked over the letter. "Thanks. Now be back here in about six hours. Don't go far though. I'll beep you if something comes up."

Exactly six hours later, I returned to discover Karst sitting at my desk. "Everything go as planned?" I inquired.

"Perfect. All systems installed and tested. Now let me show you something."

He jumped up, pushed my leather desk chair to one side, and motioned for me to join him behind the desk. We dropped to our knees and he opened the doors to a medium-sized storage cabinet at the bottom center of the room's wall unit. Now we had to lie flat on our stomachs as Karst pointed inward and upward to a series of concealed color-coded switches. It was absolutely impossible to catch a view of the switches from any other vantage point.

The agent's instructional lecture began on the floor. "Each colored switch controls the recording equipment in a different area of the office. Each time you want to record a target, you'll have to get down here and turn the correct switch north. When you're finished filming, turn the switch south."

Standing back up and brushing myself off, I was puzzled. "You mean every time a camera is turned on or off, I have to lock my office, move the chair, lie flat on my stomach, reach up, and throw the switch? Jack, I'm a chubby, middle-aged lawyer who wears three-piece suits. This will kill me! Isn't there an easier way? Ever hear of remote control?"

"You'll be just fine." Karst laughed. "Once you get accustomed, it'll be reflexive. Think of it as exercise."

For the next few minutes, with Karst's tutoring, I memorized the colors of the switches and corresponding areas each controlled. When Karst wasn't looking, ignoring his admonition that the switch locales had to be memorized, I scribbled the information on the back of one of my business cards and slipped it into my pocket.

As we prepared to leave, Karst opened Casey's closet and revealed the display within: VCRs stacked floor to ceiling, one atop the other, crowned with a box of blank tapes. All the units were turned on and displayed the time of day in bright neon colors. Karst took tapes from the waiting supply and loaded one into each of the VCRs. He then secured the closet and dropped the key into his jacket.

"You're locked and loaded, ready to record. We're gonna have a meeting with you and Andrew to go over operational ground rules. But until that meeting, stay away from those switches; don't tape anyone."

Karst exited first, leaving me behind. As I waited to head home, allowing him a bit of lead time, I pulled out the business card in my pocket.

"White is my office, blue is Andrew's office, green is Casey's station . . ."

CHAPTER TWENTY-THREE
I Think I'm Gonna Puke

DECEMBER 23, 1996—THE CORINTHIAN, APARTMENT 56E

Standing alone in my oval-shaped living room, my right arm casually draped around one of the oddly intrusive Corinthian columns plainly conceived to ratify the name of the condominium complex, I stretched my eyes due north to Westchester, past the awe-inspiring sprawl of Manhattan's unique landscape. I was making every effort to remain calm, but my efforts weren't succeeding—maybe even making things worse. I knew it was only a matter of time until the spectacular view before me was no longer my own, until the city that had been my only real home would become a matter of memories.

As for cooperating, the bullshit was now over, and procrastination no longer possible. The FBI demanded the surreptitious taping begin this night, and I was waiting for Karst, Ready, and Andrew to arrive for the first pre-briefing session. The half-expected call had already come from Andrew, saying he would be late to the briefing because of a problem with Keri, and I was finding it increasingly difficult to suppress my growing frustration at being defaulted into the lion's share of the supposedly "joint" cooperation.

Minutes before, the concierge called on the intercom and, turning my television to cable channel 120, I watched the team checking in at the front desk. To my surprise, in addition to the usual two agents, an unknown third gentleman was in the group. Leaving the serenity of the living room behind, I reluctantly walked to the front door and peered through the security peephole. Waiting for the trio to appear from the direction of the elevators, I kept visualizing the morning just before Thanksgiving when I'd looked through the very same peephole only to find a crew of federal agents, replete with battering ram, waiting to warmly greet me.

My visitors finally turned the corner of the hallway and I opened the door before they drew close enough to ring the bell. I forced a steady smile. "Come in, make yourselves at home." Reassembling in the living room, Karst and Ready quickly moved to shake my hand, and Karst pointed at the stranger. "Michael, meet Paul Roman, the third agent assigned to our team for the investigation. He's our electronics genius and he's brought some of his more sophisticated toys for tonight."

Nodding my head at Roman and motioning for the standing group to take seats around the large green-and-black marble dining room table, I asked, "I take it you've heard Andrew's gonna be a bit late."

"This view is incredible, Michael," Ready said, ignoring me as he took a seat, stretching his neck to continue gazing.

"Thanks. Every once in a while I rent the place out to movie producers for panoramic shots of the city. For some reason, the oval shape of the room makes it especially desirable."

Returning to the issue of the absent Andrew, Karst took the lead. "I'm going to have to talk to him later tonight about the whole wife thing; it can't continue. Anyway, we're not waiting for him to get things started. Michael, we're expecting you to run tonight's show with Sergio. You're much friendlier with him so we'll need you to get him comfortable, to start him talking."

Early that morning, at Karst's instructions, I'd invited Sergio to join Andrew and me for dinner. He was viewed by the FBI as the most fruitful potential initial target, as he was both knowledgeable and loose-tongued after a few drinks. Initially suspicious that some new problem had popped up at the club, Sergio pressed to know what the invitation was "really" about. Satisfied it was nothing more than a social gesture, he happily accepted, suggesting a restaurant in Westchester specializing in a mix of Italian and African foods.

Karst now enlightened me as to the goal of the night's adventure: to bring Sergio around into talking about the Kaplan sit-down: the new mafia representation by the DePalmas which resulted in Willie Marshall's selection as a new mafia presence at Scores in addition to the Sergios, and the physical mechanics of the one hundred thousand dollar payment delivered to Gotti after the sit-down.

"At this point," Karst explained, "we've only your word any of this actually happened. We need to start things off by getting Sergio to confirm these events on tape so we can begin building extortion counts for a racketeering case—a RICO. Understand?"

I smiled in response.

The initial discussion came to an abrupt end when Paul Roman hoisted his briefcase onto the dining room table, snapped it open, and started removing electronic gadgets. The first item was a perfectly normal-looking beeper. "We want you to wear this on your belt tonight, Michael," Roman opened. "Not only is it a fully functioning pager, it's also a very powerful transmitter. We'll be sitting outside the restaurant in a van and we'll be able to hear everything that's being said. It's really for your own protection because if we hear anything sounding like you're in danger, we'll come busting in. I recommend you leave your own pager at home or in the car so you won't have to explain why you have two of them. If we need to talk to you for some reason while all this is going down, we'll send a message to the beeper with a phone number followed by '911.' If you get a beep, find a way to call us back."

The next item for "show and tell" was a large and bulky cell phone. "The phone," Roman continued, "is both a fully operational phone and a highly sensitive recording device. Just put the phone on the table and it'll record every word."

Staring at the phone, I became worried. "Wait a minute. Sergio knows I use a little flip-top Motorola, why would I suddenly be carrying this big bulky monstrosity?"

"Look," Karst answered, "he probably won't even notice. But if he does, tell him your phone is being repaired, you dropped it or something, and the repair place loaned you this one. Make a joke about it being an old piece of shit."

I nodded in concession, but I didn't like the vibes running through me. *Sergio is fully equipped with sophisticated street-smarts radar,* I thought to myself. *If his defenses are up, this could prove problematic.*

"So I just put it anywhere on the table?"

"Yeah, anywhere is fine, it's a real sensitive unit. You just have to dial a number I'll give you before you walk into the restaurant. When you hear four short tones, it means the phone is activated and recording. It has about six hours of taping capacity, so we have the whole night covered."

For the next half hour, we discussed various possible ways to induce Sergio into talking about the sit-down. "And there's just one more thing." Karst's tone grew serious. "We want you to have an emergency code phrase, something you would never say in normal conversation. If we hear you or Andrew say the code, we'll know your lives are in immediate danger and we're coming in—guns drawn—to protect you. So, if you're in jeopardy, real trouble, loudly say, 'I think I'm going to puke.'"

My head snapped up. "What kind of code is that? That's something someone might inadvertently say. Are you kidding?"

"Nope, that's our code: 'I think I'm going to puke.'"

You know what, I mused to myself, *I may really puke.*

As our car crossed the border into Westchester County, Andrew and I were silent, lost in our individual thoughts. We were only a handful of moments away from our first undercover assignment, and the sudden reality of our decisions was pressing upon us, making it difficult to concentrate. The ride had started out as all business. I reviewed the high points of the pre-briefing he'd missed, repeated the list of items on the government's agenda for the evening, showed Andrew the phone-recorder and beeper-transmitter, and revealed the "puke" code in case of perceived imminent destruction.

Following Sergio's detailed directions to the restaurant, the freestanding structure with its own parking area finally came into view. I parked and, grabbing the phone and checking for the beeper on my belt, jumped out of the car. Andrew was already heading to the front door when I called after him. "Whoa, come back a second. We're not ready."

As Andrew retraced his steps, I removed a tiny piece of paper from my pocket, dialed the number written on it into the phone's keypad, and waited. After several rings, the call was answered with the four short promised tones.

I put the phone away, satisfied I had made the connection. "Now we're ready."

The restaurant entrance folded into a darkened corridor, which emptied into a bar area. We checked our coats and went searching for Sergio through the busy crowd of obviously affluent patrons at the bar. Andrew discovered our prey first, finding him seated alone on a bar stool at the far left end of the crowd. As I maneuvered for my approach, I took in Andrew and Sergio exchanging a friendly hug. Mike repeated the identical greeting with me and then picked up the drink he'd been nursing. "Let's go on into the dining room, they've been holding a table."

With Sergio leading the way, our trio passed through the press of customers toward the better-lit main dining area. As we walked, Andrew dropped back and whispered to me, "I think we're in good shape, he's halfway loaded already."

Instantly greeted by the maître d', we were escorted to a large round table in the left rear of the room. As I walked, I became flustered by the surprising décor, steeped in African tribal masks, totem-like carvings, and stuffed wild animal heads. It was all so out of character with my notions of mafia dining preferences.

After we were seated and menus were distributed, Andrew and Sergio immediately ordered martinis. As always, my predisposition to kidney stones precluded intake of alcohol, so I settled on a bottle of imported Italian sparkling water, a brand recommended by Sergio as an Old World surefire cure for those bothersome pebbles.

After a few minutes of idle gossip and a second round of drinks, I began the "script," which had been carefully concocted in the car to get matters rolling in the "right" direction. "Mike," I said to Sergio, "whatever happened to our friend Tori Locascio?"

"Didn't he go to jail with Gotti Sr.?" Andrew interrupted, right on cue.

"No, Andrew," I responded patiently, "you're thinking of the father; I was talking about the son, Tori, our onetime Scores captain."

As Sergio hadn't yet jumped in, I nodded toward him. "Is Tori still with us or what?"

Sergio frowned, revealing wide, injured eyes. Shaking his head slowly, wearing a sour grimace, he croaked back, "Whatta you think? For years this guy picks up cash every week to be the family's representative at the club, my boss. Then the first time we need him, the first time we have real trouble, he runs away. He don't want no part of no sit-down, he's too legit now, too rich, just walks away without looking back."

Keeping to plan and playing stupid, I turned to Andrew. "That's how we wound up with the DePalmas, you remember."

Before Andrew could render his next rehearsed line, my beeper went off. Pulling it from my belt, I pressed the incoming button, and a telephone number, followed by 911, lit up the small screen.

"Who is it?" Sergio asked.

"It's Mark Pastore. He's been sick all day today. I'm gonna call him back."

Picking up the cell phone from the table, I walked into the front vestibule of the restaurant and dialed the number on the beeper. It answered on the first ring.

"Michael, it's Paul. We've lost the connection on the phone; it's not recording. Hang up, and dial the hookup number again. After the four tones, go back to the table."

"Paul, can you hear us on the beeper transmitter?"

"It's a bit rough, probably a lot of metal in the ceiling, but we're getting most of it."

Having followed the instructions, I walked slowly back to the table, replacing the phone on the table between Sergio and myself. As I sat down, the waiter arrived with yet another round of drinks, and another bottle of water for me.

"Everything all right with Mark?" Sergio inquired. "I like him."

"He's feeling a little better. He just wanted me to put some people on the guest list at Scores tonight. Don't tell Andrew," I winked, "but I gave his friends a generous tab."

Trying to get matters back on track, I turned to Andrew. "Have you ever met this DePalma fellow, has he ever been to the club?"

"I don't think I've ever met him. What's his first name, Greg or Craig, I can never get it straight."

As anticipated, Sergio took the bait. "Greg is the father, the real captain—he's in jail. You know the father was friendly with Frank Sinatra when he was one of the owners of the Westchester Premier Theatre in Tarrytown."

Playing "Gracie Allen" for my own amusement, I broke in. "I didn't know Sinatra owned a theatre club in Westchester."

Thoroughly annoyed, and missing the humor completely, Sergio barked back, "Sinatra didn't own the club, Greg DePalma did. Anyway, the son, Craig, is the acting captain."

Stopping for dramatic effect and sipping slowly from his glass, Sergio added, "And both of you have met Craig, you just didn't know it was him."

Sergio was laughing now, so we joined in. "When the hell did that happen?" Andrew pressed.

"When we picked up the hundred grand in cash from you guys after the sit-down. There was me and Steve, Willie Marshall, and Craig DePalma. He ordered us not to introduce him, wanted to remain a faceless name to youse two."

My mind went off in furious search of memories from that day. I did recall a medium-sized, fierce-looking young man who'd appeared with the others to transport the cash. I remembered thinking at the time the stranger looked to be a man on the edge of sanity.

My thoughts were broken by the beeper on my belt singing out once again. Same number. Same 911.

"Mark again?" Andrew smirked.

I stood up, grabbing the cell phone. "I'll be right back."

Returning to the now-familiar vestibule, the play was reenacted. Called the number, spoke with Paul: no connection, need to dial and hook up again. This time I stepped outside, redialed, and heard the frustrating four short beeps.

By the time I returned to the party, the waiter had delivered the ordered entrees as well as another round. "I'll be up pissing all night," I half-joked.

Sergio had now begun slurring his words, and Andrew wasn't looking that much more in control. Convinced these "loose tongues" could be used to advantage, I started probing Sergio about the sit-down, pushing for an explanation of how the process really worked, what role each participant had played. Sergio's inhibitions were gone and he now talked expansively, easily covering every item on the FBI's menu of wishes.

Listening to Sergio pontificate, implicating himself and others in past and ongoing crimes, there came a point when I felt myself tinged with a modicum of guilt. I really loved this man, or at least I'd always thought so. I felt abashed at betraying him to save my own skin, but lectured myself I was being ridiculous. Our bond with the mafia was exclusively woven out of dollars, and the Sergios had apparently been prepared to let Andrew die at the hands of their cohorts for a bigger percentage of the club's profits. The writing was on the wall: my friendships with the Sergios were not deeply heartfelt and, in the end, their loyalty to "the family" trumped our relationships.

Continuing to expound about the Kaplan sit-down and everyone's role in saving the club, Sergio leaned into the table with an air of conspiracy. "I'm gonna tell you boys something, something you have no right to know. You would have lost Scores if it'd been left up to Junior Gotti and Kaplan; the only reason you kept the place was a man named Mikey Scars. He ran the whole sit-down, he really runs the family, and he wanted you to keep the club. Otherwise . . . I don't even want to say any more."

As I gathered in the amazing significance of this important piece of previously hidden information, Sergio leaned in yet again. "And one more thing. Forget that name you just heard. If you want to go on living your happy lives, forget that name. You hear me, Michael?"

"What name was that?" I answered, as the whole table uneasily chuckled in unison.

I sat back, feeling truly satisfied. Cha-ching! Cha-ching! The night was clearly an unmitigated success. Sergio. Locascio. Junior. DePalmas. Marshall. Kaplan. Scars. Extortion. Money laundering. Tax evasion. RICO. All in the bank; all in a night's work.

Finishing up the dessert I swore I wouldn't order, I heard Andrew declare without prompt, "You know what, I ate too much. I'm so full I think I'm going to puke."

In the flash of an instant, pure white anxiety streaked through my entire body, my heart hammering relentlessly. In a rush of understanding, I looked up in an effort to discern the immediate threat we must be facing. Where was the gun, the knife, the terror-inducing act that compelled Andrew to call out the emergency code?

But as my senses gathered, and my heartbeat slowed, there appeared to be nothing afoul. Sergio was happily imbibing his dessert wine, and Andrew was leaning back in his chair, arms akimbo, eyes closed.

Oh my God, Andrew's just drunk. He's forgotten the fucking code and probably really feels nauseated from overeating. Who would believe this shit? The code probably acted like some kind of a subconscious cue in his brain. The FBI is about to come crashing in, ending our cooperation, and our ticket out of trouble with it.

With my brain firing on overdrive, I pleaded with Andrew to recant. "You're not going to puke, Andrew. Right? I hate when people say things like that when there's NOTHING WRONG! Nothing at all."

Sergio took no notice of the odd exchange, but Andrew was having fun. He leaned over and said, "No, Michael, believe me, I'm serious, you know when you eat too much and you feel like you're going to puke! What are you worried about, your new car?"

Realizing it was a waste of time trying to awaken Andrew's alcohol-repressed memory, I pushed my chair away from the table and leaned into the tabletop, my face next to the secretly transmitting beeper and six inches above my crotch. I whispered, "He's drunk, guys. Ignore him, please."

"What are you doing?" Sergio roared. "Talking to your dick, Michael? Does it talk back?"

Now Sergio and Pearlstein were uproariously laughing at the jibe. On the other hand, I was desperately trying to appear unfazed, feverishly looking from the doors to the windows and back, hoping not to see three armed FBI agents crashing through the restaurant to save me from two harmless drunks.

As the minutes passed and the restaurant remained eerily normal, I finally relaxed, cradling my head on the table in my arms.

"Are you OK?" Andrew inquired.

Lifting my head, I glared back at Andrew as if he were nuts. "I'm all right now, but I feel like I'm the one who's gonna puke."

Realizing what I had just said, I ducked back to my crotch and whispered, "I didn't mean it either. Sorry."

Walking out of the restaurant after exchanging good-byes with Sergio and paying the tab as always, into the freezing cold New York winter winds, I was covered from head to toe in clammy sweat. I felt a mixture of elation, at having accomplished all that was asked, and anger, at the repeated equipment failures and Andrew's amazing faux pas. I just wanted to get Andrew alone.

When we reached the car, Andrew was stumbling, having a problem holding his balance. With my partner standing helplessly at the passenger door, I strolled up behind him. "Tell me just one thing. What was the code tonight to alert the FBI we were about to die and needed their immediate help?"

It took Andrew a few moments of thought, but when he remembered, a look of abject horror filled his face.

"Do you realize you almost blew the whole thing for us over nothing? Imagine the agents crashing in and blowing our covers?"

Andrew looked back and burst out laughing. He draped his arm around me as his laughs reached even greater uncontrolled heights. Finally he slipped, sprawled out on the car's hood, and bounced to the ground, his legs shaking in the air and his arms flaying above his head.

He was such an infectious sight on the floor, I started laughing uncontrollably as well. We had to be the two worst undercover spies ever sent on a covert mission in the history of intelligence gathering. As our laughter, now born from simple relief, rallied unabated, a strong voice bellowed from behind my car.

"What the fuck are you two doing? Why is Andrew making a fool of himself?"

Turning around, I found myself staring at the face of Mike Sergio, holding a string attached to a dainty dangling white bakery box.

Not knowing what else to say, I replied, "Mike, Andrew's drunk out of his mind. I told him a really silly joke and he went crazy."

Starting to enjoy the situation, Sergio stepped closer. Ignoring Andrew, he said, "What was the joke?"

What was the joke? I silently screamed to my inner mind. *Jerk. Now you've really gone and done it, you can't remember jokes. A joke. I need a damn joke.*

"It was something stupid, Mike," I stalled, "not really funny except to a drunk."

"I'm pretty drunk too." Sergio's face was now inches from my nose. "Tell me the joke? I want to hear it."

I stepped back, and in my desperation—or by divine intervention—a joke surfaced in my memory. "It was about the Vienna Boys' Choir on the Titanic. When the boat was sinking, the two priests accompanying the choir were told to get themselves into a lifeboat. The first priest said to his companion, 'But what about the boys?' The companion priest answered, 'Fuck the boys!' The first priest gave it some thought and asked, 'Do we have time?'"

Sergio cracked a smile, but as he realized the point of the humor, he turned serious. "That's not funny, it's fucking blasphemous."

With Andrew still laughing away and trying to climb off the pavement, Sergio turned to leave. Obviously recalling why he had sought us out in the first place, he turned back and handed the bakery box to me.

"Here's some cheese ravioli from Arthur Avenue. They're for Keri, so give them to the drunk."

And then he walked away.

I made an independent decision during the ride back to the city and dropped off Andrew at home. We were both supposed to meet the agents for debriefing at the law firm, but Andrew was in no shape to be interviewed.

After parking the car, as I walked toward the entrance to the office building, I glanced at my watch, realizing it was already after midnight. Tired and weary as I was, I was relieved to see two dark shapes huddled to the left of the revolving doors in the shadows. As I approached, Karst walked toward me, smiled, and announced, "Great work tonight."

Passing through security, the three of us eventually settled into my office. Although spent of all energy, I happily recounted in detail everything I could remember. Karst pulled out a yellow pad and started jotting notes and peppering me with questions as the night's events were reviewed. He seemed particularly pleased and interested at the information gathered on the DePalmas and Mikey Scars, whom Karst revealed was really named Michael DiLeonardo, a very high-level Gambino captain.

As the jovial mood at the evening's success started running out of steam, Karst leaned back and said, "There's bad news too."

My heart skipped a beat, worried to distraction about some unforeseen calamity that had reared its ugly head. After a pregnant pause, Karst continued, "The phone recorder malfunctioned and we got nothing on tape. We're going to need to pull off a repeat performance on these subjects."

Startled, I looked to Ready, only to find the agent looking down, avoiding my stare. "But didn't you hear everything off the transmitter? Isn't that good enough?"

"We heard almost everything, but if it's not on tape, the information can't be used in court, so it doesn't count."

Standing in reflexive reaction, I was confused. "But how can we possibly go over it all again without arousing suspicion? He'll know something's up. I'm telling you, he'll know."

Karst motioned for me to sit down. "Listen to me. We had technical problems tonight, but you showed me something. You're a natural; your questions, your tone, your reactions were all perfect. You're a born operative and you'll have no problem getting Sergio to repeat his statements; in fact, he'll love it. We'll show you how to do it. I've got some ideas. Just trust us."

On the way out, Karst put his hand on my back. "Maybe that 'puke' code wasn't the best idea I ever had."

"By the way," Ready added, "I thought the Titanic joke was pretty funny."

CHAPTER TWENTY-FOUR
Sergio's Encore Performance

JANUARY 1997

The encore performance of Mike Sergio was underway. Instead of a bustling restaurant filled with Westchester's elite, Sergio selected a tiny Italian bistro in the northern Bronx. Red-and-white checkered cloths covered each table and a middle-aged obese waiter, with a white apron wrapped around his ample midsection, stood available to serve. Except for a small table near the front door inhabited by two burly men in cheap suits, we were alone.

The mood of the group was quiet and reserved. Claiming to have fierce heartburn, Sergio declined any alcoholic refreshment. While his abstinence had no effect on Pearlstein's intake of martinis, I was feeling more than a little edgy; something in Sergio's eyes warned me to be wary.

Unlike the first dinner, the conversation on this night was neither flowing nor expansive. My pre-scripted questions were not having their desired effect. When I asked Sergio about the DePalmas, or Junior Gotti, or Willie Marshall, the subject was brushed off.

Also unlike the first encounter, Sergio seemed tired and worn, as if he had aged ten years in a matter of days. I tried retreating through a conversational back door, but even talk of Scores and family failed to engage him. This encounter was going to be a complete failure, even if the damn recorder actually did its job.

As the virtual silence continued into a dessert of cheesecake and espresso, I decided to give the operation one more chance. "Let me ask you something, Sergio, if there's a problem at Scores, do I call you or Willie Marshall?"

Sergio picked the napkin off his lap and threw it into the middle of the table. He shook his head as if some wildly offensive odor had just wafted though. Standing up, he turned his head and nodded to the two men sitting at the front table. They stood and slowly ambled toward our table.

Sergio took a gun out of his pocket and placed it on the table. As he turned back to me, Andrew yelled out, "I think I'm gonna puke!"

"Shut the fuck up, you moron," Sergio screamed. He turned to me. "Let me ask you something. We've been friends for what? Ten years. In all that time, you don't give two shits about the 'family.' You never wanna know nothing; you never want to talk shop. Now last week, all of a sudden, you can't get enough information out of me. Tori Locascio? You don't even know him. Junior Gotti? The DePalmas? You always wanted to stay away from that side of life; that's my job. Now you want to talk about everything. I'm asking myself, why? Why, Michael? Why are we suddenly talking 'mafia' together?"

I tried to be strong, but I just wanted the FBI agents to understand the gravity of what was happening. "What could I possibly want from you, Mike? What would make you put a gun on the table and bring two tough guys to scare us?"

"Then you have no idea?" Sergio sneered.

As Sergio was reaching toward his pistol, the two thugs finally arrived at the table, each taking up a position behind one of us.

Karst and Ready sat in a dark-colored sedan outside the restaurant. Ready was listening to the transmissions from the beeper with a growing sense of panic. When he heard Andrew vocalize the emergency code, his initial reaction was a guarded, "Here we go again," but now I was mentioning guns and hit men. He pulled off the headphones and looked at Karst.

"We've got big trouble; Sergio knows what's going on. We have to deploy now or the boys are dead."

Both men pulled their guns and readied them for firing. Already wearing his armored vest, Ready reached for the handle and pushed the door open. As he stepped out of the car, a single bullet penetrated his forehead and he fell lifeless to the curb.

Before Karst could maneuver his exit, three bullets fired through the car's driver's side window. He slumped back in his seat.

Three masked men ran to the car. Karst was picked up and thrown into the passenger seat, Ready was tossed into the backseat, and the door abruptly slammed. One of the men jumped behind the wheel and the car sped away, leaving the neighborhood quiet and tranquil—as if nothing at all had happened.

The slaughter of the FBI agents took less than a minute.

Hearing the sharp retorts of gunfire outside, Pearlstein and I jumped from raging fear. Suddenly, the monster behind Pearlstein lifted him from his chair and quickly conducted a body search. Finding nothing, he ripped Andrew's beeper from his belt and removed the cover. Looking at Sergio, he said, "Body's clean, beeper's a beeper."

Sergio nodded to the other soldier, who reached down and lifted me. After the pat down, he looked at the beeper. "I can't tell; it could be funny."

"Check the phone."

The soldier picked up the phone and ripped it apart. He lifted out a round silver chip and held it up to Sergio. "It's a companion to a recorder; he's wired."

Pearlstein broke away from the large hands holding him. "I don't know anything about this, Mike. I swear to God. If he's wired he's doing it on his own. He's a traitor to me too."

Sergio grinned, raised his gun, and pumped two bullets into Pearlstein. Turning to me, gun still raised, he shook his head.

I screamed.

I opened my eyes, but couldn't see. I was lying on the floor, still crying out, my hands pathetically trying to protect my face from oncoming destruction. Moments later, shaking, I could make out the outlines of my bedroom furniture: first the bed, then the cabinetry.

It had been a dream, a stupid nightmare.

Heart still racing, I pulled myself off the floor and onto a high-backed Egyptian-style chair next to the bed. Stunned as to the vivid and terrifying nature of the dream, especially because I almost never remember dreams, I just couldn't get hold of my runaway emotions. Cradling myself and rocking, I felt like crying.

I also felt abnormally hot and sticky and, gathering my composure, I walked out onto the bedroom balcony. The cold, fierce winds raging far above the sidewalk were overwhelming, but my body heat, which had been alarming, quickly dissipated. Standing in the cold and bracing myself against the height of the confined space, I suddenly found it hard to breathe. Turning away from the wind did not improve my condition. "I'm just hyperventilating," I said out loud with the relief of understanding the problem.

With my chest on fire, I walked off the balcony, through the bedroom, and into the living room. A glance at the clock told me it was slightly after 4 AM. I plopped into my favorite chair and cupped my hands over my open mouth, breathing in and out. After about thirty seconds and fifteen breaths, my respiration normalized.

I wanted to get something to drink but, before I could act on the impulse, I fell asleep in the chair, sleeping the rest of the night in glorious darkness.

Showering and shaving in the morning, I decided not to share the dream with anyone—not Andrew, not the agents. I was still shaken, far more than the silly dream deserved. But deep inside, I knew I had been somehow changed; an unwanted metamorphosis had been unwillingly visited upon me, *A Christmas Carol* style.

The most ridiculous residual effect of the dream was that I found myself furiously angry with Andrew for his cowardly conduct. *How can you be mad at him?* I mocked myself. *Your imagination is responsible, not him. He's done a lot of shitty things, but not this time.*

As I left the condo for the law firm, a nagging dread followed me out the door. Perhaps that dread was the uncomfortable realization, previously buried, that I was playing with fire and, odds were, I was not meant to survive the blaze.

CHAPTER TWENTY-FIVE

Lights, Camera, Action!

JANUARY 1997—THREE PARK AVENUE

The rules for filming in the office were explained in repetitious detail. The government had drawn up a list of potential targets and only individuals on the approved list could be recorded. No one else! In fact, should any non-listed individuals wind up being filmed, even inadvertently, the whole operation would probably be closed down. No explanations, just rules.

We reasoned, in reaction to the stringent limitations, to treat our connected office bathroom as a "lock," like the Panama Canal. In other words, whenever filming, we would ensure our bathroom doors were locked and, in that way, the customary flow of individuals passing between the law firm and Scores via the bathroom "shortcut" would be cut off.

We also created a supplementary verbal code to assist each other. Whenever one of us needed to roll a camera, but others were present, preventing open discussion, the phrase, "Do you want to order cappuccinos?" would be invoked. The desired filming site would be identified by an additional remark. For example, "When the cappuccinos get here, I'll be at Casey's station," meant the camera above my secretary's desk should be activated.

When all was agreed, I asked Pearlstein, "Can't we work the word 'puke' into our codes for old times' sake?"

I was ignored.

Thursdays were "money" days at the executive offices; envelopes containing rubber-banded stacks of five hundred dollars each awaited distribution. Payments were splits from dancers' house fees, tips from the President's Club and Crow's Nest, and other smaller cash flow streams. Appearances by the Sergios, Willie Marshall, and senior club managers on "Money Thursdays" were ritual. It was well known that Thursday was the best day to show up at the office for any sort of financial accommodation; everybody was happy that day.

As a result, that was the prime day for filming. Because both Marshall and the Sergios developed patterns of picking up their weekly spoils directly from one of the bookkeepers, the system had to be changed to allow the cameras to capture the actual delivery and counting of extorted funds. To accomplish this, the bookkeepers were instructed to deliver the "Thursday" envelopes to Andrew or me for pickup. It would raise eyebrows, but it was necessary.

As luck would have it, on the first Thursday of filming, I was alone in the office at the precise moment Mike Sergio arrived for his weekly cash envelopes. Alerted to his presence by the receptionist, I knew Sergio's first stop would be bookkeeping, to be quickly followed by a detour to my office. I had a short window of time to do the necessary.

I sprinted to my office, opened the door to my secretary's station, and instructed Casey not to allow interruptions. I closed the door, locking it as it swung shut, and zipped into the connecting bathroom to lock the door leading to Pearlstein's side. Secure in the office, but beginning to gasp for air, I ran to my desk, pushed the chair to one side, and opened the bottom storage cabinet. Assuming a prone position with some struggle, I reached up into the cabinet and activated the color-coded switch for my office.

Just as I began restoring the desk chair to its proper place, a pounding on the bathroom door from the Pearlstein side interrupted my concentration. "Michael, it's Mike, let me in," came the unmistakable voice of Sergio. Kicking the cabinet doors closed and about to confirm I would be right there, I thankfully caught myself. Rushing with light steps into the bathroom, I called back, "I'll be right with you, Mike."

Looking in the mirror, I saw myself as a sweaty mess. Wiping my face and hair down with a towel, and after splashing on water and cologne, I reached for the door to the Pearlstein side. Catching myself once again, in what would develop into an important final step, I reached back and flushed the toilet. *Nice touch*, I congratulated myself.

Allowing a reasonable post-flush period to pass, I breathed deeply, sprayed some air freshener, and casually strolled into Pearlstein's lair. Finding Sergio seated in a red leather chair facing the desk, I sat down next to him in the companion chair.

"What's the deal with the weekly envelopes? The kid says he doesn't have them. Is this another Pearlstein game, because . . ."

"It's not a problem, Mike," I interrupted. "We've had some mix-ups lately, wrong person getting the wrong envelope. So from now on, either Andrew or I will take responsibility. Come into my office and we'll take care of things."

As we trooped together through the bathroom into my office, Sergio limping more pronouncedly than usual, he called back to me, "I wanted to tell you I really enjoyed our dinner. I even repeated your joke to a few guys."

"I thought it was great fun; we never do social things."

"You know what I think, I think we should try to get together one night every week. That way we can keep on top of things."

"You know, we were just saying the same thing. Once a week from now on it shall be. Now, how many envelopes do you get?"

Sergio went on to identify the various funds he was due from the mafia's activities at the club. In response to each named category, I pulled an envelope out of my desk drawer and handed it over. With the cameras spinning away, Mike accepted each envelope, checked the amount scribbled on the outside, counted the funds, and placed the cash in his jacket pocket.

Sergio stayed a while, hoping Andrew would show. He mentioned he needed to talk to him about a problem with Steve and the coatroom. But as Andrew's absence continued, Mike suddenly got up, noting he had to be on his way.

When he was gone, I retraced the security steps, turned off the camera, and opened all the doors, all the time thinking, *Bingo! That covers extortion, money laundering, tax evasion, and the coatroom.*

I was dictating a first draft of a brief to Casey when Andrew's voice rang through on the intercom speaker. "Michael, Willie Marshall is on his way up, do you want to order cappuccinos?"

"OK, where will you be when they arrive?"

"I'm alone, Michael; I just thought it would be nice to order cappuccinos."

Looking to Casey's confused reaction, I answered, "I'm not alone, hold on a second. Case, you want a cappuccino?"

When she signaled her agreement, I asked her to order up five and allow me some privacy. "Lock my door and keep everyone out," I called after her.

"I've got it covered in here, Andrew," I called to the intercom as soon as his door was secure. "Make sure you stay alone except for Willie." I then proceeded to lock the bathroom door and reenact the required calisthenics.

I could hear through the door that Willie had arrived. Recognizing a third voice as I opened the door, I stopped short, fearing a violation of the "prime directive." But as I strolled into Andrew's office, I recognized the unexpected person as one of Willie's usual confederates, "Fat Pete," another target on the approved list.

Andrew had already handed the weekly envelopes to Willie, who was counting the cash atop Andrew's desk. *A perfect camera view,* I thought.

Seven o'clock that evening. I found myself sitting alone in Pearlstein's office. After Marshall's departure, I'd called Karst, advising about the day's tapings. The agent seemed very excited. "Michael, I don't want to leave those tapes in the closet overnight. One of you will need to hang around until everyone is gone, and we'll make a collection."

The "one of you" turned out to be me, Pearlstein claiming an urgent rendezvous with Keri and her friends. Agent Paul Roman finally called to say he was entering the building and wanted to be met at the elevators. I met him, and together we traversed a route leading back to my secretary's closet. Opening the closet, he confirmed two of the units had recorded, retrieved the appropriate tapes, and replaced the removed tapes with fresh ones.

With little or no conversation exchanged, Roman quickly departed, reminding me to wait at least ten minutes before heading out.

Sitting behind my desk, tired and a little sore from the day's bending and rolling, I realized I'd been too busy and frantic to experience any nervousness during the filming. Concluding it was a blessing, I picked up the phone, reached Sergio, and made dinner plans for the following week.

CHAPTER TWENTY-SIX
Sergio's Real Encore Performance

My day's work had been unproductive, nervous distraction winning out over genuine attempts at concentrated effort. A pre-briefing with Karst, Ready, and Pearlstein was scheduled for six at my condo to strategize the recapture of Sergio's confession—words lost to posterity by the malfunctioning "high-tech" recorder. Tonight was the night to get it right, to set matters back on course.

As I walked through my lobby, the concierge pointed my attention to two men seated on plush leather chairs in the visitors' waiting section. Nodding and waving off the warning, I approached the men, calling out to them as I neared. Both agents rose, picked up their ample carry bags, and followed me to the elevators.

Arriving at my floor, our small caravan made a series of quick left turns off the elevator and followed the hallway to my unit. In what had become routine, the agents walked into the living room, while I diverted to the kitchen to retrieve bottles of Snapple.

Sitting around the dining room table, I looked at my guests, inwardly musing how quickly these men had transformed in my mind from evil government ogres to allies, even perhaps friends. Or was that just a deluded false reality? "So who got the call from Andrew that he's going to be late?"

The agents shot stares at each other sheepishly, revealing to my unhappy surprise that something unexpected was brewing.

175

Karst cleared his throat, a clear additional signal he was uncomfortable. "We excused Andrew from the pre-briefing tonight because there's an issue we three need to discuss. You know, tonight's gonna be different from last week; we're going with a body wire, 'F-Birds' we call them, 'FBI recording devices,' and not the telephone recorder. Well, Andrew feels it's too dangerous for him to wear the wire, he's not comfortable. He says the mafia guys are always very physical with him and he's more vulnerable to discovery."

I didn't immediately react. Instead, I picked myself up and walked over to the row of continuous windows framing the room. Suppressing a growing inner rage, I turned back.

"To put it bluntly," Karst continued, "Andrew tells us the mafia guys are more comfortable with him because of rumors about the 'gay' thing with you. He feels they shy away from you, from roughhousing, because of their macho self-images."

I was finally crossing into borderline anger. Thinking about it, I shook my head defiantly. "You know what? All the mafia guys despise Andrew; have you forgotten they were planning to kill him? In all the years Andrew's been at Scores, I've never seen any of them touch him, not even once. They'd surely slit his throat rather than feel him up. And think about what you're saying, because I'm gay, or so they suspect, the guys avoid me, but they feel perfectly comfortable playing around in Andrew's crotch. This is all so stupid, I'm frankly lost for a response."

Once I got going, I found I couldn't stop. "You know, I've really made every effort to live up to my part of our bargain. I've showed up to every meeting, pre-briefings and debriefings. I'm the one who met you guys for the camera reinstallation, I'm the one who works the crazy switches in the wall unit, and I'm the one who wore the beeper transmitter and carried the recorder phone the first time around. So be it—I don't really care if Andrew misses every meeting and leaves all the administrative pain-in-the-ass work to me. But now he wants to avoid the really serious risks as well? And worse, you two seem to be buying into his crap. Do you really believe this is all about jostling around with mafia guys, or about his inability to control his girlfriend? Is the wool so far over your eyes he now has you doing his dirty work? Tell me, is there some justification for me to be the only one to wear a wire?"

Karst walked over to me. "You really want to know what I think? I think Andrew is lazy and scared to death. I think he lacks the courage and guts to strap on the F-Bird and walk into a room with mobsters. So the question on the table right now, and the reason we needed to talk to you alone, is can this investigation proceed on your back alone or not?"

I was surprised at Karst's directness and honesty; it made me feel moderately appeased. Since the experience of the dream, I'd been living on the edge, in a world of dread laced with fear. And now I was being asked to walk with my fears alone, Andrew stealing even the comfort of sharing the danger. I began feeling myself inching toward a breaking point; why would anyone think I was strong enough to go it all alone?

"Jack, I already have serious personal doubts I can continue with this undercover stuff. Don't you think I'm scared out of my wits too?"

"You'd better be plenty scared! Fear is important and useful; without it, you'd become careless. And I've told you already, you're a natural at this kind of stuff; it shows. Andrew's not made for undercover work; he got himself drunk the last time as an escape from his terror. Our targets trust and respect you; you have history with them. They'd never confide in Andrew the way they confide in you. Think about it, you know I'm right. You're the only one in a position to make this investigation work, without you we might as well pack it in right now."

Lifting my hands, I rubbed my fingers up and down the bridge of my nose. Before I could respond, Karst jumped back in. "I'll tell you something else, between us. I've sat through all the proffers so far, yours and Andrew's, and there's a difference between you two—you have a conscience. You understand you've received a second chance from the government; you've been invited to become a 'patriot.' When all this over, your sins are being forgiven, your wrongs outweighed by your courage and contributions. Instead of going to jail for a long time, you're getting your life back. Not in New York, of course, but you'll be on top again in some different place."

Karst was doing his job, motivating me to perform for the government's benefit. How many times had I heard motivational speakers expound on these techniques? Yet Karst was hitting all the right chords, striking all the notes I wanted to hear, needed to hear. Dammit, I did want to make things right, to be forgiven and redeemed for the Florida debacle. And if risking my life was the price demanded, if I could truly make amends by risking my very existence, I'd do it.

I stared back. "I'm committed to the investigation, you know that. But I'm scared and worried. Scared I'll be killed, worried that after all of this Carol

Sipperly won't keep her word. Can you imagine how stupid and betrayed I'll feel if I keep up my end and then the Florida case never comes here and I wind up with a long stretch in prison based on my own proffered words?"

"I can't guarantee what a court will do," Karst shot back, "but I can share my experience. One, the Southern District always keeps its promises to cooperators; don't give that issue a second thought. Two, if this investigation reaches as far into the mafia as I believe it can, I can't see any federal judge anywhere in the country giving you any time in jail at all. Even if things never get that far, you're never going to be in jail for more than a year. No way. And you'll be in a country club, so get visions of Attica or Alcatraz out of your mind."

I quickly digested Karst's words. I could manage, worst-case scenario, enduring a year in a country-club jail. But I had other concerns gnawing at my insides: What about my family and friends? What about my law license? What about Scores? But those were questions, I knew, for another day in another forum.

Karst put his hand on my shoulder. "Just remember, when you feel the taste of fear rising, remind yourself you're a patriot, a man who had the courage to do what most would find unthinkable. You're a patriot taking the ultimate risk for the ultimate reward. Whatever you did before, whatever the wrongs, they are overwhelmed by what you're doing now. Think about all the people you're saving from extortion, beatings, and even murder; think about the grief you're saving their families. What's that worth? This is a no-lose proposition: for you, for the government, for the country."

After the pre-briefing, I picked up Andrew and together we drove to Westchester County. Ready had given us directions to a motel about five miles from the restaurant, and we would all meet up before proceeding to dinner with Mike Sergio.

For better or worse, I decided not to verbally spar with Andrew over the F-Bird issue. I wanted to avoid any unproductive distractions, keeping my mind focused on the night's assignment. If it were possible, Andrew seemed even more moody and distracted than the first time around, showing absolutely no desire for small talk anyway.

The motel was situated in a rural, wooded track off the main upstate highway. It was easily located and, searching for the specified room, we discovered the door ajar on the second floor of a garden-apartment-like complex. The first order of business was the attachment of the wire to my torso. "Drop your pants," Karst directed with the slightest hint of a smile.

"Can I trust you won't be doing anything 'funny' down there?"

When Karst pulled out a roll of silver duct tape, I stepped back and looked at him as if he were deluded. "What are you planning to do with duct tape? Tie me up?"

"I'm about to tape the F-Bird to your leg, what else?"

"That's what you're gonna use to secure the wire? Sticky, crappy, greasy duct tape? Ever hear of surgical tape? Tell me, have you ever done this before? Because this is *not* how they do it in the movies!"

Karst proceeded in a semi-huff to affix the F-Bird, about the size of a bar of soap, to the inseam line of my thigh, inches below my crotch. Two minia-ture microphones, attached to thin black wires, ran from the device and were taped to my chest at a level just below my nipples.

"Wait, Jack," I interrupted the procedure. "Can we leave the microphones down by my waist for now? Then when I feel safe, I'll visit the bathroom and raise them."

Karst shook his head. "I don't like that idea. Why complicate an already-complicated night?"

"Because I'm asking, because I'd feel better."

Karst relented and the microphones were lowered. He also cautioned that the F-Bird might start to feel warm after a few hours, adding it was nothing to worry about.

When he finished, I took a quick walk around the room. "The damn duct tape is pulling on my leg hairs."

"Just shave those areas next time," was the only solace offered by the less-than-sympathetic agent. Karst next turned on the recorder and identified himself to my crotch.

When the arming of the F-Bird was complete, and as I re-dressed, Jack put his finger to his lips and scribbled a note on a small white pad. The note read, "No more talking until you arrive at the restaurant."

I grabbed the pad from Karst and wrote back, "You're the first person to ever formally introduce himself to my dick. Are we engaged?"

Karst read the note, shook his head, crumpled it, and tossed it in the gar-bage without comment. In a final act, he reached into his carry bag, removed a beeper-transmitter, and clipped it to my belt.

As we parted company, Karst exaggeratedly mouthed the words "Good luck."

After a short trip in silence, we parked and entered the restaurant. Returning to the same locale carried an aura of unreality, a discomforting déjà vu: same well-dressed and sophisticated crowd, same droning din, same disconcerting dead animal heads peering down sadly from the walls.

Locating Sergio seated on the same stool at the bar, handshakes and warm greetings were exchanged. Mike gently put his arm around my neck and walked me over to a quiet corner of the room with Pearlstein trailing far behind. *Good thing Andrew isn't wired, look at all that dangerous jostling going on between him and Sergio,* was my bitter thought.

"You know," he began, "my boss was really pissed off at me for having dinner with you last week. He's worried the government's gonna 'flip' you two because of that Florida thing hanging over your heads."

"What do you mean, 'flip'?" I played dumb.

"Turn you into witnesses. I told him he was talking crazy, that we'd been friends for years. In the end I had to make a compromise. I said I would search you for a wire tonight. You mind?"

Having now joined us, at the mention of a search, Andrew went wide-eyed. He said, "Don't they understand the Florida case is going nowhere and will probably just go away for lack of evidence?"

Sergio just shrugged his shoulders.

"Mike, what am I supposed to say? I'm hurt and surprised, but what the hell, if it gets you out of a bind, let's do it. On the other hand, we could agree not to talk about anything sensitive."

"I still gotta keep my promise to my boss, it's a matter of honor. I want to prove you're loyal." He turned to Andrew and said, "Go get us a table, we're gonna hit the head."

As we entered the restaurant's bathroom, Sergio made a quick tour of the stalls to ensure privacy. Once satisfied, he returned to the entry door and locked it with the small dead bolt.

I was facing an instant decision: stay and fight, or turn and run. I opted for the former and broke the ice. "So, no one ever did this to me before. How's it done?"

"I just have to make sure you're not wearing anything under your shirt."

Feeling the sweat beginning to bead on my back, and experiencing a wave of mild dizziness, I glanced longingly at the room's locked door, eternally grateful I'd moved the microphone wires lower than Karst wanted.

There's still time to get the hell out of here, I reminded myself. *I can run faster than Mikey Hop,* for the first time grateful for the severe limp that brought him his mob moniker.

Instead, I removed my suit jacket and hung it on a stall knob. I whipped off my tie without breaking the knot, and unbuttoned my shirt. With my chest now revealed, I turned around in front of Sergio, showing him there was nothing hidden anywhere on my upper torso.

"That's enough," Sergio said with a tone of embarrassment. "I'm sorry, I just had to follow orders. But now I can report back I was right about you."

Sensing Sergio's gross discomfort, I recklessly decided it would be to my benefit to press the issue a bit further. In what I would later recall as an "act of insanity," I raised my voice in response. "Oh no. If you're going to hurt my feelings and question my loyalty, let's do this thing right." I then proceeded to open my belt, unzip my fly, pinch down the tiny microphones, and pull down my Calvins—just enough to expose my privates.

As I walked toward Sergio, my manhood hanging down in full glory, he covered his eyes with his hands and turned away. "Get dressed, Michael. I feel like I'm getting a lap dance at a gay Scores. I've seen all I need to see, more than I need to see, you're clean."

Praying my pants wouldn't drop far enough to expose the duct tape, or the F-Bird, or the dangling microphones, I carefully raised my slacks and dressed myself slowly.

"I'm really so sorry about this," Sergio apologized, stepping toward the bathroom door. As I followed, I kept wondering whether Andrew had run away. As we reached the exit door, I stopped. "You know what? I really do have to use the bathroom. I'll meet you at the table."

I walked directly into one of the stalls and sat down while Sergio returned to the dining room. Here I was, the big brave undercover agent; I was shaking like a leaf. The wood-paneled walls around me were spinning and I was concerned I might pass out. Reaching down and removing the beeper-transmitter from my belt, I softly spoke. "Everything's OK." Feeling worse, I added, "What you're about to hear is not code, it's just an amusing irony."

I dropped to my knees in front of the toilet and began puking into the blue-colored water.

Cleaned up and feeling surprisingly giddy, I stared at myself in the bathroom mirror. As I thought about what happened, I realized my exhilaration was emanating from a sense I'd broken a barrier, passed into a rim of unanticipated safety. Sergio was never going to dare to search me again, and that was a very comforting thought.

Just as I reached for the bathroom door, I froze in place. Locking the door, I again slipped off my jacket, opened my shirt and trousers, and pulled the microphones up from the F-Bird. To my chagrin, when I tried to tape the microphones back onto my chest, the tape wouldn't hold; the small black nubs kept falling off. Try as I might, I couldn't get them to secure to my skin.

Struggling to find an option, I reached down and pulled off some of the tape holding the F-Bird to my leg. Examining the excess pieces, they seemed sufficiently sticky to do the job. It was with the greatest relief that both microphones held to my chest at their first applications. Satisfied I'd succeeded, I rebuttoned the shirt and put myself together one more time.

Walking through the dining area, I came upon Sergio and Pearlstein enjoying a round of martinis. Spying my own waiting bottle of Italian sparkling water, I announced, "I see we're right back where we left off."

After the meal was ordered and a second round of drinks delivered, Sergio raised his glass and called for a toast. We raised our glasses in return. "Let's drink to Mikey Scars, the man who gave us back Scores," I sang out.

Andrew raised his glass to his lips, but Sergio stood up with a malevolent mask covering his face. "Where the fuck did you hear that name, and how do you know about him and Scores?"

"Are you kidding, Mike? You told us the whole story of Scars and the sit-down last week."

Sergio sat down and cradled his head in his hands. After a few tense moments, he raised his head and started laughing. "Boy, I must have been really drunk last week, I don't remember saying a fucking thing about that. I can never do that much drinking again."

When he finally stopped laughing, he turned serious. "Hey, listen to me, forget that name, forget that story. It could get us all killed."

"You told us that last week too," Andrew chimed in.

"I did?"

"You did," Andrew reaffirmed.

"Then why did you say his name?" Sergio yelled at me.

"I forgot to forget," I answered wearing a robust smile.

The balance of the evening passed as sweetly as a summer breeze. Having passed the search, and realizing Sergio had no recollection of the prior week's conversations, the group covered all the topics lost to the malfunctioning recorder. As Andrew pumped Sergio with an endless array of alcohol, the stories of Steve Kaplan, Willie Marshall, the DePalmas, Tori Locascio, Mikey Scars, Gotti Jr., and the one hundred thousand dollar sit-down extortion spilled from Sergio's lips with expanded detail and priceless admissions.

The only personal annoyance I increasingly encountered was a burning sensation kicking up from the F-Bird. My leg was becoming painful, although I forced myself to ignore the distraction I was forewarned might occur.

With a triumphant feeling of glorious success, the dinner came to a quiet end. We paid the check and traded farewells at the front door.

We'd been warned by the agents to always monitor for the possibility of being followed after leaving the scene of an undercover meeting. According to Karst, "The departure is always dangerous and the time most cooperators let down their guard. It's also the moment the mafia will most likely strike if they suspect you've been compromised. So always check to ensure you're never being followed after a taping."

This admonition was on my mind as we pulled out of the restaurant's parking lot. It would be an easy matter to monitor any vehicles trailing us because traffic was light and the area was borderline rustic. It was several blocks away when I noticed a car behind us, keeping a steady distance. I mentioned the vehicle to Andrew, who suggested making a few turns to judge whether it was in fact a "tail."

I turned the car left, then right, and then left again. At each turn, the car behind mirrored our movements. Sharp panic ruled the moment and we started discussing the best methods of ensuring escape. I started furiously punching keypad buttons on the dashboard phone to reach Jack and Bill. "Maybe they're close enough to help."

As the phone kept ringing without response through the car's speaker, I made another turn in a vain hope the tail would just disappear. When the car behind again followed suit, such hopes faded and my agitation mushroomed.

Finally, Jack Karst answered the phone. "Jack," I was half screaming, "where are you? They must be on to us because we've been followed since we left the parking lot. Tell us what to do!"

After a pregnant pause, during which I actually thought I heard laughing, he responded, "That's us behind you."

Disconnecting the call, we looked at each other in open disgust, feeling as ridiculous as two men could feel. We started laughing, and kept laughing as I dropped off Andrew at home. I was on my way to keep the standard debriefing appointment with the FBI; Andrew was going to sleep.

Jack and Bill were waiting for me in front of the building. As I approached, Jack held his finger to his lips, apparently trying to ensure no conversation took place while the F-Bird continued to record. Both agents were smiling like Super Lotto jackpot winners.

After settling into my office, Karst proceeded to turn off the F-Bird, again verbally entering his vital information and the time of day. With the session at an end, Ready blurted out, "We heard almost everything, and it was amazing."

"We couldn't have dared hope for a more productive night and you squeezed every bit of information out of that man," Karst added.

I then retold every part of the night I could remember as the agents took extensive notes. When the bathroom confrontation was reviewed, Karst just dropped his pen, leaned back, and said, "It's just too easy, it's like shooting fish in a barrel for you."

When the F-Bird came off my leg, I simply stared at the red, nasty-looking rectangular welt left behind on my inner thigh. "I can't believe it," I complained, as I gingerly rubbed the wound. "I felt it was burning, but I never dreamed it would be this bad. You think it'll leave a scar?"

"I don't think it's that bad," Karst responded, "but we're doing something wrong. Let me think on it."

The following week, I received a call from the agents advising that they'd been instructed to conduct a proffer-interview with me on the subject of the Florida insurance frauds. Sipperly and Miller needed to know all about the frauds so that negotiations between New York and Florida on the issue of our promised sentencing transfers could finally be initiated. We quickly agreed on a time and place, and although it would be years before I understood most of what had really transpired, I was determined to honestly present everything I knew at the time of the interview.

I'd first learned of National Heritage Life Insurance Company—referred to as "NHL"—in 1990, when a loan broker referred three strangers to me. Facing an extreme deadline, the trio explained they were seeking a short-term, high-interest bank loan of three million dollars, which together with an additional million they'd already raised on their own, met the four-million-dollar purchase price for NHL from its existing ownership. In fact, if they couldn't close the desperately needed loan within a month or so, NHL would be permanently closed by government regulators and the trio's contract to purchase the company voided.

At first, I found the NHL loan difficult to sort out. Although the company's only office was located in Orlando, Florida, it was an insurance company incorporated and licensed by the Commonwealth of Delaware, under the supervision of the Delaware Department of Insurance. So while everyone I knew referred to NHL as "the Florida Company," it was Delaware's final approval that was required for the sale.

Through my banking connections, I was able to arrange timely approval of and commitment for the loan. This was something I'd done many times before through a banker I'd known and worked with for decades. Filled with relief, my clients moved their families to Orlando, committed to home purchases, enrolled their children in new schools, and took up employment at NHL. But, on the day before the scheduled closing, the banker called to tell me that the bank's president had vetoed the loan, declaring it was outside their lending area.

The borrowers angrily turned to me, as if I were somehow responsible for the bank's extraordinary about-face. According to the trio, as a direct result of "my" bank's default, all three men would now be unemployed and bankrupt; their families hopelessly displaced in Florida without assets or hope for the future. They begged me to come up with a solution, and I honestly did feel some measure of responsibility. After all, I'd assured them there would be absolutely no problem with the loan, as approval had been confirmed verbally at a meeting between the bank and the borrowers.

In a night filled with recriminations and tears, the buyers pleaded with me to fly to the closing on the following morning and present the sellers with a "rubber" check from my brand new and woefully inadequate escrow account. They explained that, since NHL had millions of dollars in a corporate account in the same bank branch as my escrow account, a quick transfer from NHL to my account following the closing—before my check could possibly be presented by the sellers to the bank some fifteen hundred miles away—would cover the escrow check and save the sale.

In an act of insanity, I acquiesced—and the plan amazingly succeeded. My check cleared after the NHL transfer, and the sale closed without incident. What I didn't realize at the time was that I was now "in bed" with some truly troubled and unethical folks.

After the men took control of NHL, one of the buyer trio, David Davies, the man who would later become one of the driving forces behind the creation of Scores, in his role of NHL's chief financial officer, began issuing mortgage loans to "friendly" borrowers at inflated values. Here's what that means: NHL would, for example, loan three million dollars on a piece of undeveloped land worth one million dollars. Two million dollars of that loan would be approved for planned future construction on the property. But instead of paying out that two million over time as construction proceeded, as is the norm, Davies paid the two million at closing to the buyer, who funneled the money back to Davies. On paper the loans looked legitimate, but Davies was secretly pulling millions out of NHL.

Davies's intention was to use eight million dollars of excess cash from these loans to purchase another insurance company for merger with NHL. Once this purchase was completed, he would be in control of significantly greater assets, and the fraudulent loans, as well as the initially stolen three million dollars, could then be made "right"—at least in theory.

I regret to say this, but Davies recruited my full participation by promising to buy out a failing restaurant I owned in California, enabling me to pay off all of the restaurant's debt with the purchase proceeds. The restaurant was seriously underwater, and I was on the brink of declaring personal bankruptcy. Davies's offer would save me from the bankruptcy filing and all of the horrific ramifications that would have flowed as a result to me, to my investor-clients, and to my law firm. In return, I agreed to support his loan scheme by assisting in acquiring the properties, closing the loans on NHL's behalf with his recruited borrowers, and defending the loans within the company and with regulators. Unlike the initial three-million-dollar loan fraud, which I enabled out of sympathy and guilt, and without compensation, this second phase of the NHL frauds marked my voluntary passage to the "dark side."

Davies's plan was interrupted, however, when it was discovered he'd concealed a prior European criminal record from the Delaware regulators in his purchase application. He was ousted from NHL by Delaware regulators, and another of the original threesome, Patrick Smythe, took over the reins of the company. But, in the end, Davies departed with the great bulk of the undiscovered excess loan cash in his pocket, and NHL was now secretly in debt for about ten million dollars. I admitted to the agents I'd been aware of these activities and had profited from them—though not at the levels of either Davies or Smythe.

NHL now began successfully selling annuity policies at an aggregate face value of approximately one million dollars a day, and was headed toward a billion dollars in assets under its management. With time, NHL would grow sufficiently to cover *all* the missing funds from earned profits. But NHL's success led to more regulatory scrutiny and, at this point, it became increasingly impossible to hide the ten-million-dollar hole. The company had too many loans in which the loan amount exceeded regulatory maximums for a fledgling venture with insufficient capitalization. NHL was on the brink of being prohibited from selling further annuities in Florida—its largest market—unless the offending loans were reduced or removed from its books immediately.

Lloyd Saltzman now entered the picture. Saltzman and Smythe came up with a complicated plan to rescue NHL. They arranged a credit line for one of Saltzman's companies from an international bank, secured by NHL assets secretly assigned to the bank by Smythe, and Saltzman utilized the credit line to purchase sufficient interests in the offending mortgages to bring the company back into compliance. Smythe also arranged a second loan to a different company of Saltzman's, also secured by NHL assets, and those funds were used to increase NHL's capital base to avoid another regulatory threat of closure. These rescues were in violation of Delaware insurance law and most certainly illegal, because the loans were recorded on NHL's books as investments and not loan security, making the insurance company look far more fiscally sound than it really was. I was fully involved in this fraudulent rescue scheme with Smythe and Saltzman.

This newest fix fell apart when the international bank unexpectedly called the loans and demanded immediate repayment. The hidden asset "hole" now stood at thirty-five million dollars, and the situation seemed hopeless. In desperation, Saltzman introduced us to Sholam Weiss, a purported financial expert who was going to save us all.

The salvation plan as concocted was straightforward: We would spend one hundred sixty-five million dollars of NHL cash to purchase mortgage assets with a face value of two hundred million dollars at government FDIC and RTC auctions. These assets, being sold from recently failed banks taken over by the feds, were available at varying and often significant discounts. The plan was to purchase enough large, first-quality mortgages at a cumulative discount sufficient to cover the new thirty-five-million-dollar hole. These mortgages would next be securitized into a bond that NHL would purchase and place on its books at the face value of the mortgages.

At the time I believed the newest plan had finally solved NHL's financial issues forever, but by the time of the proffer with the agents, I knew everything had somehow gone terribly wrong. The mortgages purchased at auctions turned out to be totally nonperforming, bought at deep, deep discounts, and virtually worthless. Smythe suddenly disappeared, the bond defaulted on its first interest payment to NHL, and Delaware officially closed NHL's doors. Weiss, Smythe, Pound, and other confederates had stolen the bulk of the NHL funds designated for the original purchase; they quietly cherry-picked everything of value out of the bond for their own profit. I would not discover these truths until years in the future.

As events unfolded, it became clear that the conspiracy in Orlando was going to overwhelm me and everyone else involved. Each attempt to save NHL had only compounded the company's problems and our individual culpability. I accepted my role in all of this and I was willing, at the invitation of the United States, to risk my life in an effort to redeem myself and avoid a long prison sentence.

After the proffer, the government reaffirmed that my sentencing for the Florida financial crimes would be transferred from Orlando to New York, to be heard before a judge with experience in mob cases, who would fairly evaluate and appropriately reward my life-threatening undercover risks, as promised.

CHAPTER TWENTY-SEVEN
The Beat Goes On

During the ensuing weeks, Thursdays remained the primary days for covert filming at the offices. The Sergios, Willie Marshall, and various other targeted mafia cohorts were regularly and tediously captured on tape, collecting and counting their weekly spoils. The cameras also bore witness to conversations on issues ranging from bouncers forced upon the club, disagreements over financial responsibility for coatroom repairs, and admissions about assaults and usurious money laundering, to demands for free dinners as signs of "respect" to mafiosos.

At the FBI's prodding, we developed a pattern of confiding frustration to Sergio about Marshall, and to Marshall about Sergio. These "nudges" resulted in valuable insights into the competing mafia interests at Scores. It became evident that "Willie & Co." had grabbed the upper hand of power and the decision was made to use this struggle to our investigative advantage.

On one particular Thursday morning, after collecting his cash tribute from Andrew, Mike Sergio ambled into my office. He took a seat and impatiently waited for me to finish a telephone conversation. When the call disconnected, Sergio immediately spoke his mind. "I need to talk to you privately."

"OK, should I lock the doors?"

"Not in the office, Michael. I'm nervous in here ever since you found those bugs in the ceiling. By the way, are you keeping on top of that situation?"

"We have the offices swept for devices every week," I lied.

"Good, that makes me feel better. But I'd rather talk alone somewhere else. Why don't we go to dinner next week, just the two of us, without your prick of a partner?"

I agreed and promised to call with a proposed night for dinner as soon as my trial calendar finalized. A little apprehensive about an unexpected private meeting, I called after Sergio as he was on his way out. "You've got me curious, is there a new problem?"

"There's a couple of problems, but nothing for you to worry about."

Feeling relief, I decided to be a smart-ass. "Mike, I just wanted to warn you in advance, I may need to search you and I hope you won't be offended. This way we can keep things between us kinky."

Sergio looked back with a frown. "Go fuck yourself."

When the door slammed behind Sergio, I immediately called the FBI about the requested dinner. Unfortunately the agents were unavailable, so I left messages. A couple of hours later, Casey's voice came through the office intercom. "You have John from Peter Ginsberg's office on line twelve."

Recognizing my secretary's words as the code used by the agents to identify themselves, I picked up the receiver to find both Karst and Ready on the line. I went on to describe the morning's exchange with Sergio and the proposal for an unusual one-on-one dinner.

They were delighted, speculating Sergio might have something important to share but wasn't comfortable discussing the matter within Andrew's earshot. Karst mentioned he wouldn't be available the following week, so Bill and Paul would handle the dinner.

We selected a Tuesday night for the encounter. Asked for a restaurant suggestion by Sergio, I proposed Nanni Il Valletto, and he volunteered to call ahead for seven o'clock reservations. Ready agreed to meet me at the condo at half past five for a standard pre-briefing, and he arrived right on time.

"We're going to have to use my right leg tonight because the left one hasn't fully healed from being burned last time. In fact, if we don't get it right tonight, I'll be out of legs!"

Shrugging off my jab, Ready turned to business. Since Sergio would be dictating the evening's conversational agenda, the only pre-briefing advice was to try and pull out as many historical facts from him as possible to document the Gambino's relationship with Scores. "It would really be helpful if you were able to get him to talk about things like the grand a week paid in cash, where it actually goes, and how it gets there. We want to start reaching over Sergio into the bosses."

When we were satisfied we were viewing the night through the same lens, Ready traversed the room to retrieve the bag of electronics. He removed an F-Bird with attached microphones and a large roll of masking tape. I immediately rolled my eyes in disbelief. "Masking tape? Did they cut our budget? Bill, masking tape is even worse than duct tape. It'll never work."

Ready looked mildly embarrassed at the rebuke, his emotions not as easily hidden as Karst's. "It'll work just fine; I couldn't find any of the silver tape."

I stripped off my suit pants without being asked and watched in silent horror as Ready placed the F-Bird on my undamaged thigh, inserting a wad of gauze behind the device as supposed protection for my skin. Next, he went round and round my leg with strips of tape.

When the job was done, and after viewing the final product, which looked as if my leg had been prepared for shipment to Afghanistan, I interrupted Bill before he had an opportunity to affix the mini-microphones to my chest. Asking for the agent's momentary indulgence, I walked over to the couch, retrieved my pants, and put them back on.

Strutting before the wall-length mirror at the entrance to the living room, I did a quick double take and burst out laughing. There was a bulge sitting atop my right thigh that a stranger might reasonably mistake for a severe case of elephantitis. The man-made protuberance was so insanely invasive, my pant leg now rested some four inches above the top of my ankle-length sock.

"I swear to God," I barked, unable to get control of my runaway amusement and terror, "you're going to get me killed; only a blind man could miss this 'tumor.'"

Ready stripped off the tape securing the F-Bird, now himself smiling broadly and shaking his head, but causing such pain to the leg, my eyes welled up with tears. Remembering I was partially to blame for the pain, having forgotten to shave affected areas, I jogged to the bathroom and performed a quickie hair removal with an electric trimmer. Upon my return to the living room, "F-Bird Installation—Part II" commenced.

The second time around resulted in a markedly thinner application of tape. When the F-Bird, microphones, and beeper transmitter were all in place and we agreed they were visually undetectable, I danced around to test the strength of the tape. "I don't know about this," was all I could say.

In the elevator, as I prepared to depart the building, my mind was churning about the excursion ahead. The inventory of my cascading thoughts came to an abrupt halt when we reached the lobby and the doors silently slid open. I heard a distinct, quiet thud and, looking down, there was the F-Bird, wrapped around my ankle, peeking out from under my pants.

Extending my right arm abruptly to block any effort by Ready to exit, and pointing to my leg, I simply reached over and pressed the button to return from whence we came. Not a word was uttered until the cabin doors slid silently shut, then I turned to Bill. "How come James Bond never had these problems with Q?"

"F-Bird Installation—Part III" was a somber episode. We just stared at each other as I lowered my pants yet again. "I feel like a Scores dancer; do you feel like my regular customer?" I joked with a grin, breaking the ice.

Taking a moment to think matters through, Ready looked up and said, "I know this will sound odd, but do you have any Band-Aids?"

Initially confused about the question, the lightbulb above my head finally lit. "By Jove, I think we've got it. Band-Aids should do the trick."

And in fact, they did. As the masking tape wound its way around my leg yet again, Band-Aids were applied to support areas of particular tension and drag. By the time the recorder and microphones were in place, they felt snug and secure, the extra reinforcement holding up nicely.

Satisfied the problem was now solved, and after the adhesive bonds held secure for the elevator "stress test," Ready accompanied me to the building's garage. I drove out of the basement level and headed north, up First Avenue, for dinner with the mob.

Entering the familiar vestibule of Nanni's, I passed into a crowded bar area, and announced myself to the maître d'. Immediately escorted to what I knew to be the restaurant's VIP table, the waiter advised I was the first of the "Sergio party" to arrive, and accepted my order for a Perrier with lime.

Left alone at the corner table, memories came flooding over me. This was the same table where Andrew Cuomo and I had first met John F. Kennedy, Jr. I beamed inwardly, vividly recalling the nation's first son of Camelot, dressed in a T-shirt and jeans, greedily sucking down beers from the bottle.

It became one of those moments of morose and bitter sadness I'd been working to repress. Life as I knew it was coming to an end; all these places and memories to be brazenly wiped from my new life. Since cooperating, I'd refused to even consider the implications of my upcoming life as a federally protected witness, choosing instead to focus only on the reality of my daily dangers and the very real possibility I would never survive to reach the WIT-SEC stage of rebirthed existence.

Tears filled my eyes as I momentarily permitted a host of passing regrets to swim through my psyche. I would have made radically different decisions if I could go back and make course corrections; I would not have chosen the same turns in life's road. I was going to desperately miss my life and the people who gave me reason to live. And in a moment of rare introspection, I decided it really might not be too bad to die. After all, I'd accomplished so very much in my years, succeeded at so many things, dearly loved so many people. Perhaps my last chapters would be of such painful disappointment, it would be better not to live them, to permit things to end on a high note. These weren't suicidal fantasies; they were, rather, a simple and honest evaluation that my best days, the days worth living, might have already come and gone.

As I wondered if Harold's New York Deli pastrami was available in the afterlife, my attention was drawn to a limping man bounding down the aisle. Sergio had arrived.

The meal swelled my mood to a better place; the conversation was, unfortunately, not as pleasant. The dinner had been apparently called for Sergio to express his rabid, growing hatred for Andrew, and to warn of the rapidly deteriorating relationship between Andrew and Steve. Sergio repeatedly expressed his fear that his son was going to kill Andrew if the nonsense between them didn't soon abate. "I tell you right now," he whispered in angry tones, "Steve'll crack Andrew's skull with a baseball bat and put him in his trunk."

Sergio wanted me to use my influence with Andrew to put an end to the squabbling. "Let each of them live up to their obligations. No one says they have to be friends."

I completely agreed, but expressed my honest sense of frustration at having little influence over my partner in such matters. I did agree to try my best to smooth things over, and the gesture seemed to satisfy Sergio for the moment.

At the close of dinner, Sergio politely ignored the check and I picked it up. He suggested sharing drinks on Charles Street at a small Italian restaurant owned by one of my friends. Knowing I would feel safe there, I quickly agreed.

Sergio had imbibed several rounds of cocktails and wine during dinner and his conduct was perfect for my purposes, knowing alcohol loosened his lips. Leaving Sergio's car uptown for later retrieval, and driving mine, it took little prodding to get my guest off and running on the history of Scores and the Gambinos. During the ride, he chatted happily about securing the coatroom operations for Steve; how he had been honored at the responsibility of bringing the early weekly cash to John Gotti, Sr.'s house in Queens; how Steve now arranged for delivery of the weekly cash to Junior's home; how difficult the mafia captain on Scores' First Avenue corner had been about the valet parking; and how unfortunate the whole Kaplan-Gold Club mess had turned out for him personally. For the very first time, Sergio openly admitted the DePalmas and Marshall were eroding the Sergio power base at Scores.

Once Sergio began his remonstrations, it was as if the FBI had written the script; he was unknowingly covering every area of their interest. I was acutely aware I was capturing valuable admissions, but as was sometimes my wont lately, my heart was filled with an irreconcilable mixture of triumph and guilt. I was responsible for and bearing witness to the ruination of the man sitting next to me, and while there was no doubt that ruination was richly deserved, it still saddened me. How can you still love and care about someone who has totally compromised your life and business as a matter of greed?

We parked on Charles Street off Seventh Avenue, and strolled the few remaining steps to the restaurant. Securing a small table in the rear of the establishment, over a bottle of red wine Sergio finally revealed the true reason for our evening. "Michael, I'm worried and I really need your advice. You know the name Greg DePalma, the captain in Westchester. Well, that man has the biggest mouth in the mafia. Even though he knows his phones are bugged, he can't stop himself from talking. His mouth has put away more guys than the feds, and that includes himself. But he can't change.

"Anyway, after those murders at Scores, I got called up to DePalma's house with Willie Marshall. He tells us the family's honor has been tarnished, that murders can't be tolerated in 'protected clubs,' and he orders Willie and Steve to find the Albanian brothers who committed the murders and whack them."

The sudden change in seriousness captured my complete attention. Sergio had just possibly and unexpectedly opened the way to a full-blown murder conspiracy. "What happened next?" was my reflexive response.

"I said, 'Why don't you send your own son to murder them. I'm not ordering my son to kill anybody, I'd rather do it myself.'"

"And what did DePalma say to that?"

"He said it was up to me and Willie, that he didn't care who pulled the fucking trigger, as long as it got pulled."

Sergio poured himself another glass of wine and swallowed deeply. "Now here's the rub, what's worrying me. I have it on good information DePalma's house was bugged on the night of that little talk and, if that's the case, my words were recorded. And knowing Greg, he probably got on his bugged phone and bragged about it all night. So what I wanna know is this: since we never found the Albanians, and never tried to actually kill them, could I get in trouble just for the conversation?"

I had no meaningful experience in criminal law, but reaching back to law school memories, my instincts pushed me in a definite direction. "Mike, this is off the top of my head. Talking wasn't a crime last time I read the Constitution, not unless you take what they call 'affirmative acts' in furtherance of a conspiracy. So the real question is: Did you or Steve or anyone working with you take any actions to kill these brothers? The answer to that question answers your question."

Sergio rubbed his hands together nervously, and his eyes darted to points unknown on the ceiling. "I just don't know. I don't really understand this 'affirmative act' shit. I don't fucking know if the conversation was even recorded. Maybe I'm worrying about nothing, maybe I'm a dead man." He was slowly working himself up into a state of nervous anger.

"It sounds to me," I calmly cut in, "as if you never acted in furtherance of the conspiracy, or on the orders of DePalma. But let's do this, I'll go do some legal research on 'affirmative acts,' and you sit down with Steve and find out exactly what he or Willie or their friends did about the brothers, if anything. Then we'll get together and compare notes, figure out where things stand."

And so it was agreed. Each man had his homework assignment, and the issue was tabled for further discussion to another day.

The FBI debriefing began about 2 AM at the deserted law firm. Ready was beyond elated at the content of the night's conversations overheard through the beeper transmitter. He took copious notes as I recounted all I could remember, and Roman exchanged the recorded tapes in the closet for blank ones.

Sergio had unexpectedly led the investigation into new and fertile ground that appeared to reach to the highest tiers of power within the Gambino family. Without saying it out loud, each of us knew we were on to something potentially enormous. It's just that we were too tired and spent to articulate our hopefulness.

As we prepared to call it a night, Ready turned to me. "I have to go home with you. Jack wants a pair of your underwear."

I was slowly trying to formulate an appropriate response to Ready's bizarre request when the agent held up his hand. "Not a word. I'm too tired for one of your smart-ass comebacks."

Once we got back to my apartment, we found ourselves in the master bedroom, together going through my closet containing my boxer briefs in assorted colors. As I selected a black pair, there seemed to be some subtle impatience in Ready's body language. "Just one more second, Bill, I'm trying to find a pair without shit stains."

Ready looked up and shook his head in obvious defeat. "I knew you couldn't resist. You can't control that mouth of yours."

The following morning, Andrew and I took a quick moment to confer in our stairwell hideout. I shared the events of the evening in detail and we agreed there was substantial potential in the new murder conspiracy. Not for lack of diligence, I had no success in reaching Karst or Ready or Roman to discuss their reactions.

I was relieved the next morning when Casey announced John from Peter Ginsberg's office was on the line. When I picked up, it was an exuberant Jack Karst with a cornucopia of developing news. According to Jack, the evening with Sergio earned a "five-star" rating. The agents had in fact spent the entire prior day meeting with the prosecutors reviewing the F-Bird recording and exploring certain legal issues raised by the conversations.

"We were initially concerned that your status as an attorney, and the fact Sergio was seeking legal advice from you, might raise certain sticky privilege problems down the road."

I was caught off guard; I hadn't given any thought to issues of attorney-client privilege. But before I could mull it through, Karst explained the prosecutors dismissed the FBI's worries. "Since Sergio hasn't yet been indicted, since he's seeking your assistance in covering up a crime, and since that in itself is an ongoing crime, there's no applicable privilege. We're clear."

With privilege issues put to bed, Karst turned to Sergio's fear of whether his conversation with DePalma about murdering the Albanians had been recorded. "It didn't happen, there were no bugs in the captain's house that day."

Just as my spirits began to sink, with hopes for exploring the conspiracy fading, Karst came back. "We're not worried though. We think we know where Sergio gets his information about investigations. We're going to let that source 'discover' there was a listening device in the house that night and we did capture the exchange. We're hoping we'll light a fire under Sergio and he'll come running back to you for more advice."

"What good will that do if there's no recording?"

"Michael, tell me something, what's the difference between having the original conversation in DePalma's house on tape and having each of the participants confess the facts to you on tape?"

I couldn't think of any significant difference.

"Before we're done," Karst finished up, "we'll have Sergio, his son, Willie, and maybe even DePalma himself, all confirming to you DePalma's orders to find and execute the brothers; and that they conspired together to do it. That, my friend, is a serious federal crime."

At eight on a lazy Saturday morning, my telephone rang out. Startled to attention, I grabbed the receiver.

"It's me, Mike Sergio. I'll pick you up at ten, we'll grab something to eat and talk."

"I can't do it, I have a house full of guests and plans for the afternoon."

"Fuck your guests. Fuck your plans. Be outside at ten."

Unsure what to do, I carried the phone to the balcony and dialed Karst's beeper number. The call had triggered a potential disaster: if I met Sergio without an F-Bird and couldn't record important information, it would be a major missed opportunity; if I stood Sergio up, I'd be in a personal pickle. Knowing I needed to make a quick decision, I added 911 to my message.

Karst thankfully responded almost instantly. When he was apprised of Sergio's call, he hesitated for just a moment. "What the hell," broke the silence, "Bill and I will meet you in your office in an hour."

Despite a lack of sleep and waking with my wits discombobulated by Sergio's call, I was inexplicably calm. When the agents arrived, Karst had a wry smile plastered on his face; something was afoot.

Reaching into his bag, Karst pulled out and handed me my black boxer briefs with a flourish. Apparently having pondered the F-Bird leg burn catastrophes, and the obvious physical limits of duct-tape reliability, Karst had taken the underwear to a tailor and ordered a pouch sewn into the side. The pouch was the exact size necessary to house the F-Bird perfectly, and holes were provided for the mini microphone cables. Karst, it would seem, was not only a seasoned agent, he was a closet inventor as well.

As I opened Sergio's car door and jumped into the passenger seat, the recording device was safely and securely housed in the "Karst pouch," so named for posterity by yours truly. For the first time, my movements with the F-Bird were fluid and uncompromised, my baggy jeans also adding to the undetectibility of the mechanism. Hopefully there'd be no more burns, slippages, or movements.

"Morning," was the only word of greeting I could manage.

Looking straight ahead and obviously disturbed, Sergio pulled out of the driveway, onto the street, and parked on a deserted portion of East Thirty-Eighth Street between First Avenue and the FDR Drive. He reached for something at his side and fluidly placed a black revolver atop the storage unit separating our seats.

At the sight of the gun, I swooned; so much for a calm demeanor—immediate and terrible urgency rippled through my body. *This may be it, the jig may be up,* my mind screamed in the silence of the car.

"Are you afraid of me?" Sergio said, still looking straight ahead.

"I wasn't until now. Do we have a problem?"

"Rats. Rats are the problem. I wish these were the old days, the days when we killed rats and their families. If you don't set the right precedent, the next guy's gonna rat too. Why the hell not? I for one wouldn't hesitate to kill any rat with his family and his friends."

Paying very close attention, it became increasingly clear to me that Sergio's tirade was not being directed at me in particular; it was somehow more diffuse.

"According to my source, there's a rat in DePalma's crew. They had a wire in Greg's house on the night I was worried about, and they got the whole fucking conversation on tape. I'm dead."

Still unsure why there was a gun sitting between us, I suggested we get something to eat and discuss the matter further.

"I made reservations at The Water Club," Sergio returned.

The Water Club is a restaurant on a barge that sits on Manhattan's East River. It's chic, expensive, and frequented by the elite of New York City's trendsetters. Reservations are certainly required for weekend champagne brunch, and Sergio tooled around the FDR Drive to find the restaurant's entrance off the Thirty-Fourth Street ramp.

Seated in a large booth in a quiet dining area, Sergio gave words to his worst fears. "You know that 'affirmative act' shit you were talking about last time, let me ask you this. If DePalma handed me a gun to kill the Albanians and I took it, is that one of those 'acts'?"

"Unless you took the gun and then actually tried to kill the Albanians with it, I'd say no," I lied, and silently calculated, *Strike one.*

"OK, well how about sending Steve and a friend to the police precinct to find out from a friendly cop if they had any leads on the Albanians' whereabouts?"

"Unless the inquiry was regarding a specific plan to do the job, again I'd say no. How would the rat possibly know about that anyway?" And to myself, *Now we know! Strike two.*

"Good, I'm happy to hear you say that. And if we went out looking for them when we heard they were in town?"

"Again, unless the rat was in the car with you, how would anyone know what you had done or what was in your mind? No way that's a provable affirmative act."

Placing my elbow on the table and my head into my palm, I concluded my scorekeeping duties that morning. *Strike three, game over.*

When the agents reviewed the tape, there was uniform agreement Sergio had confessed to participation in a murder conspiracy and had outlined three specific affirmative acts. And subsequent cherries on the cake followed. In an office conversation taped by ceiling cameras, I told Marshall that Sergio was frightened to death about DePalma's order to kill the Albanians, and about his compulsive fear the government taped the conversation. Not only did Willie acknowledge the conversation, and repeat the orders issued, he mocked how frightened and distressed Sergio had been at the meeting and how stupid he considered his fears.

At yet another taped session in the law firm's conference room, Sergio and his son both described and repeated each of the affirmative acts they'd undertaken in furtherance of their intentions to execute the Albanians for the "honor" of their family.

Mike Sergio. Steve Sergio. Willie Marshall. Greg DePalma. They were all undeniable participants in a confessed conspiracy to commit murder.

Like shooting fish in a barrel.

CHAPTER TWENTY-EIGHT
The Investigation Just Keeps on Expanding

1997

The agents called to announce a meeting at a small residential hotel on lower Fifth Avenue. Without revealing their agenda, they directed both Andrew and me to be there at 2 PM for what was described as an "important strategic planning session."

At the appointed hour, we arrived to discover Karst and Ready waiting for us in a shabby junior suite. A pathetic fruit bowl, obviously supplied on a complimentary basis by the hotel, sat atop a small glass coffee table, together with a half-eaten Domino's pizza. The mood of the agents, as they pushed the rest of the pizza toward us, was relaxed and upbeat, immediately eliminating all the nervous energy that had accompanied us during our sojourn downtown.

After some introductory matters, Karst revealed that, while the prosecutors were pleased and satisfied with the investigation's progress so far, there was rapidly growing disappointment in the lack of recorded encounters with mobsters higher up the Gambino food chain.

"We need to do better," Karst opened. "We need to create a reason to get you guys talking directly with Craig DePalma. After all, he's the acting captain, so he's the next logical target."

We talked about pretending to take Scores into the public arena for expansion funding. "We've been considering the idea of doing either a private placement or an Initial Public Offering for years," Andrew opened. "Willie already knows this and we could remind him of our plans, tell him we're ready for an immediate launch, and suggest a meeting with DePalma."

The agents reacted as if they were confused, so Andrew went on to explain that one popular method utilized by successful businesses for raising additional capital from investors is an Initial Public Offering, or "IPO," as it's known on Wall Street. "We could tell Willie we intend to raise between one hundred fifty and two hundred million bucks from the public sector to open new Scores locations in new cities, and to buy existing clubs to be converted into Scores properties."

"Why would Willie react to that information by bringing DePalma to the table? Why would he be needed?" Karst asked.

I smiled wryly. "We can tell Willie we want to acquire ten of the most successful strip clubs around, in Miami, Vegas, and Texas, for example. The Gambinos already have their fingers into strip clubs in all those locations. We could say we're willing to pay up to ten million to the owners of each club we accept into the deal, and give them management contracts to run their own places as new Scores franchises. It's too big a deal for Willie, he'll recognize that, and he'll need someone of DePalma's stature to make appropriate introductions and ensure we avoid conflicts within organized crime elements. Willie will be happy just to be the hero who brings this deal to his boss."

A chorus of approval for the concept erupted throughout the room. "Being able to parcel out ten-million-dollar bricks of cash all over the United States to mafia-affiliated club owners would instantly make Craig DePalma one of the most powerful captains in the country," Ready opined.

"Not only that, he would definitely look to grab 20 percent, or two million dollars, out of every ten-million-dollar payment as a secret finder's fee," I added, "and that's twenty million in his pocket under the table."

"And the best part is," Karst weighed in with a broad excited grin, "as soon as he hears about it from Willie, Craig will want to meet with you right away because he'll know if either Junior Gotti or Mikey Scars gets wind of this, they'll blow him right out of the way in a heartbeat, taking the deal for themselves. As I see it, Craig will want to become your new best friend."

Smiling broadly, I blurted out, "It's all irresistible. And I can prepare papers to make it all look real. We tell DePalma we need to start interviewing owners of 'friendly' strip clubs; need his help in setting things up, bringing 'applicants' to the table; and safely steering us through national mafia waters without stubbing our toes. Greed will trump any possible reservations he might otherwise feel."

The meeting closed with a sense of accomplishment floating in the air, with definite articulated goals. Andrew was instructed to broach the issue with Willie at the first convenient moment, and then we'd all wait for our friends to swallow the enticing bait.

As everyone was focused intently on tempting the Gambinos into participating in the nonexistent Scores IPO on Wall Street, Sergio casually dropped yet another explosion into the investigation's lap. It all began innocently, with an invitation from him to share dinner at Rao's Restaurant, a unique culinary oddity in Manhattan. Situated on a quiet unassuming corner of East 114th Street, the shabby-looking eatery sits on perhaps the only block in East Harlem with a zero percent crime rate; where limousines and chauffeurs comfortably line up to await their dining employers. It's the only restaurant where politicians, police officials, movie stars, private detectives, and high-profile businesspersons mingle happily with mafia captains, soldiers, and associates. At Rao's, all dining is conducted cordially under white flags of truce, and even local street felons are more than aware that criminal trespasses on restaurant customers or their property are acts of suicidal insanity.

As gossip has it, reservations for dinner—which by the way is the only meal served at Rao's—in this mafia-protected playground are made by the year. As a result, one who desires a reservation must make arrangements through the table's annual "owner." There are no menus for the Italian-style home-cooked cuisine, the place is "mom-and-pop" family run, and you simply take your chances on what's being served on any given night.

So, when Sergio called and extended an invitation for Andrew and I to share in, and to pay for, dinner that night at Rao's, we quickly accepted the opportunity. When a call to Karst revealed there was insufficient lead time to set up recorded surveillance, it was agreed we'd attend nonetheless and just "sniff around" for useful information or leads. It was a "sacrifice" we stoically bore in the name of our cooperative endeavors.

Entering the small, dark restaurant, we were pointed to a tiny standing bar to the right and advised our table would be ready shortly. While waiting, we espied Sergio sitting at a table, engaged in earnest conversation with a gruff-looking Italian fellow in his late seventies or early eighties. Sergio noticed us and waved us off.

A short while later, our pleasant reverie was snapped when Sergio walked up and announced our table was ready. As we sat ourselves in a booth, Andrew excused himself to use the restroom.

"You see the guy I was talking to?" Sergio leaned into me conspiratorially.

I nodded in response. "His name is Angelo 'Cheesecake' Urgitano, he's an old-time captain in the Lucchese family. We know each other for thirty years. Follow me, I have a reason for you to meet him."

Assuming nothing more to be lurking than a social interaction, I slid out of the booth and trailed Sergio the few steps back to a small cocktail table in the bar area where Urgitano was now seated alone. After introducing me, Mike motioned for me to sit.

"Angelo, this here is my friend, Michael Blutrich, the lawyer I told you all about." He then switched his gaze back to me. "Michael, tell Angelo the name of your famous law partner."

I positively hated when Sergio did this to me. He knew full well Andrew Cuomo was no longer a member of my firm, but he wanted me to brandish the relationship to impress his confederate. Playing along as always, I quietly answered, "Andrew Cuomo," to Sergio's obvious delight.

"Not only that," Sergio broke in, "Michael's close to the governor himself and was appointed an administrative law judge at one time. Am I right, Michael?"

"You're right," I responded.

Throughout the banter, Urgitano had been coughing in deep spasms, unsuccessfully attempting to regularize his breathing. As the coughing finally quieted, Sergio again seized the floor.

"Michael, listen to me. Angelo's son is in jail on a murder rap. He's a good kid, and he's coming up for parole. Do you think maybe with a little help from your friends we could get him out?"

Talk about being put on the spot, I had been wholly unprepared for this sudden turn of events. Unlike the usual bid for small political favors, I was now being recruited to conspire in a bit of illegal influence peddling, more properly termed "bribery," to spring Urgitano's son out of jail. *Thank God this particular murderer was a "good kid,"* I thought to myself.

In normal times, my political seasoning would have led me to casually defer myself out of the conversation, telling Urgitano I would look into things, but later sharing I had little influence in such matters. I would have fallen back on common political strategy: do absolutely nothing, and hope to take credit if the kid actually managed to somehow get paroled.

But these were no longer normal times and I decided not to come back with normal responses. "Is this his first parole hearing?"

"No, he's had them before and been denied. They treat him like scum because he's got an 'Organized Crime' jacket on his prison file."

"That does make it tougher," I confirmed in Sergio's direction.

"Do you think you can help?" Urgitano asked in a raspy voice before again breaking out in a coughing fit.

Taking a moment's respite and opting for the plunge, I directed my response to Sergio. "It just so happens a very close political ally of mine serves on the parole board." (I actually knew no one on the board.) "And I have in the past been able to favorably influence parole decisions." (I'd never known or represented anyone seeking parole.)

Urgitano leaned in, bringing his face within inches of mine. "I'm not gonna live that long and I want to see my son out of jail. Cash money is no object; I'll pay what's necessary to get your friend behind us. See what you can do, please."

"I gotta be honest, Angelo, and I'm only saying this because of my close relationship with my friend here, it'll cost big bucks to deliver this kind of result. Not a penny for me, mind you, but all for the man on the board taking the risk."

Sergio clapped his hands in patent joy. "This is great. Michael, do us some magic and let me know the price tag."

"I'll check it out and get back to Mike," I said to Angelo, rising from my chair. "No promises, there's lots of factors, and you know that OC jacket is a problem."

I walked back to our table in the dining area while Sergio lingered for a few final words with his friend. Making my way, I was, as usual, filled with a bothersome mixture of elation and guilt. *This is unbelievable*, I thought, *an attempt to bribe a public official—a major felony and something new to feel guilt over. Preying on a dying old man who foolishly loves his son too much to worry about himself.*

I shuddered as I suddenly felt a hand on my shoulder. Sergio squeezed hard and said, "Thanks for that, let me know what you find out. Angelo's in his twilight now, but he was quite a killing machine in his youth, one wicked motherfucker."

That little gem of information made me feel much, much better about what I was going to do.

When I phoned Karst and Ready on the following morning, the agents listened in silence as I recounted the introduction to Urgitano, the approach to orchestrate a bribe, and the offer to pay cash to obtain the son's parole. Their silence continued as I detailed the lies I'd invented: I was a personal friend of a parole board member, I'd influenced parole decisions in the past, and the deal would cost "big bucks."

When the tale was told, Ready broke the ice. "This is unbelievable, you're turning into a 'fatal attraction' for the mob."

"Michael," Karst changed the conversation's direction, "did Sergio identify which family Urgitano is with?"

"He said he was an old-time member of the Lucchese family."

"I'll be damned, they even told you the truth about that."

After going over the facts a second time, Karst instructed me to phone Sergio and tell him the "thing" was in the works. "Tell him you'll have word on what's up in about a week and it looks good. Let's get Urgitano's hopes flying. In the meantime, we'll have to meet with Carol and Marjorie and contact state prosecutors. I'd say we're gonna be running with this one big-time."

Exactly one week later, the agents called me. There was unmistakable excitement in their voices as they brought me up to speed. "You need to call Sergio," Ready opened, "and tell him you have very positive news for Urgitano. Ask for a meeting as soon as possible. We'll tell you all about it when we pre-brief. Meanwhile you're authorized to tell Sergio you've been to Albany and there's a chance you can get the favor done if they act quickly."

I hung up the receiver, dialed Sergio's cell phone, and repeated verbatim what I'd been told to say. Sergio's reaction was nothing less than euphoric. He promised to immediately reach out to Angelo and set up a dinner within "the next couple of days."

True to his word, Sergio called back confirming dinner on the following night at an Italian restaurant in the Bronx. After I wrote down the name and address of the designated establishment, I ended the call and leaned back in my desk chair. *A small bistro in the Bronx. Great. If it looks like the restaurant in my dream, I'm not going in. I'm running away.*

The pre-briefing convened in my apartment about two hours before the Bronx meeting was scheduled. The agents brought the standard hardware: F-Bird, microphones, beeper-transmitter. I brought clean underwear with the "Karst pouch."

Before commencing the process of attaching the recording equipment to my torso, Karst reached into his briefcase and brought out a file contained in a manila folder. "This is an exact copy of Urgitano's son's file at the parole board. It has the records of his prior hearings—both the public records and the board's private memoranda. If you take a look in there, you'll see it also has the dates for his new hearing and the board members who will sit on his case this time around. That information has not yet been released to the family, or even to the prison, so he should be quite impressed and convinced you're dealing with someone deep on the inside."

I was myself impressed, and quickly reviewed the entire file, confirming it contained everything detailed. "This is really something, Jack, how did you get it?"

"Both federal and state prosecutors want to bring a case against Angelo. He's a longtime soldier with a long history of violence and sadism. A case against him, even at his age, will send the right message: no one in organized crime is safe from prosecution."

Reading the confidential notes of the board, I looked up at the agents. "Sergio did lie to me about one thing. This ain't a 'good kid.'"

Armed with an F-Bird, a manila envelope containing Urgitano's son's file, and "a song and dance," I drove north on the FDR Drive toward the Bronx. I was followed by a nondescript car manned by the FBI and, locating the restaurant in a small strip mall close to Sergio's apartment, parked to the left of the entrance.

Pulling back on the glass front door, I spied a small bar with stools, separated from the main dining area by an étagère-like wooden wall panel. Sergio looked up from a seat at the bar and rose to his feet, calling, "Michael, come with me, I have a table."

As we seated ourselves, Sergio smiled. "I've already ordered the whole dinner; I know everything you like." He motioned to the waiter to start serving their appetizers, and requested a round of liquid refreshment.

When the waiter passed beyond reasonable listening distance, Sergio peered at me greedily. "Angelo can't stay for dinner, but he'll be here soon. Tell me what's up?"

I breathed deeply, preparing myself to convincingly recount the carefully constructed tale. Monitoring my verbal tempo, I began: "As I told you, I flew to Albany and met with my friend. He thinks, despite the many obstacles posed by a murder conviction and an organized crime jacket, he can influence the parole decision to come down the right way."

Reaching for the manila envelope beside me, I removed the file contained inside. "Here's a copy of the son's official parole board file, the file used by actual members on the panel. It has all the information about his upcoming hearing. Angelo can take this home and study it, but he can't show it to his son's lawyer, he can't copy it, and I must have it back soon."

Sergio took the file and leafed through it quickly, plainly not taking the time to digest any of its contents. He placed the file to the side of the table. "How bad is the bad news? How much?"

"I'll need twenty-five thousand dollars down in cash and an additional one hundred thousand dollars when and if the kid gets paroled. If my friend fails, he gets to keep the deposit and obviously gets nothing more. That's the deal and it's non-negotiable."

As the meal started arriving, Urgitano entered the room. When Angelo drew Sergio's attention, he scooped up the file and walked with the veteran Lucchese soldier over to the bar. As I started to move in tandem, Sergio looked back at me. "Stay put, Michael."

After about ten minutes, which seemed to me like a crawling hour, Sergio returned to the table alone. "Angelo was in a rush but he couldn't believe his eyes; he says there's stuff in that file nobody but the parole board itself could know. He said you're 'real.'"

When I made no response, Sergio freely continued, "He took the file home with him, but he definitely wants to do the deal. He needs a week, so we'll meet same time, same place. He'll bring the twenty-five large to you in green."

The balance of the dinner was uneventful, but Sergio's mood was unmistakably upbeat. Perhaps his ego had been inflated as the successful go-between for his pal, or perhaps he'd worked out a potential financial boon for himself if everything went successfully to plan.

After finishing our dinners and parting ways in the strip mall's parking lot, Mike stopped short. "Where are you heading now?" he pointedly asked. It was a simple, harmless question, but the way Sergio spoke the words stabbed at me. Not able to respond with the truth, as I was heading directly for a debriefing, I blurted out the first destination to pop into my head. "I have some people to see at Scores."

Sergio betrayed no reaction and walked toward his parked car after planting a firm bear hug around me.

Turning the car's ignition, I couldn't shake the curious unease I continued to experience about Sergio's interest in my next stop. I became convinced the question was more than idle curiosity. Did he or Urgitano suspect something? Did Urgitano order Sergio to keep close tabs on my next moves? Would they have someone following me? The more I pondered, the more paranoia splashed over me.

After a couple of miles, I grabbed the car phone and dialed Karst. Sharing my concerns about Sergio's abnormal interest in my comings and goings for the evening, the agents agreed to postpone the office debriefing for an hour. In the interim, I wanted to stop at Scores, just as I said I intended.

When I pulled the Mercedes onto East Sixtieth Street, I tossed the keys to one of the valets and instructed the car be parked in front. Scores was batteringly loud as I entered, and I felt a potential migraine brewing, cursing myself for choosing the club as my next stop.

Walking into the menagerie of smoke, music, gyrating topless dancers, and inebriated customers, I was loath to engage in conversation, mindful every spoken word was being recorded by my leg. I needed to find a way to be invisible for a bit. Luck remained my companion still and, as I walked into the dining area, my favorite "massage girl" and friend, Marcie, was walking in the opposite direction. Spurning a waiting customer at my request, she sat with me at a dining room table and administered a long and luxurious foot massage. As usual, some patrons weren't overly thrilled to be bearing unwilling witness to my massage while enjoying their dinners, but I couldn't have cared less. As the woman's strong and practiced fingers worked themselves deeply into my painful arch, I could feel all the night's tensions draining away.

When Marcie remarked with a laugh on the sidelong disparaging looks the foot massage was attracting, I simply whispered, "Such are the joys of ownership. Anyway, if they were such sensitive gourmets, they wouldn't be eating here. Our food is more offensive than my feet."

After the massage, Willie Marshall stopped by the table as I was putting myself back together and preparing to depart. "I had a conversation with Andrew earlier," Marshall shared. "He told me about the Scores IPO. I sound like a broker now, right? All I can say is you guys are fucking amazing. I'm gonna set up a dinner with my boss, you know, what's-his-name." As he ended the sentence, he crossed his lips with a finger revealing his desire not to say "DePalma" aloud.

"That's good news, Willie. We're gonna need him, and you, to make the IPO work, and make us all rich."

"In your case, don't you mean richer?"

I laughed in response, walking toward the club's outer vestibule. Reaching the front door, I heard someone calling my name. Turning back, it was Steve Sergio seeking my attention from behind the cash register.

As I retraced my steps, Sergio the Younger said, "I spoke to my dad a little while ago and he said you did him a big favor tonight. He said you're the 'greatest guy in the world.' But you know he's really getting a little crazy as he gets older; he didn't want to talk to you and he didn't want you to know he called. He just wanted to see if you were here."

Unhappy at the information, I thought to myself, *If your father didn't want me to know he called, why are you telling me?* But to Steve, I replied with a smile, "I guess he was just worried about my driving here from the Bronx safely. I drank too much club soda at dinner."

Leaving Steve laughing, I retrieved my car and drove it into the night on my way back to the office. To put it mildly, I wasn't New York's happiest camper, my thoughts turning in rapid-fire succession. *Sergio has a bug up his ass about something. He has never called to check up on whether I actually went somewhere I said I was going. There's more to this than meets the eye, but I don't have a clue what it could be.*

I decided to raise my concerns as the first issue at the debriefing.

Seven nights later, I was nervously pacing my living room, waiting alone for Karst and Ready to appear for another Urgitano pre-briefing. I'd been out with the agents on multiple weekly missions for months now, and between those late-night escapades, daytime office filmings, proffers with the United States Attorney, and constant conversations with my lawyers, I was mentally and physically exhausted. The strain was becoming unbearable, and for the most part, was being borne by me—alone. I was fearful of burning out.

Noticing the FBI was unusually late, I was relieved when the phone rang and caller ID revealed my friend Marisa Anderson on the line. Anderson, a friend, law client, and practicing psychic, was one of the very few intimates with whom I shared the fact of my undercover activities. Her counsel and empathetic personality repeatedly served to brighten my spirits in my darkest moods.

After answering the call, we exchanged pleasantries. Marisa focused the conversation when she asked, "You're not going out tonight on one of those missions, are you?"

I felt a spark of panic. "Why are you asking?"

"Oh, I don't know, I've just been uneasy about you all day. But if you're going out tonight, I feel there may be trouble. Nothing you can't handle, but you need to be on alert, something is brewing around you."

I was about to launch into a vigorous cross-examination of my psychic friend when the lobby phone sang to signal guests had arrived. I asked Marisa to hold, ran to the phone, authorized the visitors through security, and sprinted back to the call. "Are you sure I'll be able to handle what's coming?"

A pause followed, throwing me into an even greater degree of concern. "Yes I'm quite sure, but be on your toes. You're too smart to get caught, but tonight's going to be a test."

The ringing of the doorbell demanded an end to the call, and I was denied the opportunity to ask the myriad of questions crisscrossing my imagination. Distracting nervousness pulsed through my senses as I regretfully replaced the phone in its cradle and walked to the front door.

Anticipating only Karst and Ready, I was surprised when a parade of strangers walked into the condo. In addition to the regular duo, Paul Roman appeared with three unidentified middle-aged women. Noticing the confusion on my face, Karst smiled. He introduced the three women as agents of the Internal Revenue Service.

"We're gonna send the IRS agents ahead to the restaurant. We want you to try to count the money in a way they can observe. They're not going to try to total the cash with you; they just need to verify that 'cash' was turned over to you by Sergio and Urgitano. Questions?"

When I shook my head, Karst sent the agents on their way. As she was leaving, one of them stopped and said, "When you receive the currency, I'll probably get up and cast a glance at you as I head to a phone or the bathroom. Don't look at me or notice me, and please don't make the mistake of acknowledging me by a smile or gesture."

Signifying my understanding, they departed and the FBI proceeded to fill my underwear pouch with the F-Bird.

The drive to the restaurant had been pure, unmitigated torture. I was sorely tempted to call Marisa back on the car phone, but that would have meant recording our conversation. The government would certainly have been mightily displeased to learn I was consulting a psychic and that she was aware of the secret investigation. Following the same road map as the previous week, I walked through the restaurant's front door and, except for a few tables, the place was empty and eerily quiet. Sergio and Urgitano were seated at the bar and, to my dismay, neither was drinking anything.

Sergio rose and kissed me on the cheek. He gestured toward a stool between them and, removing a wire hanger from a nearby standing rack, offered to hang my suit jacket. Bells and buzzers of alarm rang through me immediately. In the years of our friendship, through dozens of meals and meetings, he'd never once assisted in the removal of my suit jacket. Clearly, an orchestrated game plan was at play, and I feared I was the mouse in the maze.

Seeking to compose myself and set order to my wildly dispersed thoughts, I desperately needed a few moments alone. Removing my jacket and handing it to Sergio, I indicated a need to use the facilities. Neither one seemed to care.

In the bathroom, my bottled-up panic escaped control; fear was my dominant emotion. All my instincts screamed for me to abort the mission, "live to fight another day" emerging as my mantra of the moment. But painful reality couldn't be avoided. If I ran without accepting or counting the cash, the proverbial "jig" would be up, investigation over, trust forever gone, and legal problems up the ying-yang.

Walking into a stall, fearing one of the men would come to check on me, I lectured myself into the merest semblance of calm. *Think! Be smart! Do something!* I repeated these words as a war cry. The first move I took, in deference to my psychic friend's warning, was to open my shirt and move the chest microphones below my belt. I didn't care if the sound was impaired, it was better than getting caught.

After straightening myself up, throwing cold water on my face, and patting off the remaining beaded mixture of sweat and water with a brown paper towel, I looked in the mirror. *What the fuck, this is why you get the big bucks. Better this than a cell mate named Bubba!*

Walking back to the bar, consciously painting a smile on my lips, I had a comforting thought. *Maybe it's a mafia custom to remove your jacket when counting money.*

Resuming my reserved place at the bar between my hosts, Urgitano motioned toward the bartender, who reached under the frame and came up with a crumpled paper bag. Sergio reached for the bag and removed slipshod bundles of cash. He divided the bundles in front of himself and handed one to me. "Count it, each should be five large."

I picked up the bundle, removed the rubber band, and started to count. I hoped the small tremors in my hands weren't visible. As I continued counting, Urgitano demanded a glass of ice water from the bartender. As the glass was handed across the bar, he began coughing wildly and spilled the water directly onto my shoulder and sleeve. While a witness might have honestly described the spillage as a mere accident, there wasn't the slightest doubt in my mind that both Urgitano's coughing fit and his water mishap were intended actions.

Grabbing a towel that had been conveniently placed on the bar top, Urgitano maneuvered me into a standing position. The old man's sure hands started wiping down my shirt, carefully passing directly over areas where tiny F-Bird microphones had recently nested. When the overattention to a purported simple water spill ended, with Angelo apparently satisfied my upper body was clean, we reseated ourselves and the counting resumed.

When I reached the third bundle, a small woman approaching the bar caught my eye. She asked the bartender for the bathroom, and glanced casually at the cash sitting in front of the trio of patrons. I made every effort and ignored the IRS agent—despite a weird compulsion to do the opposite. I was actually beginning to calm down, believing the worst was now over, with the searches at an end. But as I began to count the fourth bundle, Urgitano placed his right hand on my left knee, the knee unfortunately attached to the leg bearing the F-Bird. Although the gesture was disturbingly inappropriate in any circumstance, no sense of alarm arose in me until the hand started to move in an upward circular patterned rotation.

Biting down stomach acid, and impossibly trying to maintain an accurate count of the cash, realization dawned that I was in deep shit. The massaging continued, slowly but unrelentingly, on a direct course up the leg and toward my privates. *He's fucking searching for an F-Bird,* I silently yelled, *and he's gonna find it real soon!*

It was crystal clear, I needed to do something, anything; inaction was not a viable option as Urgitano's tender touching was already merely inches from the mechanism. A dozen possibilities tore through my brain in the course of a second: another bathroom trip, a coughing fit of my own, dropping the cash, asking for a drink. But as swiftly as each thought was born, it was rejected as obvious, telltale, or just plain dumb.

Finally, an absurd and desperate notion took hold. It was outrageous, bold, offensive, insane, but perhaps a brilliant counterstrategy. It called for more courage than I believed I possessed, yet somehow I knew in my gut it was the only possible course to salvation. On the other hand, I also realized what I was contemplating might get me killed on its own merits.

Not knowing where my intended actions might lead, and moving in reaction to what could have been reasonably misinterpreted as sexually aggressive caresses from Urgitano, I leaned into the mobster's chest with my back and floated my hand into his crotch. Brushing gently at first, I located and squeezed the dick of this eighty-year-old man sitting beside me. I instantly felt waves of disgust pour over me as Urgitano's member quickly reacted to my practiced touch.

When the realization of what was actually happening hit Urgitano, he jumped so high into the air it appeared he might fall off his stool. Stabilizing his balance, he looked over at me with eyes of confused hatred and scorn, but I simply shrugged off the whole matter, returning to the business of counting the remaining cash bundles. Still concentrating on the bundles, I softly mumbled in Urgitano's direction, "I'm sorry, I thought that's what you were after." Receiving no response, I added in a louder voice, "After all, you started the whole touching business."

Sergio seemed to remain happily oblivious throughout the episode, recounting each cash bundle after me. To my relief and joy, from that moment on, Urgitano stayed as far away from me as polite social propriety would allow—certainly beyond searching range.

When it was confirmed that twenty-five thousand dollars had been delivered, I placed the bribe funds into my briefcase and prepared to leave. As I rose from the bar, as instructed by Karst, I turned to Urgitano. "Don't be concerned if your son's parole hearing gets postponed. We have to wait until we get him the 'right' panel. Understood?"

Angelo nodded in agreement, but his gaze never met mine again. Sergio approached and planted another kiss on my cheek, expressing his appreciation on Angelo's behalf. I headed toward the door and, glancing at Urgitano one last time, had the sure feeling both extreme embarrassment, as well as a fear of screwing up his son's freedom, would keep the man silent about the evening's "personal" moments.

At the FBI debriefing later that evening, the agents looked concerned; they'd already been apprised of the disjointed and confusing events witnessed at the bar by the IRS representatives. However, when I explained in detail what had taken place, my tale was greeted with wide-eyed stony silence.

Karst and Ready cast sidelong glances at each other, their unusual silence continuing. Finally, Ready said, "You actually played with his dick?"

"No, Bill, I didn't 'play' with his dick, I grabbed him, sort of. Anyway, what else could I have done? You tell me, he was inches from the fucking F-Bird!"

"I don't know," Bill countered, and then paused, "but not that, anything but that!"

Both agents simultaneously burst into unrepressed belly laughs, and they kept coming. Karst stood up with tears in his eyes, declaring, "I'm so sorry, Michael, but that's the funniest story I've ever heard."

Now I was growing angry. I jumped from my chair and yelled, "Hey, listen to me, I did what I had to do. I could've been killed and I saved the whole damn investigation. And you two are amused; this is the thanks I get?"

With each defensive declaration from my lips, the laughing from the agents grew deeper and wilder. In defeated frustration, I just sat down. As I thought about what had happened and what I'd done, I began laughing too, slowly at first but building as the moments slipped by.

In the end, I laughed without control until I became nauseated, not knowing whether I was agreeing my actions were hilarious, or whether I was just thrilled and grateful to still be alive.

CHAPTER TWENTY-NINE
Meeting with the Florida Prosecutors

1997

When the Scores undercover operations began in December 1996, New York prosecutors and Justice Department executives in Washington reached the decision not to advise Florida prosecutors of our cooperation. The need for maximum security, fueled by a certainty of our deaths if discovered, led to only a handful of law-enforcement personnel becoming aware of the covert operation.

The government's decision in favor of secrecy was a concern, because it meant a substantial delay in securing Florida's consent to the single most important precondition of our cooperation: transfer of the insurance fraud sentencing from Orlando, a district whose reputation for severe sentences is unsurpassed nationwide, to a Manhattan federal court far more experienced in mafia prosecutions. Because mob influence and crimes abound within their constituency, the New York federal judiciary is far more attuned to the risks taken by cooperators, the rarity of securing undercover cooperation at all, and the need for sentencing leniency both as reward for those who risk their lives and to encourage others to do the same. New York criminal lore is rife with shocking tales of cooperating businessmen going undercover and not living long enough to attend their own sentence hearings—a bullet to their heads their sole posthumous award for joining with the government in its war against La Cosa Nostra.

New York judges, with their urban counterparts in every major city in America, are acutely aware that fewer than 1 percent of those who agree to cooperate also agree to wear a wire. After all, those who dare to work against the mafia spend the rest of their lives looking over their shoulders in public places; their sentences are truly life sentences and their rates of recidivism markedly lower than the general prison populations. For judges in Central Florida, where mafia atrocities and intimidation are not part of daily life, the need for special leniency for undercover operatives seems beyond the scope of their understanding.

Despite this temporary disappointment, I clearly understood the government's rationale for the imposed security measures. Indeed, since the grand jury had been empaneled in Orlando, local defense lawyers had obtained steady streams of astoundingly accurate reports on the supposedly "secret" progress of the investigation. The information network was alive and well in Orlando as names of scheduled grand jury witnesses, dates for secret investigative trips out of town, names of potential witnesses earmarked for interviews, and dates and times of "surprise" search warrant raids regularly trickled back to New York through the unrelenting gossip mill.

In this environment, a bombshell piece of news such as "Blutrich and Pearlstein, owners of Scores, are cooperating undercover against the mafia in New York" would surely have spread through Orlando's defense bar within moments of being shared. And with the information spreading like wildfire, the New York investigation would have been publicly exposed and Andrew and I surely executed by our less-than-understanding underworld targets.

Even if the task force might have held their silence in this one particular instance, was it worth the risk to find out?

The government itself decided it was not.

Insecurities over the delay in obtaining Florida's consent to the sentencing transfers weighed heavily on me and I repeated those concerns regularly at ongoing proffers. Every time I expressed myself, I received the identical answer, "The transfer deal was worked out and approved at the highest levels of the Justice Department."

I'd come to take great solace in Sipperly's often-repeated 99.9 percent assurance of transfer likelihood. And I had made it perfectly clear repeatedly that, unless we were satisfied with the government's promise to transfer our sentencing from Orlando to Manhattan, there would have been no cooperation at all: no proffers, no cameras, no F-Birds, and no case against the mob at Scores. The agreement to risk our lives first, and reap our rewards later, was a conscious "leap of faith."

Word finally arrived that a meeting had been scheduled at the World Trade Center with the Florida prosecutors. On the morning of the meeting, I arrived at my office to find Andrew talking with his attorney of longest standing, Myles Malman. Joining the ongoing session, I listened to Malman sharing his worries, which seemed centered upon the personality and proclivities of the Assistant United States Attorney leading the Heritage investigation, Judy Hunt.

Talking about his experiences with Hunt, Malman recounted his view of her. It wasn't pretty.

"In my opinion, she carries prejudices and hatreds inappropriate for a federal prosecutor. She guesses at the truth in her cases and then refuses to consider conflicting facts—even when those facts turn out to be true. She lies easily, breaks her word without compunction, and despises cooperators."

Malman's last remark seized my immediate attention.

"Michael," Myles continued, "there are prosecutors, such as myself, who take their cooperators to heart, believe in them and their desire to change, welcome them to the case's team, and forgive them their prior transgressions. Those prosecutors work their butts off to ensure their cooperators get the benefits of promised deals. But that's not the kind of prosecutor Judy is; she literally hates her cooperators, never releases her initial loathing for them, views them as 'necessary evils' for the government, and harbors no concern over whether they get fairly treated in the end. In fact, she actually seems happy when cooperators get screwed.

"And in my opinion," he summed up, "knowing her as I do, she'll be off-the-wall pissed and offended at not having been told of your cooperation six months ago, and she'll hold New York's decision to keep her in the dark against you—and them—forever. I couldn't sleep last night after we learned Hunt was coming up for the meeting. Mark my words, she's probably already put together a plan to sabotage your cooperation."

Walking into the echoing chamber reserved for the meeting in the World Trade Center, accompanied by our attorneys, Weinberg, Malman, and Ginsberg, it was hard not to feel insignificant in proportion to the high-ceilinged, robustly chandeliered ballroom. I was no longer confident the meeting would bring us the long-promised guarantee of a soft landing, and a sense of dread was filling me.

Marjorie Miller was the first to arrive for the government and tersely informed us that New York's First Assistant United States Attorney, Michael Fishbein, would be chairing the meeting, and that a Florida contingent, including Judy Hunt, the lead prosecutor for the Heritage matter, had arrived.

Almost immediately, Fishbein stiffly quick-paced into the room with Sipperly and the Florida visitors, and took charge of the meeting. When everyone was seated, he opened with earth-shattering news. Apparently, after a conference between districts, it'd been agreed there would be no sentencing transfers for us. After negotiating pleas and becoming cooperators in the Heritage trial, our sentencing hearings would take place before a Florida judge.

I felt as if I'd been struck with a baseball bat. This simply couldn't be happening; our entire agreements wiped away in one unanticipated wave by someone I'd never met before.

I've been fucked with my pants on, I silently moaned.

Ginsberg was the first to respond. "You all know me from my time as a prosecutor in your office, and I'm appalled. I've never known the Southern District of New York to act so underhandedly. Our clients were induced, and it would now seem fraudulently induced, to cooperate, to proffer, to wear wires, and to risk their lives, all on the basis of one major promise. Without that promise, we would have packed up our bags, thanked you all very much, and wished you the best of luck in finding some other parties to strap on wires and tape mobsters. You convinced Michael and Andrew to trust you by promising transfers, and you now just take it back?"

Fishbein blandly responded he was aware of no absolute promise, but rather a "best efforts" agreement to obtain the transfers.

"That's a lie," Ginsberg shouted. "There was a 99.9 percent promise put on the table by your office. Would you call a 99.9 percent promise a 'done deal' with your district, or a 'best efforts' deal? You tell me?"

Fishbein wouldn't answer. He simply stared off into the distance, refusing to meet Peter's eyes. "I admit 99.9 percent was a very high percentage chance your clients took; it just didn't pan out."

With everyone in the room stunned into silence, Judy Hunt took the floor. She described a deal her office was prepared to offer: *If* we were accepted as cooperators in Florida, and *if* we fully and satisfactorily cooperated, and *if* our cooperation proved valuable in both New York and Florida, we could earn recommendations for sentences as low as sixty-one months.

I sat back, unable to gather in a satisfying breath, my mind imploding. I'd been talked into risking my life by federal prosecutors with assurances of only serving zero to twelve months in a country-club prison; that sentence maximum reaffirmed by the FBI when I was getting "cold feet" about the F-Bird; and now the number was multiplying. This time the government was throwing out "maybe" sixty-one months—more than five years—and there were a shitload of "ifs" in the new proposal.

Before anyone could say a word, Hunt stood up. "Oh, just one more thing, gentlemen. Our deal is non-negotiable, and if you don't take it, I personally guarantee no judge sitting in Florida will ever hear a single word about your mafia cooperation in New York."

For the first time, Fishbein looked embarrassed and edgy.

We took a break. As we exited the ballroom, Sipperly waved Andrew and me over to an alcove in the hall. Before we could say a word, she opened, "Don't you think I did everything I could for you? Don't you realize I was misled as well?"

Am I supposed to feel sorry for her? I thought in disbelief.

As if reading my mind, she continued, "You guys really need a reality check. These Florida people are looking to put you away for twenty-five years. If you take their deal, you get sixty-one months. With good time, that turns into fifty-two months. Now take off twelve months for a sentence-reduction program and six months for a halfway house. You're out in thirty-four months—around two and a half years. If I were facing twenty-five years, I'd grab at a chance for two and a half.

"And that's just the Florida recommendation; remember we'll all be coming down to your sentencing—me, Marjorie, Jack, Bill, and others from Washington. Your judge will hear about your extraordinary cooperation against the mafia, how you've risked your lives, and about how such cooperation is regularly recognized everywhere."

So there it was: betrayal complete. We could now either fight both districts at once, or continue to cooperate and fight for leniency later. We were completely alone and helpless.

In desperation, we took the Florida deal.

CHAPTER THIRTY

The Investigation Moves Up the Mafia Hierarchy

We were now back undercover with no sure promise of lenient sentencing, but determined to avoid the twenty-five-year sentences we faced if we'd backed out of all cooperation. Our next move in the Scores investigation was to involve Gambino family acting captain Craig DePalma in a fictionalized Scores capital-raising IPO.

Greed turned out to be the magnetic attraction needed to grease the investigation's path into the upper regions of mafia hierarchy. Having planted a seed through Willie Marshall that Scores was willing to pay up to ten million dollars to each strip club owner approved for participation in the IPO expansion, word came back of a DePalma request for a meeting. Through Marshall, a dinner was scheduled at Chin Chin, a midtown Chinese restaurant favored by DePalma.

At the pre-briefing, Karst and Ready quickly motored through all the topics the FBI wanted DePalma to discuss. I was barely listening; I already knew exactly how I intended to approach DePalma and how I would get him talking. With our plans settled, the F-Bird was attached to my leg and we readied to depart together: the FBI agents for a night in the van, Andrew and I for some Chinese food with our "friends."

Stepping into the restaurant, I paused at the front door to read a critic's review of the menu posted in the window, noting strong recommendations for vodka shrimp and barbequed pork. We found ourselves in a small, over-crowded bar area, and I spotted Marshall at the right end of the bar reaching over the heads of seated customers to accept two bottles of beer from a straining bartender.

I pressed my way to Marshall, screaming my greeting over the noise despite our close proximity. "Hey, Michael," he acknowledged with a broad, easy smile, "we got a table in the back, so grab Andrew and follow me." Bouncing in Marshall's wake, his sheer size parting the throng of patrons like Moses at the Red Sea, we made quick progress to a table where a lone man in a blue Adidas running suit sat watching our approach.

The man was Craig DePalma, acting captain in the Gambino crime family, temporarily in charge of the family's relationship with Scores while his father, Greg, was in prison. Having no detailed memory of DePalma on the day he came to the Scores office to supervise delivery of the one hundred thousand dollar extortion payment to Junior Gotti and Mikey Scars, I was surprised by Craig's appearance. He was shorter than I expected, thinner and leaner as well: gaunt, wiry, with short dark hair and brown eyes.

Knowing exactly how I wanted to open this interaction, I extended my hand after Marshall's introductions. "Craig, my pleasure to finally meet you." I next silently counted to three and added with deliberately squinting eyes, "Wow, for some reason you look really familiar. Have we met before?"

DePalma politely ignored the question, choosing to simply smile knowingly in reply. The opening gambits complete, Craig announced he was famished and wanted to order right away. The table deferred to the captain's choices for dinner, which happily included both the vodka shrimp and barbequed pork. I studied the man as he launched into a detailed and boring description of a road-paving construction job he was required to maintain in order to comply with terms of his state prison parole.

DePalma immediately made me uncomfortable. The capo's eyes were in constant motion, darting nervously in every direction, revealing a man riddled with emotional impulses requiring persistent effort to control.

As DePalma continued to casually speak, the aura emanating from him continued to disconcert me. The man's gaze had a cold cruelty to it, and allowed for no doubt of his capacity to react with violence to any threatening situation. Words like "amoral," "sociopathic," and "without conscience," kept reverberating through my mind.

This is not a man I would choose for an enemy, I thought nervously.

As rehearsed, Pearlstein raised the IPO issue and launched into a verbose, detailed description of financing mechanisms. While the spiel would have been appropriate for private bankers or brokers, it was clear DePalma was growing bored and restless, not even attempting to follow the conversation.

Breaking with the projected plan, I unceremoniously jumped into the fray. "Craig, let's get right to the point. We can raise hundreds of millions of dollars with this IPO on Wall Street. Scores is now an American institution, and a hot commodity with name recognition thanks to Howard Stern. We want to raise and use that money to build new Scores venues, and to buy existing clubs in Vegas, Florida, Texas, and Atlanta, turning them into new Scores clubs as well. We'll pay as much as ten million to each club owner who comes on board, and give ten-year management contracts to the sellers to stay and continue running their clubs. After all, there's nothing to fix in a successful strip bar—nothing's broken."

DePalma's eyes sharpened, demonstrating he was now interested in the exchange. The phrase "hundreds of millions of dollars" had obviously grabbed his attention. Putting his hand on Marshall's shoulder, he leaned back and smiled. "And why are we talking about this together?"

"Can I speak straight?" I returned.

Craig nodded his gracious assent.

"We need help in obtaining the rights to successful strip clubs in the best locations. We need to see the 'real' books of every club to set fair purchase prices. Once we own the places, we need a presence to keep leftover management honest. And most important, we need to steer clear of winding up in the middle of squeezes between families offering protection. After all, look at our business. Could there be Scores without our friends looking after us? We want you on board to handle these things."

While DePalma may have been a professional enforcer, moneylender, and shakedown artist, savvy in the ways of family sit-downs, his eyes and body language transparently revealed he was drooling to be a part of our plan. His eyes were spinning like slot machines with dollar-sign icons. So I decided it was time to spring the trap, to gather admissions that would seal DePalma's fate.

I softly slapped my hand on the table and pointed at DePalma's chest. "Craig, I think I remember you now, it's been bothering me all night. You came to the office with the others for the sit-down cash. You helped out Mike Sergio. Am I right? You were Sergio's assistant!"

I strained to keep an innocent look on my face. I'd intentionally stabbed at the captain's pride, hoping to produce an ill-considered reflexive reaction, but fearing a slap in the face. And using the elder Sergio as the hammer only deepened the wound.

I didn't need to wait long.

"Did you just say I was Mike Sergio's assistant?" DePalma seethed, gripping the dinner table with both hands, knuckles immediately whitening.

Looking pleadingly at Marshall, and then back to Craig, I projected pure confusion. "That's what Mike said. Did I just say something wrong?"

Marshall quickly sidled to Craig's ear. "You know Mike, he's an old man, he don't mean things the way they come out sometimes."

DePalma looked slightly mollified by Marshall's words, but glared back at me anew. "Tell me what else Mikey said."

I was mightily gratified; DePalma's reaction was just what the doctor ordered. Trying to look nervous and embarrassed, I lowered my eyes. "I can't remember anything else."

"Michael," DePalma boomed back, "look at me."

I complied slowly.

"You tell me the truth. I'm not mad at you and I couldn't give two shits what that old man said. I just want to hear it."

Taking an exaggerated deep breath, I circled for the kill. "All I know is the original captain at Scores was Tori Locascio, but when Steve Kaplan called a sit-down over the club in front of Mikey Scars, Locascio dropped the club like a hot potato. That left Sergio to pick up the ball and he saved us at the sit-down. He convinced everyone we were right."

Of course my story bore no relation to reality, but neither DePalma nor Marshall could know that. And to add salt to the inflicted wound, I ended my recitation with a real kicker. "He did say you helped him a lot, Craig."

I shifted my weight and waited for an explosion.

DePalma stood up, looked at Marshall, and half-screamed, "Do you believe this shit? I should smack this old man up the head. He saved Scores? I helped *him*?"

Marshall made no further defense, he just shook his head, casting his palms upward, not daring to raise his eyes to meet his boss's glare. After a pause, DePalma sat down, twisted his neck awkwardly a few times, and leaned toward his guests. "Let me just set the record straight."

He then launched into an explosive diatribe recounting how Sergio sent Marshall to him "begging" for help with the sit-down. "There was nothing he could do alone, he's not senior enough to even attend a sit-down." DePalma next recounted how he agreed to be our representative; how he attended a series of meetings in the middle of the night to arrange things; and how he—and he alone—convinced Scars to deny Kaplan's claims. For his grand finale, DePalma revealed he'd also been the one to negotiate the lowering of the demand from an original two-hundred to one-hundred grand.

"And your friend Mikey Hop had nothing to do with nothing. He was home in bed sleeping while I was taking care of what had to be done. And believe me, I don't need no credit, I just don't want you guys misunderstanding what end's up in this world."

I had by now pulled out every admission I'd ever dreamed of obtaining that night, but while the dice were still "hot," I dared to try for just a bit more.

"What I don't understand then, is why didn't you introduce yourself to us at the office that day?"

"Because I'm a low-profile guy, ask Willie. I don't shit where I eat. I just came along to make sure the cash got safely delivered to Mikey Scars and Junior. At that time, you didn't need to know who I was. You just needed me to do things."

Bingo! was the single word flying through my satisfied thoughts, and I contentedly let the issue drop.

Andrew, Willie, and Craig headed out to Scores after departing the Chinese restaurant, the dinner tab my responsibility. I begged off, citing an early morning court appearance but, in reality, I was heading to an FBI debriefing. After the F-Bird was turned off and the beeper-transmitter returned, I recounted my recollections of the night's events and the important exchanges traded with DePalma.

Ticking through the high points, Karst and Ready enthusiastically concluded the excursion had brought us to a whole new investigative level. DePalma, an organized crime acting captain, son of a full capo, at a power station far above either Sergio or Marshall, had openly admitted Gambino family involvement at Scores. More importantly, he took personal credit for his part in the sit-down extortion scheme and confirmed the active participation of Scars and Junior as well—the two men running the international family.

The "cherry" on the evening's sundae was, of course, the unexpected admission that Marshall and Sergio, together with DePalma, had hand-carried the one hundred thousand dollars in cash from Scores to Mikey Scars and Gotti Junior.

The FBI agents were delirious; they well knew we'd crossed beyond a barrier into the realm of family bosses. We'd gotten ourselves into territory few undercover operations ever reach. After these targets, there was nowhere higher to go in the Gambino clan!

"From what we heard on the transmitter," Karst said, "if we can put you into Craig's confidence, this could turn out to be one of the most productive operations in FBI history."

His words filled me with an undeniable sense of pride. Despite my gross disappointment with the Florida meeting at the World Trade Center, I was riding a wave of excitement that night along with the agents, eager to find new and additional ways to keep the investigation progressing. As long as I was active, I wasn't in Idaho or witness jail.

But as I walked alone down Park Avenue toward home, my adrenaline rush ebbed and stark reality returned to engulf me. I began talking out loud to myself, arms flailing up and down in birdlike motions, as I strode down the deserted Manhattan streets. To anyone watching from a window above, I would have seemed like an escaped mental patient.

Michael, why are you doing all this? It's all a cruel joke; you're a joke. The only thing you got out of tonight was some terrific shrimp and pork; the government got Marshall, DePalma, Scars, and Gotti. Fair trade, you think? No one but me would be stupid enough to risk his life with absolutely no concrete guarantees for a soft landing in the future. For God's sake, the government even made us pay the check.

By the time I reached home, I was all wound up and severely depressed. There was no seeming way out of this mess, and I felt myself slipping away.

I reached for the bottle of Xanax on my bedside table.

In the middle of the next week, Pearlstein strolled into my office and took a seat in one of the red leather chairs. The look on his face mirrored the cat who'd swallowed the canary. "You're never going to believe who called me."

When I steadfastly refused to guess the name of the caller, he added, "Steve Kaplan."

It took a few moments for the impact of the information to register. "Steve Kaplan from the Gold Club in Atlanta?"

"That's the one."

"Steve Kaplan who went to Angelo Prisco and called for the sit-down against the club?"

"Yup."

"Steve Kaplan who tried to take Scores from us, and cost us one hundred thousand dollars?"

"The very one."

"What the fuck does he want?"

"He wouldn't say. He just said he thought it would be to our mutual benefit to have a conversation."

"And what did you say?"

"I said I'd think about it."

After advising Karst and Ready of the unexpected approach from Kaplan, there was no doubt Pearlstein should accept the invitation. "Do you think he's learned about the IPO project from DePalma?" Andrew asked.

"Could be," Ready guessed.

"Who cares?" I chimed in. "It gives us another chance to sit down with DePalma. It wouldn't be right to meet with Kaplan without permission."

Through Marshall, an urgent meeting was requested with DePalma. Two nights later, Andrew and I found ourselves in the same restaurant, at the same table, eating the same food, facing the same man, in the same running suit.

Andrew repeated a word-for-word account of his telephone conversation with Kaplan. "After all that's happened, we didn't want to entertain his offer for a meeting without getting your advice."

DePalma was closed-mouthed about Kaplan, unwilling to share whether, in his opinion, the call was in any way connected with the IPO capital-raising efforts. DePalma's silence signaled, in my opinion, that he'd been unaware of the Kaplan approach and would be checking with his bosses about the genesis of the odd call from a former enemy.

In the end, DePalma's advice was simple: "Do what you want. I don't care."

Andrew phoned Kaplan the next morning to accept his invite. According to Andrew, Kaplan seemed delighted and they agreed to share a cup of coffee at a small cafe in Penn Station.

"Did he say what it was all about?" I asked.

"Not a word. He said we'd cover everything when we got together."

The meeting was set for the following afternoon at three. We all assumed Andrew would finally be convinced to strap on an F-Bird but, to the group's collective surprise, he adamantly refused to even consider it. He complained he'd be too nervous wearing the wire and Kaplan would surely suspect he was up to something. As no amount of prodding could change his mind, a compromise was reached: Andrew would try to make the visit a quick one, and would attempt to schedule a full meeting back at the office, under the watchful eyes of hidden ceiling cameras.

When Andrew set off for Penn Station on his first solo mission, he made a mighty effort to maintain an appearance of serenity. Knowing Andrew as I did, I could see he was terrified.

Andrew returned exactly one hour after he departed, carrying himself like a conquering hero.

Sitting in his office, on the phone with the agents, Andrew related his brief encounter. As the tale was recounted, Kaplan opened the conversation with an apology, claiming the sit-down had been a total misunderstanding. He hoped there were no hard feelings and expressed a desire to do business with Scores.

"Did he mention the IPO?" Karst asked through the speaker.

"He didn't, but I did. I told him all about it. I had the feeling he knew all the details but wanted to hear them from me."

Andrew went on to say Kaplan revealed he'd been visiting Scores on a regular basis, as a matter of "professional interest," and had a few "million-dollar ideas" for us. He was purportedly respectful, contrite about the past, and enthusiastic about the future.

"How did you leave it?" Karst interrupted.

"It worked out perfectly. He claimed to be pressed for time and suggested he'd stop by the office one night this week. He wants to meet Michael and apologize personally to him as well."

"Did you set a date?" Ready asked.

"No, but I bet I get a call tomorrow."

Andrew was clearly pleased with himself and we agreed to share dinner at Smith and Wollensky on Second Avenue. I like the pea soup there.

During the dinner, while making every effort to ignore our depressing plight for a few hours, my beeper started vibrating. Pulling out the contraption, I stared at the screen in horror. The message read: "Call Bill Ready. 911."

Ready answered on the first ring. "We don't know how it happened, but the undercover investigation has been leaked to the press. There may be a story tomorrow linking Scores to an active sting against the Gambinos. You may have to be ready to leave New York early tomorrow morning."

I could barely speak. "Bill, this can't be right. You promised us two years. We can't leave at the drop of a hat. There are a million details to attend to."

"Michael, if this story leaks in the newspaper, there will only be one detail to attend to—your funeral. But listen, the US Attorney herself is meeting with the editorial board of the *Daily News* tonight. They may agree to kill the story. So stay in touch because if things don't go as hoped, you and Andrew have to spend the night packing."

I reported every word to Andrew, who stood stiff and pale in the shadows of the restaurant. Hard to comprehend, but I might have just eaten my last cup of Smith and Wollensky pea soup.

I spent a wretched sleep-deprived night. Pacing around my living room, watching the darkened city begin to stir, I was forced for the first time to confront the reality and ramifications of my cooperation. It had been one thing to give passing lip service to "someday" entering the Witness Protection Program; it was a horse of different color to be actually packing bags.

The impact of what could be happening in the next few hours was crushing: leaving behind family, loved ones, businesses, and partners; changing names, abandoning a complex personal history, and replacing it with a sterile manufactured past without substance or comfort; never coming home, never again dining in a favorite restaurant, shopping in a familiar store, calling a trusted doctor. And even worse, spending the rest of my days looking over my shoulder, fearing the next face I saw might be of the man who would kill me.

Losing an identity is no small thing, yet I had agreed to do so without ever taking in the full implications of the decision. *A little late now, buddy,* I forlornly counseled myself.

Questions piled upon questions as my anxiety grew thick: Was I really capable of no longer being Michael Blutrich? Was I strong enough to never return, to never make contact, to cease to exist?

While my questions were many, answers were painfully elusive, and the personal confidence that had always guided every step of my life suddenly left me.

What the fuck have I done?

At 7 AM, with paranoia at full throttle, Bill Ready told us that the editorial powers at the *Daily News* had agreed to "kill" the story in order to avoid both prematurely ending an important undercover investigation and potentially endangering the lives of its cooperators.

When the conversation ended, and realizing I was still me, and still controlling my life—not being immediately shipped off to the boondocks—I was overcome with waves of emotion. Collecting myself, I vowed to use every additional hour granted to better prepare for the "Day of Judgment" on the horizon.

CHAPTER THIRTY-ONE
Hemorrhoids to the Rescue

SUMMER, 1997

Making home movies for the government in the office continued like monotonous clockwork. At least once a week, one of the FBI team would rendezvous with me after business hours and retrieve the tapes. On this particular evening, after completing the exchange, Karst sat himself down in front of the desk that dominated the room. "Have you heard anything about one of your managers getting threatened at gunpoint by a 'made guy' from another family?"

"Not a word. Are you sure it happened? Because that kind of gossip usually gets back to me."

"We recorded Sergio on a phone tap saying something about an incident with another family. I'd love to know the story."

"You know, Jack," I knew I sounded frustrated, "we can kiss good-bye those days when Sergio spilled his guts at the drop of a hat. Ever since he found out about our new 'friendship' with DePalma, and ever since Willie Marshall began asserting himself at the club, Sergio's gotten tight-lipped. I think he's afraid of getting pushed out of Scores completely and losing his weekly cash."

Karst stood up and paced around the room, rubbing his hands together slowly. "It's true. Sergio probably got called on the carpet by DePalma after

233

we savaged him as a big-mouthed washerwoman. He's definitely scared and we've got to get him into a new environment where he'll feel safe opening up all over again. Any ideas?"

Nothing immediately came to me and silence filled the office. When an idea struck, I held it back, at first unsure I wanted to creatively assist the FBI in expanding its probe. But it was a really good idea, too tempting in the end to keep to myself. "What about this, I've been complaining to Sergio about my inflamed hemorrhoids. I've had a lot of pain lately and some blood . . ."

"Michael," Jack interrupted, "this is more information than I need to know."

"Fine, I didn't realize you were so squeamish. Anyway, Sergio keeps offering to take me to his proctologist friend in Connecticut. I could accept the offer and maybe Sergio would start talking on the ride."

Karst thought the matter over. "There's a problem. You can't wear a wire if the doctor's gonna examine your privates."

"I know, but we can wire up my limo and capture conversation on the road."

"You know what? Let's do it. Call Sergio and ask him if he'd take you to the doctor. If he's willing, we'll bring your limo into the FBI shop."

As I suspected he would, Sergio agreed to make the appointment and accompany me to the Connecticut proctologist. The FBI promptly picked up the vehicle and outfitted it with several backseat microphones. When it was returned, I received instructions in the procedure for controlling the recording equipment through a switch behind a rear seat cushion. All we needed was a date from Sergio.

On the morning of the appointment, the limo picked me up at home and headed up the FDR Drive north to Sergio's Bronx apartment. As there were no body wires involved, I was on my own; no trailing team of FBI agents. As we pulled off the highway, and with the passenger cabin concealed from the driver by the limo's divider panel, I reached behind the seat cushion, located the recording switch, and rolled the tape. The operation took longer than anticipated and I barely had sufficient time to replace the cushion and assume a relaxed pose before Sergio ripped open the door and bounced into a seat in the spacious vehicle.

He was in a relaxed, gregarious mood, plainly pleased to be spending an afternoon with me away from the city. His conversation opened with reassurances the Connecticut doctor was first-class, followed by a usual spewing of hatred for Andrew, and concluding with some harsh words for the way he was being treated at Scores by the DePalmas.

As we crossed over the state border into Connecticut, I casually raised the circulating rumor about a pistol-whipping incident outside the club with one of the managers. Without hesitation, Sergio launched into a recitation of the lurid tale, and of the manager who foolishly opened his "big mouth" to a mafia soldier from another family—almost getting killed in a backlash. He named names, times, and the steps he'd been constrained to undertake to smooth over interfamily waters.

"Sometimes these guys," Sergio shook his head, scowling as he spoke, "they just don't think before they speak. The jerk-off was scared shitless, but maybe he learned something from a gun in his mouth."

I breathed a sigh of relief, having accomplished the day's investigative goal without breaking a sweat. All that was left was a quick consultation with the Connecticut "ass man," and back on the road for some extra bonus admissions.

The proctologist's office was located in a small, unimpressive, white, boxlike medical complex. The office we were seeking was on the ground floor and, as we entered, Sergio received a boisterous greeting from the receptionist.

"You seem to be really popular in Connecticut anal circles," I whispered as we took seats.

"You're another one who never knows when to shut his piehole."

After filling out insurance forms and sitting through a reasonable wait, I was called and escorted through reception portals on my way to an examination room. As I entered the room, I was startled to find Sergio trailing directly behind me. Turning to my escort, I pointedly said, "Whatta you, my mother now? I can't see the doctor alone?"

"Will you please just be quiet? I want to say hello and hear what the man says about your problem." Our continuing banter was interrupted when a nurse opened the door and handed me a standard paper gown, instructing me to trade it for "all" my clothes.

After a while, as I sat uncomfortably on a freezing cold table, and Sergio rested himself in a plastic chair, the doctor entered with a flourish. Once again it was Sergio who was the center of attention as he and the physician traded exuberant personal exchanges about family and politics.

With the pleasantries over, I explained about the pain and blood spotting I was intermittently experiencing. "Well let's take a look-see," the doctor responded with a broad engaging smile.

Now on my knees atop the examining table, with Sergio standing above my head and the doctor making a rear assault on my upturned, helplessly exposed bottom, I quietly withstood a degree of uncomfortable prodding as the physician went about his business. With everyone holding their respective positions, the doctor finally said, "You have a series of common hemorrhoids, which are causing all your pain and blood. Lucky thing is they can readily be treated and I can perform the surgery right now."

I gulped deeply in response. I'd been perfectly willing to endure an embarrassing examination to further the investigation; it was a different matter to undergo surgery.

I twisted my neck around severely to meet the doctor's gaze. "To be honest, Doc, I wasn't really prepared to have any procedure performed today. I'd like to think about it."

"Think about what?" Sergio roared, causing me to lose balance and crash my upper torso into the table. "We come all this way, you've got the best doctor in the world, so stop being a chickenshit and let him fix your ass."

Remaining on all fours between the two men, my rear facing the heavens and all sense of privacy now abandoned, I attempted to quickly learn about the procedure being foisted upon me. "Doc, can you explain to me exactly what you're proposing to do?"

Once again it was Dr. Sergio who jumped in to preclude any meaningful doctor-patient exchange. "He takes rubber bands, wraps them around the damn hemorrhoids, kills off the blood flow, and burns the things off. I've had it done and it's no big deal; it don't hurt."

The surgery seemed to be proceeding as described, with special supervision by the esteemed mafia medical consultant. My bottom was spread beyond any reasonably anticipated human level by devices better suited to an Inquisitor's torture chamber, and the proctologist actually wrapped rubber band-like straps around each offending nodule.

To avoid the reality of what was impossibly happening behind me, I lowered my head into a cradle of my folded arms and silently lectured myself in growingly outraged thoughts. *It was bad enough I burned and scarred my inner thighs wearing the F-Bird. I thought I'd reached the limits of humiliation when I was forced to lap dance naked in a restroom. And of course, new standards of sacrifice and disgust were surpassed when my only way to survive an undercover sting turned out to be grabbing an eighty-year-old, overexcited penis. But I gotta admit, lying here on this table, my ass spread far enough east and west to drive a truck through me, this is the worst one yet. It's too much; things like this cannot be expected by the government from cooperators. Were I a betting man, I would bet the ranch I'm the only witness in history to have his butt cut open in the name of cooperation!*

As shots of pain rippled through my body, I just moaned forlornly and mumbled out loud, to no one in particular, "This really really sucks the big one."

Walking back to the limousine, I was holding a rubber donut, the size of a child's toilet seat, which I'd been instructed to sit on for the next few days. Life just kept finding more and more humiliations for me.

After opening the limo door, I asked Sergio if he would mind getting in on the other side. As he walked around the vehicle grumbling, I dove into the back seat, my ass screaming in painful resistance, and I managed to pull out and reengage the recording device.

Sergio plopped himself into the cabin, laughing and looking at me.

"And what's so funny now?"

"I was thinking about how much your first crap is gonna burn. But you'll be thanking me in a few days."

As summer unceremoniously marched on, a problem developed between the New York prosecutors and us. The problem concerned our New York plea deal. The government was still of a mind that we should plead guilty to various crimes in New York deriving, for the most part, from our relationship with the mafia at Scores. Our counsels argued ferociously that being extorted by the mob wasn't a crime.

Sipperly and Miller were callously unrelenting; they wanted their "pound of flesh" from us in New York in the form of guilty pleas, arguing the pleas would make us more effective witnesses. Tempers flared to unanticipated heights and, acting as if it were a labor dispute, the prosecutors temporarily "locked us out" from continuing the cooperation. The entire investigation was put on hold, over rabid objections from an appalled FBI, until the matter of pleas could be straightened out.

A summit was called in the hopes of negotiating a settlement.

The peace conference was scheduled in the now-familiar upstate hotel. All the players were invited: the two prosecutors, the two lead agents, our two attorneys, and the two of us. When I entered the reserved suite, everyone had already seated themselves around a circular cluster of arranged chairs. Carol and Marjorie seemed to be in unexpectedly wonderful moods; in fact, they seemed to be suppressing chuckles.

As all eyes bemusedly focused directly on me, little goose bumps appeared on my arms. Although I already suspected what was coming, I realized I was being compelled to "ask" to be humiliated.

"All right, I'll bite. Why is everybody looking at me like I have a booger sticking out of my nose?"

That did it. The entire room lost control and laughter erupted in boisterous spurts. Finally gaining a modicum of control over herself, Sipperly shook her head and cleared her throat. "The agents and your lawyers were telling us for the first time about your intimate encounter with Urgitano . . ."

"And your recent surgery," Miller threw in as a kicker.

Once again the gathered group burst into rolling yelps as I tried my best to preserve my pride and bearing. Sensing my seething reaction, which was actually feigned, Peter Ginsberg leaned toward me. "We're laughing with you, not at you. But you have to know this is the stuff legends are made from."

Then the meeting turned serious. The same old tired arguments were exchanged on the plea issue. It appeared little progress was going to prove possible, until Sipperly made a startling statement. "For the life of me, I can't understand why you're fighting us on this point. Your New York sentences are going to be minimal, a matter of months, and will run together with any Florida time you receive. Don't you understand, a New York plea is the only way for you to keep Scores?"

"What is she talking about?" I literally screamed in disbelief in the direction of the attorneys. "No one has ever said a single word about losing the club!"

Sipperly, plainly sensing she'd hit a nerve, went on to explain that Florida was readying a motion to seek immediate forfeiture of Scores. "And you know where that motion will be heard and decided, don't you? And you know what your chances are in front of a Florida judge, don't you?" Sipperly lectured. "The one and only way you're going to keep that from happening is to forfeit the club to us first—that ends the issue in Florida, but requires a New York plea agreement. Things are going to get a whole lot worse for you guys really fast unless you start seeing things our way."

The possibility of losing Scores to Florida was beyond threatening and took the wind from our sails, our New York plea resistance movement coming to an immediate collapse. After all, without the significant income from Scores, we would be unable to pay mounting legal bills or maintain our lifestyles. More importantly, without the club as a "front," the undercover cooperation would be blown to oblivion. The preservation of our ownership and control of Scores had just become the only focus of real importance.

Perhaps if I had allowed myself a moment of quiet introspection, it might have become obvious the New York prosecutors had an equal, if not greater, vested interest in keeping Scores under our control. Had Florida actually managed to wrestle away ownership, either closing Scores' doors or installing new owners, the New York investigation would have surely been terminated. A detached, dispassionate observer would have recognized neither New York nor the FBI was about to let that happen, not when they were perhaps only months away from "nailing" the most powerful members of the Gambino and other families.

Unfortunately, and rather than utilizing the government's equally compromised position to our advantage, we reacted again out of fear, thinking exclusively of ways to preserve the "cash cow" club. We missed an opportunity to bring the government to its knees, or at least get fair rewards for our effort and risk.

Sipperly and Miller must have shared a fine laugh, watching their two prized cooperators, unaware of their own value and power, gratefully dancing to the government's music of pure unadulterated self-interest.

Over the next few days, Pearlstein and Ginsberg participated in a series of meetings on the forfeiture issue. Out of those negotiations, an accord was finalized: we would plead guilty in New York with an agreement to immediately forfeit Scores; actual turnover of the club to be held in abeyance until we surrendered into custody to begin serving any time; until then, presumably years away, we would continue to act as owners, with all profits earned from the club's operations being ours to keep and utilize as we saw fit.

There were caveats: 1) during the period before physical turnover, we agreed not to diminish the value of the club, no "stripping the cupboards bare," so to speak; 2) the government would have the right to conduct discreet audits of the books to ensure its value was being maintained; and 3) prior to actual forfeiture, we would have the option of selling the club to buyers "of our choice," for a price not less than two million dollars, the money going directly to the government.

We were satisfied. Although it was never openly discussed, our right to sell the club to buyers "of our choice" was an open invitation to put together a "friendly" group of new owners to maintain caretaking operations during our brief prison terms.

It finally seemed the Southern District of New York had found its way to rewarding and recognizing the enormity of our sacrifices. Plainly, this was the promised "soft landing" waiting at the end of the nightmare.

CHAPTER THIRTY-TWO
Money Laundering and Florida Craziness

With plea understandings drafted and signed, I was now back in the saddle, undercover activities fully resumed. And as for subject matter, a cornucopia of new mafia crimes continued to arrive at our doorstep. For example, Willie Marshall announced to the world his intentions to take his longtime girlfriend as his bride. An official wedding date was set for November 1997.

At a planning session for the investigation, Karst suggested that Andrew urge Marshall to use his wedding to engage in some old-fashioned money laundering of illegally earned cash he'd hidden from past loan-sharking activities. If successful, the agents reasoned they could capture him both admitting his role in loan-sharking and engaging in new financial crimes to avoid federal and state taxes on ill-gotten gains.

I broke the group's train of thought. "I'm getting just a little confused. Don't we have enough on Willie already? Do we really need more than extortion of Scores, the Kaplan sit-down, transport of extortion proceeds to Gotti, and murder conspiracy with DePalma? What I mean to say is, is it worth the risk of getting caught and being exposed just to get Marshall snagged in one more crime he's not even thinking about committing?"

Karst and Ready held a quick private discussion in reaction to my queries. After some animated hand gesturing between them, they broke their impromptu huddle and returned their attentions to us. "We think you deserve an overview of our long-term goals here," Karst opened. "Michael, you're absolutely correct, we've got more than enough right now to convict Willie of twenty years of federal crimes. The same is true for the Sergios certainly, and we're getting close to that point with Craig DePalma. But as of now, our aim is to turn those three into cooperating witnesses in the future.

"Unlike you guys, they can take us directly to Gotti, to Scars, and to a bunch of other major players in several crime families. So, if we get Willie to now admit he's been into loan-sharking, when he turns into a witness down the road, he'll have to give up all the names and details involved in that operation."

"That's how an undercover investigation sometimes blooms and mushrooms," Ready interjected. "You guys are the roots; without you we'd have nothing. But when the Sergios, Marshall, and DePalma each find themselves facing thirty years behind bars, they become the next tier of cooperators."

When the opportunity arose, Andrew called me on the office intercom. "Michael, I'm here with Willie Marshall, wanna order cappuccinos with us?" I recognized the code signal to start the ceiling tapes rolling.

"Sure. Where do you want to have them?"

"Your office in ten minutes."

I sighed deeply, thinking about all the physical machinations I had to accomplish in the next few moments. When the cameras were finally rolling, I placed my chair back in its normal position, retraced my steps to the bathroom and, after flushing the toilet and spraying air freshener, opened the dead bolt, and walked back to my desk.

Moments later, with Andrew holding two large cups, he and Willie Marshall strode into my office. Andrew opened, "Michael, Willie and I have been discussing the opportunity his wedding presents to wash clean a bunch of his cash. Here's the plan: Willie brings cash to the office, you deposit it into your attorney escrow account, and we issue back-to-back checks to Willie as wedding gifts from Scores, or you, or myself."

"I wanted your opinion about all this," Willie said, pointing his chin at me. "I'd like to be able to use the cash I've got in the house, but I don't wanna get in no trouble."

I feigned a measure of deep thought. "It's virtually foolproof. Cash going through my escrow account in reasonable amounts would raise no eyebrows, and checks as wedding gifts are not taxable to the happy couple. I'd say you've got a rock-solid money laundering plan at no cost to you."

Everyone smiled knowingly.

Exactly one week later, the "Marshall Money Laundering" episodes began in earnest. With the office properly prepared for filming, in a scene that would be repeated over and over, Marshall entered my office and, after locking all doors, removed cash from a paper bag. He counted the stacks and I double counted him. The cash was then placed in my wall safe and I pulled out the escrow checkbook. On some checks on some days, we filled in "wedding gift," and on others we substituted "reimbursement of expenses."

"And I won't have to put this on my returns or pay no tax on it, right?" Marshall was recorded asking.

"Not at all, neither gifts nor recovery of expenses are taxable events. Don't get me wrong, none of this is legal—obviously—but I can't see you getting caught either. All in all, a reasonable risk."

After each cash delivery and check disbursement, the FBI photographed the currency overnight and returned it to me the next morning for deposit in the bank. When all was said and done, Willie was signed up for forty thousand dollars in money laundering and tax evasion charges.

It was a hot, muggy, New York summer afternoon, and I was in line at the Citibank ATM machine on Park Avenue, near the office. As I waited my turn, the beeper at my belt began vibrating. When I casually removed the machine from its holder, the message startled me. The message was from Bill Ready and it read "911."

Staying in line at the bank, I grabbed my cell phone and dialed his number. He answered after several rings. "Are you on a landline?"

When I said I was not, he shot back, "Go to a pay phone immediately and call me from there."

"What's wrong?"

"No danger, just some unexpected activity in Florida."

It turned out Judy Hunt, the Florida prosecutor, had unsealed an indictment that morning in Orlando for the Heritage insurance case and Andrew and I were named among the listed defendants.

It was an unexpected event as it was clear Hunt wasn't anywhere close to being ready for an immediate trial; her case would require a great deal more investigation and preparation. Rumors abounded through the local defense bar in Orlando that Hunt, fearing New York would indict Pearlstein and myself on Heritage counts in New York in order to insulate us from any Florida prosecution, jumped the gun to ensure we could not be wrestled from her control. Of course, New York never considered any such course of action, but Hunt had no way of assuring herself of this.

Hunt seemingly couldn't have cared less about the New York undercover case against the mafia or our safety. Her exclusive priority seemed to be that her prosecutorial powers would be preserved. But the indictment was dangerous; it would place us under intense mafia scrutiny as potential cooperators.

According to the New York agents, it was only at New York's insistence, and over Hunt's objections, that we weren't physically arrested. Instead, we were, along with all the other defendants in the new case, directed to surrender the following week in Florida for bail hearings. Again with New York's intervention, our bail hearings were severed from the rest—announced by the court clerk as a matter of simple administration. The severance was imperative to avoid any possibility of inadvertent discovery of our cooperation status, and immediate slaughter.

When Andrew and I arrived in Florida on the morning of the bail hearing, our retinue of attorneys in attendance had much to share. There were going to be two hearings that day: a sealed, secret hearing where the magistrate would be advised of our status as undercover cooperating witnesses in New York, and a public hearing at which bail would be set. The unexpected news was that Judy Hunt was demanding one million dollars collectively in bail for us, secured by real estate.

The Hunt bail demand was extraordinary. In normal legal discourse, white-collar covert cooperating defendants are always released on signature bonds—with no requirement for posting of collateral.

Waiting for the sealed hearing to conclude, and as we had been excluded from attending, Andrew and I shared a swim in the pool on the roof of our hotel. Pearlstein was agitated because it had been discovered that an outstanding warrant was pending against him out of Nevada for his failure to pay a small casino marker in a timely manner. Unless the misdemeanor warrant was cleared by the end of the bail hearing, he would be held overnight in county jail.

"Why didn't you pay that marker, Andrew?" I joked. "Did you think Steve Sergio owned the casino?"

"Screw the jokes! Why aren't you making sure the warrant gets cleared? You don't care if I spend a night in jail?"

Remembering our similar conversation in my law firm library on the day of the New York search warrants, when Andrew had failed to lift a finger to ensure I wasn't under arrest, I simply turned to him, and repeated back his own words, "I'm just leaving the issue of your freedom to the lawyers."

And then I swam away, already aware the warrant had been cleared, but with no intention of informing him of that fact just yet.

The attorneys appeared after the sealed hearing looking agitated. They related that New York had sent an impressive letter to the magistrate informing him of the ongoing undercover investigation and the importance to the government of setting reasonable bail, if any. Hunt vehemently opposed any bail below her million-dollar demand, claiming we were multimillionaires, arguing the amount sought was "chump change" to ensure our court appearances.

Sadly, we again failed to recognize the power we had at our fingertips, waiting in vain to be exercised. If we'd simply refused to post the extraordinary bail and voluntarily surrendered into custody, New York would have busted a gasket and gone running to Washington for intervention. More importantly, since Hunt wasn't anywhere close to finishing her investigation and was years away from being able to commence a trial, our surrender would have invoked "speedy trial" rules and she would have been ultimately required to dismiss the indictment at great cost and embarrassment to her office. But of course, and still hoping to receive fair treatment, we plodded along, ignoring the inconsistent rumblings of a government now seemingly fighting itself.

The public proceeding lasted well into the night. The magistrate allowed everyone with something to say to say it—at length and repeatedly.

While the fact of our cooperation remained a guarded secret and a taboo subject, the magistrate decided at the close of argument to "split the baby." He ruled bail would be set at three hundred thousand dollars for each of us, a bit more than half of Hunt's request.

The magistrate went on to shock the tired and exhausted defense team by announcing, of his own accord and with no request from Hunt, that he was imposing bail conditions on our conduct: there would be a 10 PM nightly curfew and a daily requirement to report to a federal probation officer.

"Is this man trying to get us killed?" I whispered to Sandy. "We'll tell the mafia guys all dinners have to be over by nine. Before they start!"

No cries of foul or dissent could move this magistrate, who apparently hated cooperators—or just us. He wouldn't relent, even after being reminded no such conditions had been imposed on any defendants in the case the week before by another magistrate in the same building. It seemed, in the Middle District of Florida, magistrates treat undercover cooperators more harshly than non-cooperators.

As these bail restrictions would both seriously impede the New York investigation and actually endanger our lives, the New York prosecutors quickly advised us that the magistrate's conditions had been amended. The curfew would be monitored and regulated by the FBI (which meant it no longer existed) and the daily reporting requirement was changed to weekly by phone (as imposed on all the other defendants). I suspected these modifications were worked out with a helpful probation office in New York, the Florida magistrate never becoming the wiser.

I could no longer think clearly as my world had turned irrational. In my mind, no one could be believed, no one could be trusted. Everything I did for New York pissed off Florida, but if I stopped what I was doing in New York, I would lose all my support for sentencing leniency in Florida.

CHAPTER THIRTY-THREE

Cooperation Complications, and How Leonardo DiCaprio Saved My Life

Steve Kaplan, owner of the Gold Club in Atlanta, was a Gambino associate of standing. He was also the man who'd spearheaded an unsuccessful coup to wrestle control of Scores from us through an ill-conceived sit-down presided over by Gotti's chief advisor, Mikey Scars. Yet, despite this attack aimed at our lives and livelihoods, Kaplan was now working with a new agenda. After his brief afternoon conversation at Penn Station with Andrew, he quickly arranged a more substantive meeting with both of us at the Scores executive office. He explained he was making a pressing quick trip back to Atlanta, and would be available to stop in for a short meeting on his way to the airport.

His choice was, from an investigatory perspective, perfect. It would allow for utilization of the ceiling cameras, and the conversational exchange would be captured and preserved on film without the necessity of employing F-Birds. On the other hand, it was also the first time we'd be engaging in undercover work without a familiar face in attendance. At least with the Sergios, Marshall, and DePalma, there'd been history, a time-tested period where trust had been built and securely implanted. Between Kaplan, Pearlstein, and myself, there was only a blank page, with the exception of the prior nasty ambush. Kaplan was sure to be more suspicious and guarded than our usual targets.

Karst and Ready were more than pleased over this latest unexpected expansion of investigative horizons. Long suspecting Kaplan to be an important mafia associate, and believing him to be actively involved in significant money laundering, the opportunity to turn him into an active target could potentially catapult us even further into organized crime's usually unreachable "royalty."

Realizing we would have to be especially convincing in this night's episode, nervousness began coursing through me when Pearlstein's beeper rang out, signaling Kaplan's arrival. Andrew rose and made his way toward the elevator banks to intercept our guests, and I began the ritual of starting up the cameras.

With everything in readiness, I found myself alone, pacing in Pearlstein's office behind the familiar desk. Looking out through the array of windows at a Manhattan skyline bursting with lights and color, I hadn't the slightest inkling the scene about to unfold was destined for notoriety. Had I suspected the next thirty minutes of dialogue would be repeatedly scrutinized and reviewed for interpretation of every word, with lives hanging in the balance, and that the film of the encounter would be replayed hundreds of times on international television, in courtrooms, and at grand jury proceedings, my attitude and demeanor may have been severely altered, and my performance and the value of the evening greatly diminished.

For me, it was honestly just another uncomfortable evening sponsored by the friendly neighborhood FBI. All I wanted was to get things done, run through a quick debriefing, and head out for dinner.

Kaplan entered the room, along with two unexpected sidekicks. He looked typically mafioso: medium height, dark hair and eyes, five o'clock shadow in full bloom. Wearing a nylon running suit, gold chain, watch, and bracelet, he could just as easily have been heading out to a casting call for *The Sopranos*.

Our guest seemed instantly at home, taking one of the seats in front of Andrew's desk, leaning back, and spreading his arms as if it was a comfortable and familiar spot. One sidekick plopped himself into the other chair facing the desk, while the second commandeered a chair on the far wall beside an immense fish tank. Andrew grabbed his own seat and I elected to remain standing, steadily pacing up and down the side aisle of the office.

Kaplan introduced himself and his associates. Smiling continuously, he opened with regrets for being a bit late and for needing to push on to the airport very soon. His smiles and self-deprecating attitude notwithstanding, I unexpectedly found myself alarmed by his projected aura. There was something about Kaplan's eyes; while his lips were smiling and his body language was intended as familiar, his eyes were piercing, hard, and most of all, dead. Unlike DePalma, who betrayed vibes of a sociopath fighting for control to contain his inner demons, Kaplan was definitely in total control. I was convinced this man could not be trusted, and I was dealing with someone with a hidden, and potentially malignant, plan.

Our guest's presentation began with a profuse apology for the long-ago sit-down, and his assembled coterie immediately joined in. Looking to change the negative conversation into a positive field, Kaplan now revealed he'd secretly been visiting Scores as a customer over the past few weeks, explaining he'd taken time "as a friend" to evaluate the operation through professional eyes. "By the way," he smiled broadly, repeating what he'd told Andrew at Penn Station, "I have a million-dollar idea for you."

As the entire room waited in expectation, he went on to suggest every cab driver delivering a fare to Scores be handed a five-dollar tip by the doorman—compliments of management. "You can bet the next time that cabbie is asked to recommend a club, he'll be pushing the hell out of Scores—and only Scores."

I looked at Andrew and he stared back, smiling. We both turned back to Kaplan, and Andrew said, "That *is* a million-dollar idea." And from that night forth, every taxi driver delivering a fare to the club received a tip and, indeed, the club was the talk of the Big Apple's Yellow Cab world for some time to come.

It was clear Kaplan was leading up to some kind of business proposition, but first wanted to impress us with his strip bar acumen. In practiced remarks, he informed us we were "missing the boat" on millions of dollars in potential revenues, and he was willing to share "special" practices he'd invented in his own club. According to Kaplan:

- Dancers are required to solicit and cajole patrons into buying expensive cocktails for them, which, unbeknownst to the customers, are severely watered down. In this way, liquor profits soar.

- Patrons are too intimidated to solicit sex from magnificent lithe exotic dancers, most of whom are lesbians anyway. Instead, the Gold Club employs a bevy of "cocktail waitresses," with the emphasis on "cock," who are readily available for sexual encounters. "They're a bunch of cows," he proudly declared, "but any customer can fuck the crap out of any one of them all night long for the right price."

- The "right price" is paid to the club when a customer secures a booth in the rear of the establishment and purchases a mandatory bottle of champagne for each thirty minutes of occupancy. The benefit to the club is that a one-hundred-dollar bottle of mediocre bubbly is sold at a price of one thousand dollars.

- It is prudent practice to allow celebrities use of these booths without charge, as it encourages others to follow suit. He shared that his "celebrity booth policy" is regularly taken advantage of by NBA, NFL, and MLB professional athletes.

I silently stared back at Kaplan in horror. While he probably believed we were rendered speechless by the dollar signs dancing in our heads, quite the opposite was true. First, everything Kaplan proposed was grossly illegal. Aside from the obvious disregard for prostitution and solicitation laws, New York statutes specifically prohibited any club employee from "pandering" to a customer for the purchase of drinks. I casually mentioned this fact in passing to our guest, who showed no reaction to the information.

This man is just nuts, I thought. *Why would we ever commit untold numbers of felonies, and thereby endanger the most profitable club in all of Manhattan? With vice cops in Scores every night, we'd be closed in ten minutes.*

More significant, however, was the fact Kaplan was unexpectedly and voluntarily confessing on videotape to untold numbers of crimes. Without the slightest prodding, he was eloquently digging a hole from which he could never extricate himself. *Talk about being in the right place at the wrong time,* I thought. *This is the unluckiest night of his life.*

After completing his self-destructive soliloquy, and asking the Scores owners to mull his suggestions over, Kaplan reminded the assembled group of his need to get rolling to the airport. He proposed a follow-up dinner to continue discussions, but took time to cover one further matter.

Kaplan extended an invitation to us to travel to Atlanta two weeks hence for a major weekend he was sponsoring where there would be tons of "friendly" strip club owners to meet from across the country. He promised us a complete tour of his club, and an opportunity to see his profit suggestions in action.

We immediately indicated our gratitude and intention to attend, subject to clearing existing appointments.

Karst and Ready were stunned as I described the night's events at the formal debriefing. When their incredulity persisted, I just sat back and said, "Guys, just go to the videotape!"

The next day, Karst called to say the prosecutors were "blown away" by the Kaplan recording. "The man actually confessed to a mind-boggling number of felonies," Karst added, sounding borderline giddy. "We're reaching out to the United States Attorney in Atlanta to see if he wants us to accept the invitation for the weekend."

When the subject next arose, Karst reported the Atlanta prosecutors were enthralled with our results on the undercover tape and desperately wanted us in Atlanta to work covertly at the invited weekend. "They've had their eyes on Kaplan for quite some time, believing him to be a man with strong mafia ties. Until now, they could never get close enough to build a solid case."

Eyeing the trip to Atlanta, the FBI formulated a plan whereby three FBI agents would accompany Andrew and me into the "belly of the beast." As usual, I would wear the F-Bird and Pearlstein would run interference, presumably by getting drunk. Only one small, bureaucratic problem needed to be resolved. The bail conditions set in Orlando contained travel restrictions limiting us to New York, New Jersey, Connecticut, and Florida. In order to proceed to Atlanta, we would technically need permission from the Florida judge.

"Is it a problem?" I asked Karst.

"You're going to Atlanta with the FBI. It's a technicality."

With all plans set, a few days before our departure for Atlanta, Karst called. "The Atlanta trip is cancelled, Michael. The Florida judge, Conway, refused our request to take you there."

"Are you kidding?"

"Unfortunately not."

"But, Jack, doesn't the judge realize she's killing an undercover operation by the bureau with far-reaching potential benefits? What possible problem could she have with our travel in the company of federal agents?"

"She didn't say, Michael, she just denied the request. It has to be the first time in history that a federal judge has refused to allow defendants on bail, cooperating in an undercover mafia investigation, to travel under FBI supervision. It's just inexplicable to everyone here because the judge is violating settled public policy.

"We're sending a letter requesting reconsideration," he continued, "but as of this moment the Kaplan trip is a dead issue. You can't believe how disappointed and unhappy the Atlanta prosecutors are feeling."

I hung up the phone with a mixture of conflicting emotions. On one hand, I was relieved at the cancellation because I'd been quite frightened at the prospect of the trip with its inherent unknowns and dangers. On the other hand, the judge was acting outside reasonable judicial roles. Her ruling was frightening in that it was actually protecting the mob from a federal probe.

Judge Anne Conway issued no ruling on the government's request for reconsideration of her decision. Waiting in vain until the very last possible minute, we finally called Kaplan to express regrets at our inability to attend.

To the frustration of all, the Kaplan initiative was abandoned in New York and shipped off to Atlanta for further evaluation and investigation. Instead of obtaining recorded confessions and firsthand testimony documenting the illegalities being perpetrated nightly at the Gold Club, the ruling set the government on a course that would eventually require the expenditure of millions of tax dollars, over a number of years, to reach a result that could have been attained in a single night of covert recording at virtually no expense.

After the window of opportunity had forever closed, Judge Conway issued a surprise order on the following Monday reversing field. She'd now decided to allow the Atlanta trip to proceed, even though the meeting to be taped had already taken place. The prosecutors and agents, finding themselves more confused and frustrated than before, could offer no plausible explanation for the judge's prior or new decision. Needless to say, there were a substantial number of disbelieving heads shaking furiously in the halls of the Department of Justice that day.

At the close of this most unhappy episode, I could not divest myself of a disconcerting feeling that, notwithstanding Sandy Weinberg's reassurances to the contrary, Judge Conway was not going to prove to be the ideal choice for two cooperating witnesses from New York City. In my heart, I worried a judge who would actually subvert an FBI undercover sting operation might *not* be prepared to reward its participants generously, or even reasonably.

With perfect clarity I understood, between an openly hostile prosecutor, and a seemingly indifferent judge, I was up to my neck in a deep pile of shit.

With a heavy heart and waning enthusiasm, my attention was turned without warning to an unexpected meeting with the acting head of the Colombo crime family, Alphonse "Allie Boy" Persico, a man with a well-earned reputation for violence and mayhem.

Relying upon intercepted wiretap information, the FBI learned Persico was scheduled to attend a birthday fête being thrown at Scores. I learned of the party from the agents, and was directed to reach out through my own contacts to request a meeting with Persico at the event. I was also told I would be strapping on my F-Bird for the encounter.

The plan went off without a hitch and, under the guise of seeking permission to open a new Scores in the heart of Persico's turf in Brooklyn, the requested private meeting during the birthday party was confirmed. With the F-Bird planted in the "Karst pouch," I headed out to Scores on party night. Upon arrival, I unhappily discovered an entire group of some of my closest friends dining in the restaurant. I made the instant decision to keep far away from them, even if it meant raising some eyebrows. I feared an inadvertent remark about some casual illegality might get recorded and wind up opening an unwanted can of worms for one of the folks I cared most about in the world.

The Persico party was assigned to the President's Club, which we'd closed to the public for the evening. I busied myself with preparations for the bash, constantly checking my watch in anticipation of our target's arrival. As the hours passed, all of the invitees made appearances, with the exception of the Allie Boy crew.

At ten o'clock, with still no Persico in sight, one of the managers approached me and whispered, "Boss, Leonardo DiCaprio just arrived with a small party. He's asking for you, and I seated them in the Champagne Lounge."

"Perfect, just let him know I'll get over there as soon as I can. Meantime, everything he wants is on the house."

Leonardo DiCaprio was my absolute favorite celebrity guest at Scores. He'd been a regular for years, and I'd come to enjoy the actor's sense of humor and sharp intellect. DiCaprio was never permitted to spend his own cash at the club, and all of his guests were accorded celebrity status.

Again concerned some undesired remark might find its way on to the recording F-Bird, I slowly approached the lounge area with a sense of trepidation. "Hey, kid," I opened, hugging Leonardo, who'd stood in reaction to my presence.

Pointing to the young men to his right, he said, "Say hello to Tobey Maguire, he's one of my best friends and an actor, and to David Blaine, the world's best magician." As these were the days before they achieved fame and celebrity in their own right, I honestly paid scant attention to the introductions in the midst of the crowded craziness and obscene noise level of the club.

Virtually shouting to a man standing six inches away, I asked Leonardo whether he wanted to remain in the lounge or preferred a private party in the Crow's Nest. With a broad smile, probably remembering prior escapades in the club's most sequestered area, he opted for the private facilities, whereupon I motioned for the trio to follow me.

With drinks and dancers quickly arriving in the Nest, I excused myself for a moment to learn whether Persico had yet made an appearance. Told he was still missing-in-action, I made an immediate decision. I wasn't going to risk recording an innocent friend for a meeting with Persico that probably wasn't going to happen. In quick succession, I climbed the spiral staircase, told Leonardo I'd be back to set up dinner, and dashed down again and out the front door to find the FBI van that I knew to be parked around the corner on a deserted stretch of quiet street.

When I tapped on the van's passenger's side window, both Karst and Ready jumped in surprise. I met their concerned stares by motioning to the rear of the van: "Let's talk in the back." In the quiet of the vehicle's rear chamber, which was stacked with shotguns and recording equipment, I explained Persico was now more than three hours late, and the party was itself winding down. "Nobody still expects him; I think we're wasting our time."

Admitting to their own fatigue, the agents agreed it would be prudent to abort the evening's operation. Given the go-ahead, I handed over the beeper-transmitter, and stripped off my suit pants as the F-Bird and mini microphones were removed.

"Don't worry about it," Ready remarked of our first investigative disappointment, "every night can't be a home run. We'll get Persico some other time."

As the van began pulling away from the curb, it suddenly stopped and Karst rolled down the window. "I meant to ask you, how's your postsurgical ass feeling? All healed?"

I heard loud laughter escaping the cabin as the van quickly pulled away. I shouted after them at the top of my lungs, "You know, the two of you can just go screw yourselves!"

With the official portion of the night now ended, I retraced my steps to the club. No longer concerned about inadvertently capturing private conversations, I stopped at my friends' table to smooth over my initial poor manners. Satisfied all was well, I headed back to the Nest for a bit of much-needed decompressing. Leonardo and I quickly conferred over the menu and ordered a combination of finger foods. As we were waiting for the order, he turned to me. "I think your club is boffo."

"Well, I appreciate that and you know you and your friends are always welcome as my guests."

Smiling wryly, Leonardo asked, "By the way, do you know what 'boffo' means?"

"Hey, kid, listen, I knew what it meant before you were born, although I've never heard anyone not collecting social security actually use the word."

He laughed, but before he could shoot his next barb, a club manager appeared at the top of the spiral staircase with a large, muscular, swarthy stranger. The two made their way directly to me.

"Say hello to Dom," the manager began. "He's here with our friend."

As I stretched out my hand, "shit" was the single word that pierced my pained mind. Persico had finally arrived.

"Nice to meet you, you got a great place. He's in your office waiting."

Nodding, I mumbled excuses to Leonardo and headed off, without benefit of F-Bird or beeper-transmitter, to a now useless meeting with the head of the Colombo crime clan.

The route from the Crow's Nest required following a path through the restaurant to the club's office, passing a side door leading to the employees' bathroom and a private exit to the street. As I passed the side door, Dom grabbed my left shoulder and pushed me aggressively though the portal. Startled and disoriented by the surprise maneuver, I stumbled into the usually deserted hallway only to find two more brutes awaiting me. Fearing the jig was up, my cooperation somehow uncovered, the blood drained from my head as I stared in silence at this welcoming committee. When I noticed one of the men was brandishing a revolver, I felt myself passing out of consciousness.

One of them grabbed me and held me up against the nearest wall, another proceeding to open my shirt and rip my slacks and underwear to the floor. An immediate search of my entire body indelicately began.

The gun-toting leader closed the distance separating him from me and whispered, "Nobody sees our friend without being fully searched."

Initially failing to remember the F-Bird had been removed, I shut my eyes and waited to be carted out to a car on the street for final disposition with Jimmy Hoffa. I could think of nothing to say or do to save myself, and was proud of the self-control I was demonstrating in the face of my end of days.

Despite this steely resolve, I began uncontrollably shaking until I was mercifully flooded with the realization there was nothing to hide and I would actually pass this inspection with flying colors. I cursed at my own stupidity, when new stabs of fear raced through me. *What if Karst didn't get all the tape off my abdomen? He always leaves some. What if this idiot below sees the scars from the F-Birds on my thigh? Will he know what he's looking at?*

After what seemed an eternity, bile building up in my throat, the searching mechanics finally ended and a surprisingly high-pitched voice came bellowing from the direction of my crotch. "He's clean."

As they all waited for the leader to give the next order, I felt myself growing uncontrollably elated. Looking down at the stranger still positioned in front of my privates, I needed all my self-control to suppress what would have been a most untimely episode of laughter. Stretching my neck, I silently mused, *Here I am again, with another mob guy introducing himself to my dick and ass. I'm beginning to suspect this whole mafia thing is a closet gay organization.*

Holding on to control for dear life, I snapped back into reality when the armed fellow returned his gun to its shoulder holster and smirked. "Sorry about all this, you can go on in now."

What to do, what to do? I decided I needed to react in the way any innocent club owner would respond. I also wanted to find a respectful excuse to avoid the scheduled face-to-face with the head of one of the five international families as I was bare of F-Bird.

Pulling my pants back into place and rebuttoning my shirt, I turned to the trio. "Please tell your boss I'm going to get my message to him through intermediaries. With all due respect, and I understand a need to protect and insulate him from rats, I can't allow myself to be treated like this in my own place. A simple request and I would have willingly submitted to a search, but I never expected a surprise attack. Please let him know I'm not insulted, just not up for any business tonight."

Without allowing time for retort, I straightened myself up, exited the hallway into the restaurant, and made my way directly back to the Nest, legs wobbling and equilibrium in total disarray.

Reaching the top of the Nest's circular staircase, I laughed out loud at the sight unfolding before me. The only patron there was Leonardo, who was sprawled out in a lounge chair, three topless dancers attending to him. "Last time I saw anyone getting this much attention, it was from a mafioso and a proctologist," I joked out loud for my exclusive benefit as I took a seat on a couch and helplessly fell asleep.

I'd no concept of how much time passed when Leonardo shook me back to life. Standing before me, now sporting a sweatshirt and knitted cap pulled below his ears, I would never have recognized him but for his uniquely piercing eyes.

Extending his hand, the film star said, "Michael, we're all taking off, we promised to stop at a party and we're already late. Thanks for everything."

I stared back at my guest and newly crowned personal savior, overwhelmed by feelings of gratitude. Had Leonardo not come to Scores for dinner, sought my attention, and provided me with a personal motive to abort the covert recording of a high-profile target, I might not have decided to ditch the body wire. And, had I still been wearing it when the Persico crew searched me, there's little doubt as to what would have ensued.

Without knowing it, intending it, or even now realizing it, DiCaprio had, by a chance decision to drop in at his favorite Manhattan strip bar, and by simply being himself, single-handedly saved my life.

When I reported the night's disturbing turn of late-breaking events to Karst in the morning, my words were greeted with unusual total silence. "We were very, very lucky," he slowly intoned.

"Jack, make me feel better, tell me if I had been wearing the transmitter when all this went down, there would have been ample time for you and Bill to bust in and save me."

Karst didn't answer.

"Jack?"

"To tell you the God's honest truth, probably not, Michael. One of the reasons we agreed to abort was we weren't getting a peep of reception out of the beeper and it was worrying us."

"So I would have been completely on my own and in trouble?"

"More trouble than you probably realize. Part of Allie Boy's street reputation is he takes killing responsibilities personally."

"And you decide to tell me this now?"

I hung up the phone, my hands shaking.

CHAPTER THIRTY-FOUR
The Rule of Threes

Ancient superstition warns that evil always rears its head in episodes of three. Wary of this teaching, soldiers in foxholes under enemy fire refuse to light cigarettes with "three on a match" to ward off this time-proven curse. After the disappointment in Atlanta, and the escape from Persico's surprise shakedown for body wires, it took scant time for my third bout of ill fortune to arrive. It all began about a week after the Persico party, on a relatively unremarkable day.

Harvey Osher, my friend and Scores "right-hand man," decided to conduct an impromptu meeting with Andrew. Osher had invested some of his family's money in a boxing event that ended up being cancelled back in November 1996. The investment had been guaranteed by Scores and, after waiting for Pearlstein to voluntarily honor the guarantee, Harvey became increasingly disgruntled. He decided to confront Andrew on the issue.

When Osher voiced his demand and need for immediate payment of the long-overdue obligation, Pearlstein's blithe response went something like: "Listen Harvey, you made an investment, it didn't pan out, that's what's called doing business in the real world. Scores isn't covering your losses."

Now, it's never been clear whether Pearlstein just didn't remember, or chose at the moment not to remember, that Osher held a written guarantee for the debt from the club. But hearing Andrew's answer, Harvey's usually mild-mannered temperament snapped like a dry twig. Losing control, he banged his closed fists on the keyboard of Andrew's laptop computer and, raising the unit above his head, smashed it to smithereens on the closest available wall.

Exiting through the shared bathroom, and now in my office, he screamed something indecipherable in my direction about "killing" my "asshole partner," and departed before I could wring any sense out of him.

As fate would have it, Harvey jumped into his car and drove to Brooklyn to find our mutual friend and Scores ownership nominee, Blitz Bilzinsky. Knowing Blitz dined every evening at the same time in the same restaurant, he headed directly to that establishment.

Blitz happened to be in the company of a Scores investor, Marcus Woodall, when Harvey arrived in a whirlwind of angry emotion. Ignoring Woodall, Harvey described his earlier confrontation with Pearlstein, vowing to collect what was owed to him. He then unthinkingly made a statement of potentially monumental significance: "Hey, Blitz, I wonder how Andrew would like it if I called Sergio and told him Andrew was cooperating with the feds against him!"

At that precise moment, Blitz was called from the table for an emergency telephone call. The call was from me: intuiting Harvey may have headed over to see Blitz, I wanted to ensure that Harvey learned the loan problem had been resolved between Andrew and myself and he would be repaid shortly. Blitz assured me that Harvey had in fact safely arrived, and promised to calm him down.

When Blitz returned to the table, Woodall excused himself. As Blitz shared the "good news" from the call, Woodall headed to the basement level of the restaurant where he picked up one of the public telephones, dialed Mike Sergio's number, and told Sergio he had just learned from Osher that Pearlstein—and so probably yours truly as well—was cooperating with federal authorities against him.

As all this was happening, I was working late in the office, alone and plodding my way through a mountain of paperwork. When my phone rang, I almost didn't answer it but, as the insistent ringing persisted, I picked up the receiver. It was Mike Sergio.

"Are you gonna be there for a while?"

"At least a couple of hours. Why?"

"I'm gonna leave from the Bronx right now. I need to talk to you about something important."

I stared at the clock on the desk, reading the time to be 6:45 PM. After thinking things through, I decided I would film the unexpected encounter. Doing some quick calculations about a trip from the Bronx, I decided to turn on the cameras at around 7:10.

Less than three minutes later, with no time to activate the ceiling equipment, Mike Sergio walked into the office. No smile, no handshake, just an angry stare.

The call had obviously been a ruse. He wanted to know if I was in the firm, and he didn't want me to have time to prepare anything, I thought to myself. To Sergio I said, "I thought you said you were in the Bronx."

"I thought you were my friend."

"Listen, Mike, what's this about?"

Sergio pulled down the zipper of the light yellow jacket he was wearing. Reaching to his waist, he pulled out a gun and placed it on the desk.

Feeling the now-familiar ring of anxiety radiating through me, not knowing whether to try to grab the gun, or run out of the office, or throw a paperweight at Sergio, I just sat frozen in time.

Sergio stood and started pacing. "Michael, I'm from the old school. You know I believe you not only kill cooperators, you kill their family and friends too. I don't go for this shit about leaving the others alone. Know what I mean?"

I didn't respond. Without knowing the source of Sergio's anger, I feared I might make things worse by guessing.

Sergio reached for his weapon, picked it up, and pointed it at me. "If what I heard on the phone is true, we're all dead men. But you're going to be the first."

I stayed still, afraid any sudden move might jump his trigger finger. "Mike, just tell me what you heard."

His eyes flared in intensity. "I just heard Andrew Pearlstein is a federal cooperator."

The words emptied my lungs, but I knew I had to maintain control. Crinkling my forehead in disbelief, shaking my head, and lifting my eyes to the ceiling, I said, "If Andrew were a cooperator, I'd know. We're codefendants in Florida and they'd have had to reveal that information to me."

"Listen, Michael." Sergio sat again. "If that's true, great. But that's exactly what you'd say if you were cooperating alongside him. And if you two are rats, I'm dead because I vouched for you with the family."

It was clear Sergio didn't want to believe we were cooperating, but he'd need more than words to turn aside his strong tide of suspicion. I also knew I needed to glean more information to attempt to make things right.

I leaned forward. "Mike, just tell me where all this nonsense is coming from." I then held my breath, hoping the source wouldn't be law enforcement or defense lawyers, hoping it would be someone impeachable.

Seeming to decide on his next move, he answered, "I just got a call from Marcus Woodall; he said he was having dinner with Blitz and Harvey when Harvey blurted out Andrew was cooperating with the feds."

I felt as if I had been hit with a bolt of lightning. Realizing this was surely not any form of betrayal, but more likely a remark spoken in anger, my mind recognized some possible wiggle room. I understood what I had to make happen.

"Mike, let's call Woodall together right now. I want to hear it for myself so I can put this crap to rest."

Sergio wanted to be convinced the story was bogus; I could feel it with every fiber of my being. He actually seemed pleased at my request for a confrontation.

He read out Woodall's cell number and I dialed it on my speakerphone. When Woodall came on the line, I told him I was with Sergio and we both wanted him to repeat exactly what happened.

Woodall nervously told the story and ended with the quote from Osher: "I wonder how Andrew would like it if I called Mike Sergio and told him Andrew was cooperating undercover with the feds against him."

I felt myself going into cross-examination mode. "Marcus, you know don't you, Harvey had come to the restaurant directly from a fight with Andrew?"

"That's true; that's what he said."

"And he was still really angry at Andrew, wasn't he?"

"I think he could've killed Andrew if he was there."

"So, was he saying he *knew* Andrew was cooperating or he could get Andrew in big trouble by *saying* he was cooperating?"

There was a long pause before Marcus said, "To tell you the truth, it could have been either, but it was more likely just a spiteful remark."

Knowing my questions had just destroyed Woodall's credibility, I glanced over at Sergio and frowned. He drew his pointer finger under his neck, signaling for me to end the call.

For the next fifteen minutes, we talked matters over and the meeting, which began as an assassination plan, ended up as a lovefest.

As Sergio departed, he added, "I'd rather you didn't mention this to Andrew; I don't want to look stupid."

Once Mike left, I was annoyed I hadn't captured the confrontation on tape. But on reconsideration, I realized it was actually another lucky turn of events. In fact, I counseled myself, I couldn't even mention this Sergio confrontation to the FBI. I needed to pretend nothing had happened as the telling, of even a cleaned-up version, would raise "danger" issues and possibly terminate the investigation. Anyway, without a taped confirmation, the information would be of no significance to the government.

"Almost died for nothing," I mused out loud to the empty room.

Deciding to call it a night, I rose and packed my briefcase; I was feeling very sad, overwhelmingly dejected, and quite alone. More alone than I'd ever felt in all my days.

CHAPTER THIRTY-FIVE

Descent into Madness

I'd lost count of how many times I'd strapped on that F-Bird, how many times I'd flipped the recording switches in my office. I'd lost track of how many dangerous conversations I'd conducted, how many times I'd narrowly escaped death.

And I was struggling with personal loss. Over a period of eighteen months, I'd buried my mother, my father, and my brother-in-law: three funerals, three eulogies, three blows to the heart. I never had time to truly grieve; the undercover investigation had been underway and my focus was on simple survival.

I'd reached my limit. I hadn't experienced a day of absolute peace since the illegal purchase of National Heritage in Orlando in 1990. Stress and fear were my life now, and my thoughts spiraled destructively. I thought endlessly about how I'd be executed by the mob: Would it be a bullet, a knife, or a pair of cement shoes? Everyone's luck eventually runs out, everyone craps out and throws that seven even after the roll of a lifetime. How many narrow escapes does one Jewish kid from Brooklyn get?

Through all of this, I'd outwardly maintained my composure and the mafia suspected nothing; the FBI kept telling me I was a "natural." And I did manage to keep my head in very dangerous situations. But the truth is, I was going crazy. I wasn't the "good little soldier" marching mindlessly and unscathed from one undercover episode to the next: fearless, reckless, indestructible. Away from the mobsters and the feds, when the cameras were off and the tape wasn't rolling, fear and loneliness overwhelmed me, and my behavior became increasingly erratic.

Every day I struggled with the compulsion to find a hidden corner and cry my eyes out or, at least, call the agents and insist on an end to the madness. The ones who loved me had no inkling what was truly going on, and the ones "using" me couldn't give a rat's ass about my emotional health. Believe me, if I were killed, the agents and prosecutors would feel sorely aggrieved, but mostly because their precious investigation would be mightily inconvenienced.

But at the same time, I didn't want the investigation to ever end. The day the plug was pulled would be the day I died, the day I morphed from under-cover operative to witness, the day I bid farewell to all I knew. I ruminated endlessly on what it would be like to actually lose everything: identity, family, and friends. The more I dwelled on these thoughts, the more panic set in. Yet how could I complain? I'd agreed to all of this.

I started asking myself: *Why am I saving money? The government will take it all anyway, except the club. What can I do to help myself? What can I do to have some happiness in the brief space left to me?* I was on Death Row, but I was free and rich. That potent combination allowed me to plunge as deeply as I could stand into waters of the grotesque. I began a feverish implosion of conduct aimed at exhausting any potential way of staying alive; filling my remaining time with satisfaction, and avoiding my guilt and regret at hurting and disap-pointing those I treasured.

Driven by loss, guilt, and fear, I passed the point of no return before realizing I had lost myself. My fear of eventually losing my identity caused me, for a time, to throw it away.

I'd hosted an AM radio call-in show for many years, first on WOR and then WEVD, with my psychic friend, Ron Bard. The show, named *Psychic Eye*, was a one-hour exploration of all things spiritual, alien, and otherworldly. Ron would give telephone "readings" and counsel each caller about the three never-varying topics of psychic interest: love, money, and health.

After I made the decision to start cooperating and the undercover assign-ments were underway, my attempts at detached analysis began to seriously erode. I couldn't resist questioning each weekly guest psychic about my future. At each show I would squirrel myself away in a private office at the station during a commercial break with an unsuspecting guest and seek out his or her intuition about my nonspecific "legal problems."

Slowly but surely I became an obsessed psychic groupie. With psychic advice pouring in from every quarter of the Big Apple, I engaged in bizarre ritualistic endeavors, and the deeper I traveled into the world of the self-deluded unknown, the more of myself I left behind.

Following instructions from a renowned psychic, I purchased a large eggplant and spent days holding it and meditating my fears out of myself and into the vegetable. I next drove a hundred miles to a point on the coast of the Atlantic Ocean and tossed that eggplant into the waters; supposedly all my problems were thus deposited into the recesses of the deep.

I attended private sessions at which chickens were sacrificed for my well-being, their blood smeared on my face.

On a cold night in February, I visited a small cemetery in New Jersey at midnight and selected the gravesite of a military man. I left an offering, enlisting him in the spirit war against those seeking me harm in the living world.

Covens of witches were charged with casting spells to foil those seeking injustice against me.

I took baths in disgusting, foul-smelling liquids to purge my aura and cast out demons.

I submitted myself to spiritual cleansings performed by groups of obese Jamaican female seers. They sang, laid on hands, scrubbed the air over me, and prayed.

I was advised to obtain a pure-white dove and interact with it in my home for several hours. I was then to release the bird—along with my woes—from the balcony of my apartment on the fifty-sixth floor. I followed the instructions to the letter and threw this poor unsuspecting animal into the air. We must have developed a deeper relationship than I realized because that dove wouldn't leave the premises. For days it prowled my balcony and windowsills, leaving mounds of green shit behind in its wake. It was only with the kind assistance of the city's emergency animal control service that the dove and I ever parted company.

I knew these activities stretched the credible, and I was certainly too embarrassed to share them with any of my intimates. But if there was even the slightest possibility a ritual could influence the outcome of my fate, I wanted to invoke it. I can see now that I could barely tell reality from insanity.

Comfort from the psychic world soon found itself accompanied by pleasures of the flesh. Before my cooperation began, I lived a quiet, semi-closeted, gay lifestyle; it had taken me most of my life to understand what I now know to be my genetically inherited sexual preference. I spent many quiet years building a group of intimate friends whom I loved with all my heart.

But now, my feelings of loss, regret, and fear drove me to mindlessly seek out an astounding number of sexual encounters with virtual strangers. At my insistence, friends began introducing me to those of their friends who'd caught my eye. For the first time in my life I began frequenting gay bars, picking up strangers, and answering personal ads. I gained a reputation among visiting models as a generous gay businessman seeking one-night stands. I became a regular at The Gaiety, a club featuring amazing nude men dancing onstage. As the owner of Scores, there was never a night when two or three performers could not be cajoled back to the club and then on to my condo for private parties.

I indulged myself recklessly, trying to fill my life with enough sex for a lifetime in each passing month. Alas, my quest to drown my pain in the loving arms of the world's most beautiful specimens was a complete and total bust. I was feeling no better at the end of each day, probably worse; in the end, it brought me no solace or comfort. In fact, it led me to neglect the friends I'd loved for years, leaving me with a growing fear that without the endless array of bodies prancing before me, I would be utterly alone. I'd abandoned reason for absurd rituals and genuine friendship for mindless sex. I needed to get hold of myself, but I didn't know how.

Sitting in my living room, looking out over the most awe-inspiring skyline in the history of mankind, I had no idea how to make things right, or if they could ever be made right again. I could confide in no one, and everything I did to heal myself only made me feel worse. I could find no pleasure in acts of pleasure. I spurned advice, offered no explanations to anyone for my moods or behavior, and could not exert control over my raw impulses outside the spheres of daily work and nightly FBI tasks.

I was burning up in a silent, invisible protest that no one could hear, and not even I could understand.

―――――――

I'd just completed yet another F-Bird operation, this time at Willie Marshall's wedding, which had a guest list that read like a "Who's Who" of the

Westchester County mob. When the usual debriefing exercises were at an end, Karst put his hand on my shoulder. "You'd better sit down for this next part."

Cold white fear rose instantly through my entire body, as I instinctively knew my world was about to be forever destroyed.

"Michael, the investigation is over as of this minute. We're not happy about it, but the prosecutors have pulled the plug. You have three days to pack up and move out of the city, and you need to be in Orlando by that time for a proffer. We're all going to assist you and Andrew in every way, including relocation money, and in finding safe houses to live in until the indictments are issued and the trials completed. Don't think now, we'll go over everything tomorrow."

The room started spinning. *Did he say "pack up"? We were promised at least another year. Pack up what in three days? Pack up my life?*

"It can't be done, Jack, I won't do it! I want to talk to Carol and Marjorie!"

"You will," Karst retorted, wearing a hard stare. "You knew this day would come, and within three days the mafia will know about your tapes. You can either stay free and work with us, or they'll make a motion to revoke your bail and ship you off to witness jail for your own protection."

"Holy shit." Those were the only words that would come to my numbed and frozen mind.

PART FOUR

Becoming Irrelevant

CHAPTER THIRTY-SIX
Shock and Awe

NOVEMBER 1997

After eleven months, 110 taped conversations with twenty-three mafia targets, and hundreds of additional hours expended in briefings, debriefings, and proffers, the New York undercover investigation was history. We now needed to be packed, out of New York City forever, and on our way to Orlando for proffer interviews as the first step to becoming witnesses in the Heritage insurance fraud case—all in three days!

During this new proffer process in Florida, we would be under the exclusive supervision of the FBI in a sort of unofficial Witness Security Program. We'd be hiding in plain sight with new identities, and would so remain until the cooperation in New York and Florida was complete, including the trials. Only at that point would we surrender into federal custody to serve whatever minimal jail sentence was imposed by the Florida court. After that, we'd enter the official WITSEC program run by the United States Marshals Service, and begin new, anonymous lives.

Sipperly and Miller let it be known that if we deviated, even slightly, from the outlined schedule, all deals in Florida would be "off the table." We would find ourselves prosecuted as defendants there, and we would never have another opportunity to earn short stints in country-club jails. In other words, New York would become impotent to help us and our undercover achievements would go totally unrewarded.

"What you're demanding is crazy and probably impossible," Sandy Weinberg screamed into the phone at Sipperly during a conference call. "Could you sort out your entire lives, and find new places to live anonymously, on seventy-two hours' notice? Think for a second about what you're doing to these men!"

"What we're trying to do is keep your clients from going to jail for the next twenty-five years." She further explained that, at the behest of her office, the powers in Washington had performed serious arm-twisting in Florida and obtained agreement for us, subject to acceptable proffer interviews, to become cooperators in the Heritage trial and earn the rewards offered at the World Trade Center meeting.

"But what guarantee do we have Hunt won't just set us up to fail?" Andrew interrupted. "That's exactly what she's been doing since the beginning."

"Because Hunt won't be the final word. Her boss, the district's first assistant, will be running the show. Hunt will be there, but we've been assured it will be her boss's decision as to whether you're being honest and forthcoming. The only part of all this we can't change is the timing that must be underway before Thanksgiving."

During the course of protracted exchanges with the agents in the following days, reasons for the recent events emerged. Apparently, the New York prosecutors finally convinced the attorney general in Washington that Florida's refusal to accept us as cooperators, and their threat to prosecute us as defendants instead, would destroy our credibility as witnesses in the mafia case in New York. After all, why would a jury in New York believe anything we said after mafia defense attorneys argued we'd been rejected as witnesses in Florida because local prosecutors branded us as liars?

Washington suddenly came to the realization that Hunt's decisions held potentially far-reaching ramifications beyond her local fraud case. If the situation wasn't satisfactorily resolved, the probable result would be disaster for the most important mafia prosecution of the decade, and embarrassment of the Department of Justice on center stage before a worldwide media audience.

The next day, my last in New York, I ordered a taxi to the airport. A sense of numbness overtook me as I locked my door, stepped into the elevator, and passed through the always glorious lobby. My mood turned mournful as I drank in the sights of the city, trying to memorize details of the Empire State Building, the United Nations, and all the landmarks that had become my backyard. I even sneaked one last look at the Scores exterior.

As depression was enveloping every part of my psyche, I suddenly willed all thought processes to a screeching halt and began lecturing myself. Yes, I was losing much to the moment, but who knew what lay ahead? I decided I could only survive by anticipating the future as an unmitigated adventure. After all, how many people get a new life, a new name, and endless opportunities? So long as I was able to sell Scores to a friendly buyer, so long as I was protected, so long as the minimal jail term in a "hotel" jail was not one more broken promise by New York, I could definitely make things work.

I was now determined to make it a beginning. No more self-pity, no more loathing, no more complaints. I decided not to measure my life by what I was leaving behind but, rather, by the possibilities ahead.

As I boarded the plane, it was not with the sadness and hopelessness that overwhelmed my last hours in New York; those emotions were replaced with a genuine sense of wonder at the life stretching before me. I would be renewed.

CHAPTER THIRTY-SEVEN

A New Life Begins, Maybe

NOVEMBER 1997—A DISNEY THEME PARK HOTEL, ORLANDO, FLORIDA

I was so out of place, a lone shadowy figure walking amid vacationing families radiating sheer joy. As far as I could tell, I was the only person in a business suit; all around me were mothers and fathers in T-shirts and shorts, and kids with Mickey Mouse ears and stuffed Disney character dolls in their clutched arms. I wished I could change places with any of them for just a little while.

Sitting in the hotel's lobby restaurant at eight the next morning, wearing the same blue pinstripe suit and red tie I'd worn the previous day, and picking unenthusiastically at a plate of bacon and runny eggs, I was already feeling telltale signs of nervous exhaustion. Glancing at my watch for the tenth time in five minutes, I sighed in relief upon catching sight of my new lawyer retained for today's proffer, Norman Moscowitz out of Miami. I rose to greet him, and together we headed out for the short trip into Orlando proper.

In response to security concerns voiced by the FBI, it was agreed the interview would not take place at the prosecutor's offices in the Orlando federal courthouse. Instead, the government's plan was to secretly gather at a downtown hotel called the Harley. Andrew's proffer was scheduled for a week later, and probably in a different place.

Norman and I encountered light morning traffic and quickly reached the hotel. Ascending an inclined walkway at the entrance, passing through a pair of glass doors, and climbing a set of interior stairs, we were greeted by a medium-sized man with broad shoulders, dark hair, and glasses, sporting an impressive suit and a firm, confident handshake. This was Mike Siegel, Hunt's superior, and the man designated to run the day's show.

Siegel was the only glimmer of hope I held for potential fair treatment in Florida. He was a transplanted urbanite, having arrived in Florida after completing a prosecutorial stint in New York's Organized Crime Task Force. We would finally be subject to review by a Florida prosecutor who understood the dangers we'd endured, one sympathetic to the rewards for leniency that traditionally flow from extraordinary life-threatening cooperation.

With a sweeping arm motion, Siegel led us back down the same stairs we'd climbed, through a glass-paneled corridor looking out on the hotel's pool, and into a medium-sized conference room dominated by a large glass-topped rectangular table.

And so my Heritage proffer began. Each member of the task force had been seemingly assigned a chronological area within the complexity of frauds perpetuated on Heritage and its policyholders, and I was going to be questioned by each member within the particular assigned zone of responsibility. The pressure on me eased as I honestly did my best to fill in the factual gaps that had eluded the team in the course of its work. Questioning went on for many hours. The excitement coursing through my body kept me mentally acute, and I started to actually enjoy the process of unburdening myself. By the end of the session, every participant was spent, but it was clear I'd won over the opposition—with the exception of one obviously displeased Judy Hunt.

Siegel walked my attorney and me out of the conference room and into the hotel's vestibule. Shaking hands with Norman, he said, "I don't see a problem here. It turned out to be a good day, far better frankly than I anticipated. Pending completion of Andrew's proffer, I can say they're on board as cooperators and they will have the leniency deal from us as offered."

He looked up at me and winked. "Feel better?"

There was an amiable silence as Norman and I walked to his car. This natural quiet continued as we drove away from the shadow of downtown Orlando.

I was completely focused on my inner thoughts. I didn't even ask where we were heading.

It's actually done, my mind screamed. *I have my deal in Florida.*

After a time, while I was falling in and out of sleep, Norman turned the car sharply right into the awkward driveway of the Marriott Harbor Beach Hotel in Fort Lauderdale, identified only by a thoroughly unimpressive flower covered wooden sign. Passing his car keys and my luggage to an attentive team of valets in uniform, Norman marched through the hotel's revolving front door and turned to the check-in on our right. Trailing behind, I followed him to a station on a long reception counter and watched as he pulled out his American Express card and handed it over to one of the clerks.

"Reservation for a single room, pool view, in the name of Norman Moscowitz. Departure open."

The paperwork for the transaction successfully completed, Norman handed me the room key. "Michael, you're never to use any of your credit cards or your health insurance again. By the way, I'm going to need funds to cover your expenses on my card."

The magnitude of having my name and credit erased in a single swipe felt like a cold slap across the face. Stunned, I obediently opened my briefcase and removed $5,000. With a quick nod, Moscowitz accepted the currency and was gone.

By 11 PM I was antsy. I haplessly channel-surfed, and wound up on the phone with Mark Pastore, my friend, nightlife partner, and radio show producer. As the FBI instructed, I placed my calls through a calling card purchased at the airport, precluding any trace back to me. Before ending the conversation, Mark gave me a list of local gay bars, which I jotted down on a small hotel pad.

I decided it would be good to go out; after all, it was Thanksgiving weekend in a party town. Walking through the lobby to the front door and taxi line, I pulled out the list and selected the top name—"Johnnies"—the bar Pastore accorded his highest "libido" rating.

A few minutes later, after a short ride, I frowned at the small, rundown establishment facing me. Shrugging my shoulders and muttering something about not judging a book by its cover, I approached the entrance.

Unlike familiar trendy clubs elsewhere, this place was dark and dank—seedy, even. I could've furnished the whole establishment for the cost of a few lounge chairs at Scores. The men were old, poorly dressed, deathly quiet, and in need of a squadron of emergency dental surgeons. Taking in the twangy country music groaning out of a filthy jukebox, I made the instant decision to leave, and to recommend Pastore have his libido examined professionally.

As I turned to exit, the bartender looked up and his gaze turned to obvious amusement.

"Hey, Sunbird," he said, motioning me over.

"Sunbird?" I asked, obscurely insulted.

"No offense, Sunbird," he countered evenly, "it's just that you're about the whitest white guy I ever did see. Didn't you fly in for sun?"

After a pause, I nodded, deciding the truth—that I was here hiding from the mafia—was perhaps a bit much.

Satisfied, the bartender pointed to a door on the other side of the room: "I would say you're looking for the other half of the bar, right through there." Ignoring the cackles from the toothless studs at the bar, I headed through the newly revealed escape route.

The owners of "Johnnies" seemingly retained the same team of interior decorators for both halves of their club. A tiny, cheesy stage occupied the far end of the room, and generic stripper music blared. But the crowd *was* pronouncedly younger, better dressed, and plainly well-heeled. Mingling with the clientele was a bevy of "entertainers," all bare-chested and in shorts or jeans. I kept to myself, taking stock of the circulating flesh: 19-25 years old, all very attractive and very tan. "Maybe Pastore's libido is fine," I revised.

I ordered a mix of cranberry and orange juices from the bartender, and found a seat on a stool against the wall. I was curious, but I'd yet to figure out how this operation worked financially.

The first entertainer to dance himself over to my chair was comically uncoordinated, but had other attributes: platinum hair, blue eyes, and beautiful skin.

"Hi. You know, today is my anniversary. I started working here seven days ago."

"How nice," I answered, settling in for some pleasant small talk.

As the young man leaned in between my legs, I noticed with a start that his penis was nestled on my pant leg.

"We usually get a dollar for each encounter," he whispered.

A dollar? I reeled to myself. *What is* this *all about?* But, never one to turn down a bargain, I pulled out a dollar and handed it over.

And then he vanished; replaced by an effeminate Latino lad who repeated the "encounter" and was away in about 10 seconds with his dollar.

"This is crazy," I muttered to no one in particular. "I'm not gonna sit here all night passing out singles just to give my jeans a cheap thrill."

My next dollar seeker was an absolute knockout: a blond, blue-eyed, pointy-nosed dancer who introduced himself as Ryan. This time, once the cat was out of the bag, so to speak, I spoke up—this had to be the most ridiculous business model I'd ever run across, and as an industry expert, I felt I couldn't keep silent in good conscience.

"Look," I said, as Ryan waited for his dollar, "wouldn't you rather spend 20 minutes with me for a hundred bucks than run to the next hundred customers trying to get a dollar out of each of them?"

Ryan thought for a moment and then broke out in a broad and engaging smile; the lightbulb had powered on. "Yes, I would prefer to do this."

"Your accent sounds French Canadian."

"*Oui.* I'm from Quebec."

As I spent the next twenty minutes talking to Ryan, enjoying a dance and a pleasant massage, he plainly began to relax. When I handed him the agreed payment, he planted a soft kiss on my lips and turned to go. And then he turned back. "Michael, would you like to spend twenty minutes with my roommate, Troy?"

I watched Ryan run over to an exquisite dark-haired dancer wearing a patterned red bandanna. He whispered in his ear, showed him the hundred, and pointed me out. Troy instantly headed across the room with a growing smile.

After paying Troy his due, I decided to call it a night. I had done my good deed for the day by sharing my business acumen—and in fact, I'd later discover, the standard operating procedure at Johnnies would never be the same.

As I stood to leave, my first platinum blond entertainer danced awkwardly over to me once more.

"Hi! You know, this is my anniversary. I started working here thirty days ago. One month today and I love it."

As he started to make his move, I skirted away. "You know what's even more amazing? I was here on the night of your one-week anniversary. And it seems like it was only an hour ago."

The next day, I made an appointment at the hotel's massage center, and arrived at a cabana-like structure filled with small rooms and the unmistakable aroma of massage oils. The receptionist had to call my name three times, but eventually I remembered that I was Mr. Moscowitz, and was escorted into Room 4. After a few minutes, a white-clad gentleman entered the cubicle. He was no more than 5'4", white haired, and somewhere in his late sixties. He looked at me. "Mr. M., please get undressed and lie face down on my table."

He left while I took my assigned position and returned a few moments later. Unfortunately, as one who prefers to avoid "massage small talk," this fellow was quite gregarious. In minutes, I knew his name was Joe Cappalini, he was from Manhattan, worked thirty years as a stenographic court reporter in federal court in Manhattan, and had retired to Florida with his wife last year.

I was only half-listening until about halfway through the massage, when Joe leaned over and whispered with a giggle, "I know you're not Moscowitz. I know you're Michael Blutrich from the Cuomo law firm."

I sat bolt upright, not believing my ears. *When did I become a celebrity?* I silently moaned.

"Lie back down, Mr. B," Joe said. "If Mr. Moscowitz wants to let you get a massage on his nickel, why do I care? I get paid just the same."

"Sorry, I was just surprised to hear my name. How is it you remember me?"

"I remember all the attorneys in my cases, especially the good ones like you. I remember one case you handled in particular...."

I tuned out again, thoughts pouring into my consciousness: *This guy is an old school Italian from New York. Does he have ties to the mafia? Will he make a phone call home? Have I blown my cover? Should I check out?* This was turning into a full-blown anxiety attack, but I did all I could to keep my rapidly fraying nerves from showing.

When the massage was over, I thanked Joe, and tipped him handsomely. As he turned to leave, I stopped him. "I'm staying in Orlando and came down just for the day to visit a friend. If I decide to head south again, what days do you work?"

"Sorry, Mr. B., this is my last day. The wife and I head to Europe tomorrow for three months. Been saving twenty years for this trip."

I departed the massage center and literally ran to my room. Sitting in a corner, I tried to decide if Joe was really going abroad, or if he was suspicious and wanted to provide me with a false sense of safety. Pacing the room, I pulled out my cell, dialed into the calling card, and called the hotel. When the receptionist answered, I asked for the massage center. "Good afternoon, I'll be arriving on Saturday. I'd like to book a massage with Joe Cappalini."

"I'm sorry," came the response. "Joe is on extended leave. Can I suggest Mario?"

I hung up the phone and slumped against the wall in relief. *This disappearing business is going to be a lot harder than I realized.*

A few days later, I was sitting in the hotel lobby when a massive creature jumped up and began licking me. I tried to push the heavy animal flesh away, but to no avail. When I heard a woman scream, "Princess, get off him," I realized I was receiving a royal greeting from my favorite dog—Princess Lynch-Pearlstein. The monstrous Doberman took my hand in her mouth and pulled me to her owners.

I was pleased to see Andrew and Keri, now newly married. They appeared exhausted, and in no mood for dalliance. After exchanging pleasantries, Andrew indicated they would be house-hunting for a place for the three of us to reside while in Florida, and would stay in touch. As the Pearlsteins headed to the door, Keri handed me a paper bag. "A little gift," she announced with a sly grin, and they were on their way.

I shook my head and opened the gift. I didn't know whether to laugh or cry as I read the words on a printed T-shirt: "Participant in the Federal Witness Protection Program."

The next morning, sleeping on my stomach, dead to the world, I heard that ever-annoying sound of my vibrating beeper dancing across the hotel room's nightstand. I was so comfortable, so content, I decided not to answer. Finally, at long last, the humming and scratching faded, and I happily drifted back into oblivion.

But it came again. And again. Conceding defeat, I lifted my head and found myself drawing a series of desperate breaths, almost as if I was drowning. Reaching out, I resentfully grabbed at the little box, pressed the button, and read the brightly lit green-colored screen: "Call Bill Ready. 911."

"Figures," I cursed, "the fucking FBI." I picked up the phone and dialed Ready's number.

"What's doing, Bill?"

"Jack and I just wanted you to know we're making the undercover investigation public today, that's another reason you needed to leave town. We're gonna drop in on Mike Sergio and Willie Marshall at their homes, bringing both holiday cheer, and a reel of video clips showing them committing and confessing to crimes."

"My God," was all I could gasp, my mind reeling in anticipation of the reactions Sergio and Marshall would have to the tapes. The list would include: disbelief, denial, horror, fear, hate, betrayal, and worst of all, a desire for revenge.

"I just wanted to give you a heads up, to tell you to turn off your phone, and stay well hidden. We'll call later."

It was time for my first check-in with Casey back at the office. Pulling out an untraceable calling card, I reached the firm. "Michael, help me, the phones are out of control!"

My reaction was a hearty laugh. "Take a deep breath and start at the beginning."

"I don't know where to begin. We've had repeated calls from the *Daily News* and the *New York Post*. Mike Sergio called at least fifty times. All of your friends called as did several of your clients. Everyone wants to talk to you, everyone wants you to call them."

My heart was racing even though the news was exactly as I'd anticipated. "Case, the lawyers will handle the reporters. Tell Sergio he can reach me through Bill Ready at FBI headquarters. And just tell my friends you're waiting to hear from me."

Later that week, accompanied by his attorney, Pearlstein dutifully attended his proffer with the Heritage task force. Again chairing the gathering was Mike Siegel, and the question-and-answer session went off without a hitch. Just as with my proffer, Siegel declared that Pearlstein would be allowed to serve as a cooperating witness in the Florida prosecution, and reiterated we would be receiving the sentence reduction recommendations from his office as outlined at the meeting in New York.

During this same time period, a major media furor began unfolding back home. The first hints came as our Scores public relations agent called to say the *Daily News* was preparing a major story about the Scores investigation. It was after midnight one night when we learned the piece would be in the paper's morning edition. Andrew secured a copy by driving to Miami in the wee hours and, when he returned, tossed one to me: "The article is on page two."

I opened the paper and found myself gazing at a giant-sized picture of my face—my image consuming no less than one-third of the entire page. Indeed, the article wasn't "on" page two, it was page two, and it took my breath away. "Serial murderers don't get pictures this big," I moaned.

New issues were also brewing in unexpected corners. Rudolph Giuliani, then mayor of New York City, embarked upon a moral purge aimed at excising Manhattan of adult entertainment. Somehow feeling he was the man to set the proper tone for the city, His Honor intended to banish all adult movie theaters, bookstores, and strip clubs to a rat-infested zone adjacent to the West Side Highway, an area where prostitutes and drug dealers ruled the roost.

When the measure passed the City Council, no one in the legal community expected the courts to uphold such abridgement of free speech. But everyone was proven wrong; every stage of judicial review floated down on the side of the new banishment plan. The personnel back at Scores, and at every other high-end lap dance club in the city, grew nervous. While there would certainly be lengthy and complicated court battles ahead, the writing was on the proverbial wall: Scores either needed a new theory of defense, or new premises in the mayor's nether zone.

With nothing but time on our hands, Andrew and I threw ourselves into tackling the problem by sitting poolside and reading every word of the laborious new law. After days of arguments going nowhere, we finally identified an issue worth debating. Even playing devil's advocate, we became suddenly excited, believing we'd actually found a hook on which to fight. We concluded that the language of the law itself could be turned against the city.

Specifically, the law defined an adult bookstore as one where the square footage devoted to adult (meaning sexual) subject matter was more than 40 percent. "So tell me if I'm wrong," I mulled out loud, "if a store only uses, for example, 39 percent of its total space for sexy magazines, books, and peep shows, the law doesn't apply."

"But it doesn't help us," Andrew complained, "we're not a bookstore."

"Au contraire, the drafters of this particular law were lazy. They defined adult clubs, like our Scores, by reference to and incorporation of the language applicable to bookstores."

"And if we," Andrew was excited now, "limit topless dancing to less than 40 percent of our total square footage, the law can't touch us?"

"Bingo!"

We immediately went to work on the club's floor plans with a local architect. The big question was whether the club could still function if 60 percent of the lease's square footage was put to use in ways outside the realm of topless dancing. After consultation with the professionals, the answer was an unqualified affirmative!

With independent ratification and endorsement from our experts, I picked up the phone and shared the fantastic news with the underlings running the big show back home. To a man, everyone opposed our new tactic. They were much more enthusiastic about completely different strategies being adopted by most of our competitors. In the end, I made the final decision. Scores would part company with other clubs in the city, and we would make structural changes to comply with what would soon become universally known as the "60–40 Rule."

In the months and years that followed, 60–40 proved to be Scores' salvation. Virtually every lap dance club in the city outside the new zone was eventually closed by judicial fiat. The state appellate courts, on the other hand, unanimously upheld 60–40.

CHAPTER THIRTY-EIGHT
The 156-Page Plea

JANUARY 21, 1998

The Manhattan federal prosecutors scheduled a press conference, summoning a worldwide media audience for an announcement of great import. The Honorable Mary Jo White, Manhattan's United States Attorney of long standing, spanning the terms of multiple presidents, took center stage to confirm the unsealing of the "Scores" indictment against, among dozens of others, John A. Gotti, Jr., the acting head of the Gambinos. According to White, the indictment contained charges of racketeering, murder conspiracy, extortion, and loan-sharking; and included captains, members, and associates of multiple crime families.

We'd received no advance warning of the announcement. We grabbed every newspaper carrying the story, printed every available Internet article, watched news telecasts, and slowly put together the pieces. Among the other named defendants were Mike and Steve Sergio, Willie Marshall, both DePalmas, and Tori Locascio.

Ms. White, her small torso partially hidden behind rows of microphones, declared the case was a major blow to organized crime nationwide. Applauding the work of her staff and the FBI, she went on to remind the public how rare it is for law enforcement to penetrate into the highest tiers of the mafia, and how the indictment was nothing less than a giant step toward eliminating the mob's extortion of innocent working people and businesses. Her closing words were, "What this case graphically shows is the power, profit, and reach of the Gambino crime family in business and industries, both legitimate and illegitimate, throughout the metropolitan New York area."

There was a sense of long-delayed satisfaction in Palm Beach as we watched clips of the press conference on repeated national news broadcasts. We collectively roared upon spotting Carol Sipperly, Marjorie Miller, Jack Karst, and Bill Ready snuggled on the stage behind White and their superiors, all seeking credit and acknowledgment for the mob prosecution of the decade.

When a copy of the indictment itself appeared on the Internet, we read it through. We laughed mightily at some of the nicknames attached to familiar figures. Mike Sergio was appropriately listed as a/k/a ("also known as") "Mikey Hop" and his son was branded with a grammar-school nickname, "Sigmund the Sea Monster."

"No one calls Steve by that name," I declared.

"Who cares?" Andrew bellowed in reference to his long-standing nemesis. "No matter what happens, Steve will forever be recorded in mafia history as 'Sigmund the Sea Monster.' It was all worth it, just for that."

When Bill Ready called a few days later, I teased him about how badly I felt at being ignored on the very day the undercover efforts reached fruition. I also laughingly suggested that Mary Jo White should have acknowledged the loss of my hemorrhoids as part of the undercover operation.

"The truth, Michael, is that Jack and I haven't slept for days. We were in charge of rounding up the defendants for arrest and we had little else on our minds."

"So everyone's behind bars?"

"Absolutely, and they'll all stay there for the duration. We don't think any of them will get bail. And while I can't talk details about the prosecution anymore, Jack and I both know there would've been no case at all without you and all the risks you took. No one may have said it on television, but you are a real hero in all this."

At the first Florida debriefing following the New York press conference and subsequent media splash of attention, we were treated to lunch at a local barbeque restaurant by members of the task force. It was clear our months of sessions with Florida prosecutors were winding down as we'd already shared most of our secrets and insights. The mood was pleasant and relaxed, the barriers of formality and distrust having long ago eroded over months of interaction.

At one point during lunch, one of the agents casually turned to me. "That was some press conference back in New York. I don't think we realized just how important an investigation was going on at Scores."

"It sure pissed off Judy," one of the other agents chimed in, then stopped, quickly realizing he'd misspoken.

As the group strolled back to their cars, I slid next to the agent who'd revealed Hunt's negativity about New York. "Why would Judy care about our mafia case?"

The agent looked around furtively and, confirming we were out of earshot of the group, quietly returned: "Pissed is the understatement of the century. She was downright livid, filled to overflowing with piss and vinegar. I heard her complain about the unfairness of all the publicity New York gets while our work down here is ignored."

"Doesn't she understand that a major indictment against the world's largest crime family, including its boss, always gets extraordinary press attention? It's not about the case—mafia stories sell papers!"

"She doesn't care. She hates the New York prosecutors, she hates you two, and she's not impressed with your undercover work."

About two months later, I received an emergency beeper message from my lawyer, Norman Moscowitz. I returned the call with a burning coal in the pit of my gut.

"Michael, I'm sitting here staring at your plea agreement from Hunt. I've never seen anything like it in my life."

"I don't understand, Norman, what are you talking about?"

"Well, I've tried several times to read it, but I just can't make any sense of it."

"You're talking nutty. What's the big deal about a plea agreement?"

"For one thing," Norman stuttered, "it's 156 pages long!"

I dropped the phone.

It took me five nights to read through the maze Hunt had constructed. Hunt's mind-set seemed to be that all participants were responsible for the entire fraud. As a result, she hadn't bothered to specify which crimes I'd knowingly participated in, and which were perpetrated by others without my knowledge or participation. In essence, the plea recounted every act of every crime committed at Heritage, and held me responsible for all of them. I was suddenly reading all about crimes I never knew took place, but now, I seemingly "owned" them all.

We were also being required to plead guilty to the commission of alleged "new crimes" during our cooperation with New York—which was an outright lie. Hunt acknowledged as much in a call with us, but claimed that if we didn't agree to this and sign the plea, Delaware was prepared to indict us in its state courts, a claim which also turned out to be completely false. But in the end we had no choice. The prosecutors had all the cards and, if we didn't accept the plea agreement, all of our cooperation in both districts would be ignored at the Florida sentencing.

These "new crimes" had in fact been part of a puppet show directed by the prosecutors during our time in New York, who'd wanted us to pursue a vigorous defense in both a civil action commenced in the Southern District of New York by Delaware, and in an insurance insolvency proceeding for Heritage filed in Delaware, so that it wouldn't appear we were cooperating with the FBI at Scores. With permission of the federal judge presiding over the Delaware civil case in New York, and against my better instincts, we filed false affidavits in the New York civil action, and false Proofs of Claim in the Delaware insolvency, opposing all relief the insurance company sought. If we'd undertaken any other strategy, all the mobsters and our insurance co-defendants would have known (or seriously suspected) we'd been flipped into cooperating. Everyone in law enforcement understood the life-threatening situation presented, and how important our approved filings had been to the eventual success of the mafia investigation—with the solitary exception, whether real or feigned, of Hunt.

CHAPTER THIRTY-NINE

Surrender

1998

Over the ensuing weeks, an eerie wall of silence developed. Calls to Orlando seeking status reports went unacknowledged, messages left for the New York prosecutors about a rumored recent Hunt meeting with the New York team were ignored, and even calls to the FBI sat unreturned. To my mind, the deafening silence was a clear signal of impending catastrophe.

A flow of rumors emanating from both Florida and New York confirmed my worst fears. According to sources, Hunt arrived in New York with a coterie of task force members and proceeded to make incredulous inquiries, based on wholly false facts, as to how it was possible the New York prosecutors allowed their cooperators to burn a quarter million dollars a month in Scores profits on lavish living, while the insurance company they defrauded was in a multimillion-dollar hole. Needless to say, none of this was true. Most of the money from Scores went right back into the club to pay its debts, and we were hardly living high on the hog. And, of course, this had all been negotiated long ago. But on the phone with Marjorie Miller after Hunt's visit, she was icy.

"We gave you money for living expenses when you left New York," she said.

"Are you kidding?" I scoffed. "Your office handed us a grand total of $12,500. We appreciated it, but that didn't even cover the security on the house in Palm Beach the FBI insisted we lease."

"I didn't know that," Miller shot back.

"What are you talking about? Jack and Bill flew to Florida to approve the house, and one of our lawyers has been sending Carol monthly reports on our expenditures down here paid by Scores."

Hunt had read Carol and Marjorie the riot act. She threatened to formally complain to their superiors, or to take the matter to the attorney general in Washington. She shared "inside information" that the State of Delaware, the victim, was so outraged, it was considering initiating a very embarrassing civil litigation against the New York United States Attorney for improper dissipation of stolen assets. Hunt was again invoking the Delaware Insurance Department as the battering ram for her threats.

As it turns out, the Hunt threat was made up out of whole cloth. Delaware officials had no intention of litigating against the New York prosecutors, and no conversations between Hunt and Delaware had ever taken place on the subject. Unfortunately, however, Sipperly and Miller were apparently fooled and took the empty threats seriously.

Appealing to Hunt as a fellow prosecutor, Carol and Marjorie sought to mend fences. Hunt's response was simple: Scores was to be sold immediately, and we were to be incarcerated as soon as possible. She would then handle Delaware.

A meeting between the New York prosecutors and our attorneys took place a week later. It was chaired by Sipperly's boss, Mark Pomerantz, the new First Assistant United States Attorney. A trio of our attorneys, Sandy Weinberg, Peter Ginsberg, and Myles Malman, attended. As each of the attorneys was a former prosecutor, each knew Pomerantz well and held him in high regard.

Sipperly opened the meeting by stating that we had violated our plea agreement, pointing to the uncontrolled spending of Scores' profits in Florida. Ginsberg quickly interrupted. "Let's hold it right there, Carol. Together with Andrew, I personally negotiated that issue with your forfeiture department and the deal was simple: our clients retained control. The only condition was they couldn't reduce the club's resale value."

"That was not the deal, Peter," Sipperly angrily snapped at Ginsberg.

"It was, Carol. I was there. You weren't, but your two FBI agents, Karst and Ready, were present." He turned to Pomerantz. "Mark, I suggest you ask them what they remember."

"I already have," Pomerantz answered, shooting a derisive glance at Sipperly.

"If I may," Weinberg jumped in, "Michael and Andrew are living on a fraction of their prior incomes in a strange city where they were required to start their lives over from scratch. Despite substantial profits being earned by Scores, they've used those profits to settle corporate debts. Since the club is worth a great deal more today than it was a year ago, I fail to understand your complaints. As I see it, they deserve your praise." He handed papers to Pomerantz. "We've been sending Carol monthly statements accounting for all the Scores funds being expensed out in Florida."

Pomerantz looked over the monthly expense reports, then tossed the bundle to Sipperly. "I've never seen these before, have you?"

Sipperly looked at the reports and turned very pale. "They look familiar; they're probably buried in a pile on my desk."

In the end, our attorneys' efforts resulted in few benefits. Pomerantz made it clear he disapproved of the forfeiture deal struck over Scores. "Of course your clients needed to retain complete control of the club while they were undercover. But after the fact of their cooperation became public and they left for Florida, it's hard to understand why they were left in control."

"Maybe because they would never have gone undercover and there would have been no Scores case if that concession hadn't been made by your office," Ginsberg responded, the veins on his neck popping as he spoke. "Maybe because they were falsely promised a transfer of their sentencing from Florida to New York, a promise which your predecessor refused to honor. Maybe because they were promised a tiny amount of jail time, which you can no longer guarantee. Bottom line, you used our clients, hung them out to dry, and ensured their continuing cooperation by promising to leave them with the only asset you had under your control. Taking it away from them now would be immoral."

"You may be right, Peter," Pomerantz answered contritely, "but shit happens, and you know that's true." Forfeiture rights in Scores would be transferred from New York to Delaware through Florida.

But it was Pomerantz's final point that would be the hardest to swallow. We were being asked to surrender into custody by August first.

"Now who's violating the plea agreements?" Weinberg angrily vented. "Your office promised our clients would remain free until their cooperation was complete here and in Florida; the Florida pleas are identical. Our clients didn't expect to be incarcerated for years to come, and you want them to surrender in thirty days? Do you people intend to keep even one of your promises to these men?"

Pomerantz frowned, shaking his head slowly. "I can't disagree with you that this whole case is a mess. I've never seen successful undercover cooperators treated so shabbily. And I'm not ordering them to surrender. I'm urgently asking them to do so. And I'm certainly not declaring them in default of their plea agreements here in New York. But I can't let them take any more money from Scores. If we get into a big fight over this, it will make their Florida sentencing ugly. They know they're going to do some time in Club Fed, so let's get it started and concentrate on getting them out as quickly as possible."

Following a final meeting with Hunt back in Orlando, as I was preparing to leave, she casually mentioned the upcoming surrender.

I willed myself to be polite. "Let's just hope things go as planned and we're in and out quickly," I said.

"Well, I don't know about that one," Hunt returned with her broadest of smiles.

"What does that mean?" I asked, trying to conceal my mounting hysteria.

"Well," Hunt shook her head, "I know you and Andrew are hoping it's going to be a quick fix, six months or a year in jail, and then out. Ta-da! Trust me, that's not going to happen."

"What do you mean? The Florida plea agreements have specific recommendations, and you agreed other districts and states could argue for even less time."

"That's true, I did," Judy said, "but I know this case and I know this judge. I was just trying to soften the blow on its way to you."

AUGUST 1998

Surrender Day. After being searched, fingerprinted, and cuffed, Andrew and I were ushered into separate cars, accompanied by a total of six federal marshals. The moment the motorcade entered the New Jersey Turnpike, it began to rain. It was the most torrential downpour I'd ever witnessed, and we were forced to pull over several times for lack of road vision. For the multi-hour trek, the rain never let up, never faltered.

Sitting in the backseat, on the way to a WITSEC facility, I couldn't help but think the gods were crying.

CHAPTER FORTY
Sentencing, Parts I and II

NOVEMBER, 1998

Our sentencing hearing in Florida was scheduled for November 13, 1998. Typically, cooperating witnesses are sentenced based on agreed-upon terms of incarceration and so the whole affair is usually mundane. After the crimes of the defendant and his cooperation are reviewed, the government confirms its recommendations and the judge imposes the recommended sentences.

But somehow our judge, at the urging of Judy Hunt, decided to impose sentences upon us as scheduled, but to defer consideration of pending government motions for massive time reductions until *all* our cooperation was *completed*—probably years away. The prosecution would now immediately be seeking the most severe sentences possible, as if we weren't cooperators at all, although it was legally committed to recommend maximum leniency at a later date when the reduction motions were heard. This procedure actually violated federal law, and the resultant publicity would be terribly prejudicial to us.

We sat through a full day of motions for leniency from our side, opposition from Hunt, and denial of all relief by Judge Conway. Even sentence reduction motions granted by other judges in the same courthouse to other defendants in the same case were denied.

Tired, weary, and beaten, I simply listened without reaction or emotion as Conway pronounced three-hundred-month prison sentences on both of us. Twenty-five years: an unprecedented sentence in American justice for extraordinary undercover nonviolent cooperators. Even Sammy "The Bull" Gravano, who never wore a wire, received only four and a half years behind bars after testifying against John Gotti, Sr., despite confessing to eighteen murders.

We were sentenced to twenty-five years, and any reduction in that sentence was deferred until the various trials and legal actions were complete and our usefulness was officially ended, years in the future. In the meantime, all I could do was continue cooperating, and pray for eventual leniency from a justice system that had yet to show any.

Just as Karst and Ready predicted, Mike Sergio and Willie Marshall, when confronted with the extent of their criminality captured on tape, quick-marched into the open arms of the prosecutors, voluntarily enlisting as witnesses to the extortion of Scores by the Gambinos.

Although facing life imprisonment for a litany of crimes, both men were afforded extraordinary leniency in recognition of the dangers they now faced as witnesses against the mafia. Marshall received a nine-month term and was already home by the time I'd surrendered; and Mike Sergio, owing to a prior conviction, was serving out a twenty-two-month sentence.

Between September 1998 and April 1999, the New York prosecutors amassed a universal plea from all defendants indicted in the Scores investigation. At a splashy news conference, the world learned that John A. Gotti, Jr., acting boss of the Gambino family, the largest crime family in the world, together with thirty-eight other members and associates of his and other families, were pleading guilty and heading off to jail.

Hailed as a major victory for the federal government in the war on organized crime, the plea received massive national and international media coverage. As for me, I watched the spectacle from a prison cell, waiting endlessly for my cooperation to be presented and my sentence drastically reduced.

During this same time period, the Atlanta case against the Gold Club began heating up. I was transported, as had become the norm, in body shackles reminiscent of Hannibal Lecter, through airports, onto commercial airliners, and into solitary confinement cells in county jails. Andrew and I testified for days on end before a sitting grand jury, recounting the tale told in the recordings with Kaplan, of his participation with the Gambino crime family in the extortion at Scores. Based on our testimony, and information from others who agreed to testify because of the damning undercover tapes, the Atlanta grand jury indicted a host of defendants.

Unbeknownst to me at the time, it was the testimony of Gambino acting captain—now cooperator—Craig DePalma, before that same grand jury, that implicated Mikey Scars DiLeonardo, one of the most powerful mafia figures in the country, for his role in the shakedown. The indictment of Kaplan, the inclusion of Mikey Scars, and the anticipated testimony of several NBA superstars all raised national eyebrows.

After the Florida criminal trial finally ended, I again began my active cooperation with Delaware. It had been Delaware's insurance fund that quickly repaid every Heritage policyholder his or her total investment, ensuring that not one person had lost a dime in the whole sad and heartbreaking fraud. Each individual investor having been made whole, I was now cooperating to make Delaware—and other later contributing state funds through their association, NOGHLA—whole as well.

Months of lonely waiting for the filing of sentence reduction motions turned into tedious years. A WITSEC facility is a maximum-security federal prison for witnesses—cushy by prison standards, sure, but "cushy by prison standards" is hardly a ringing endorsement. I sadly learned that a jail by any name is still a jail.

As my cooperation had continued—in New York and Atlanta, and in criminal and civil forfeiture cases for Delaware—Hunt had stealthily maneuvered behind the scenes, resisting every effort to schedule our hearings.

Finally, in mid-2001, a newly appointed Florida United States Attorney wrote to announce our hearings would be scheduled, and her district would be recommending the maximum reduction under the Florida plea agreement.

Invitations were extended to prosecutors in New York and Atlanta to attend, and to submit their own independent recommendations for appropriate departures—which would certainly be "time served."

In that euphoric moment, after almost three years of incarceration, it seemed the time for redemption and reward had arrived. But when the government's actual motions were received, authored and signed by Hunt, it was apparent we'd been betrayed yet again. Hunt's motion was transparently designed to further pollute the judge against us, and to subtly lobby against granting the relief sought by her superiors. Hunt again raised the issue of "new crimes" committed while cooperating in New York, a fiction we'd agreed not to contest because we were left no choice.

The hearing convened. With the exception of Judy Hunt, the government representatives from New York, Georgia, and Delaware more than lived up to their promises to emphatically urge maximum sentencing leniency.

New York submitted an extensive letter of endorsement. It apprised the court of the cooperative risks undertaken, describing them as "incapable of being overstated," noting the targets of the Scores investigation were dangerous career mobsters who "would not have hesitated to have killed [the cooperators] had it been discovered [they] were wearing body wires." New York asserted that comparable cooperation had frequently resulted in reductions exceeding Florida's recommendation from federal courts across the nation.

FBI agent William Ready addressed the court. He summarized the successful capture of 110 recordings, over a year's time, resulting in the indictment. He reserved special praise for me, telling the judge I'd worn the F-Bird wires, had taken most of the risks, had been patted down in searches for hidden recording devices on at least three occasions by armed gangsters, and would surely have been executed "on the spot," but for my guile and bravery under what most others would find unimaginable stress and fear.

The then chief of the New York Criminal Division, Alan Kaufman, one of the most respected, influential, and hard-nosed prosecutors in the country, rose in solid support of massive sentence reductions. He categorized our assistance as: "The most extraordinary cooperation law enforcement can hope for." He explained that, for those who wear wires and enter WITSEC, their lives are "forever changed"; danger of retribution follows them into their new identities. And importantly, the ability of government to enlist future cooperation depends on judges honoring prosecutors' promises.

Arthur Leach, the Atlanta prosecutor leading the pending Gold Club case, advised Conway that his prosecution in Atlanta would not have been possible without the undercover recordings and our extensive testimony to the grand jury. He also stressed that our testimony in the upcoming trial merited great weight.

The Insurance Department of Delaware, in a rare and impressive move, also appeared and rose to support maximum leniency. Few if any defendants ever achieve such recommendations from their "victim."

After hearing from me and our attorneys, the courtroom held its collective breath awaiting Conway's ruling. She opened by agreeing our cooperation was extraordinary, but revealed for the first time she'd secretly set a limit for cooperation sentence reductions at one-third below the mandatory guidelines. Conway went on to lower the original sentences from three hundred months down to two hundred months (or sixteen-plus years).

In so ruling, Conway ignored the unanimous chorus of governmental recommendations (seventy months or less), the original grid agreement she approved at our plea hearings (sixty-one months), the sentences she and other judges had imposed on other Heritage cooperators (one hundred and fifty months), and the national standard for rewarding extraordinary cooperators who wear wires against mobsters (70 to 90 percent reductions from guidelines).

The courtroom erupted.

Our attorneys first undertook to remind Conway she had, just a few months earlier, lowered the sentence of Patrick Smythe, a codefendant and chief financial officer of Heritage, to one hundred and fifty months from three hundred months—a 50 percent reduction. He'd done nothing more than testify about his own crimes, he'd not undertaken cooperation against the mob, wouldn't be entering WITSEC—and his sentence reduction exceeded the just-announced "secret" limit of 33⅓ percent.

Conway looked startled. She ruffled through her notes, turned several pages, and then declared, "Perhaps Mr. Smythe got more than he should have."

"Perhaps he got more than he should have?" Andrew furiously whispered to me. "She gave him that sentence."

When asked to explain how an ordinary cooperator like Smythe could receive a greater reduction than cooperators who risked their lives and faced a lifetime of retribution, Conway responded:

"I understand that. But it's the defendants, themselves, that put themselves into a position where they were able to give that kind of cooperation. Mr. Smythe, as far as I was advised, was never in a position to have done any of those things."

This logic was breathtaking in its absurdity. Because we "were in a position" to be extorted by the mafia and were willing to accept the government's offer to risk our lives and cooperate in exchange for leniency, we were not entitled to the promised rewards. But Mr. Smythe, because he was not in a position to provide undercover cooperation and did not do so, would receive the greater reward.

As the arguments grew heated, Conway refused to listen further. She announced there were no words that could ever convince her to alter her course and she would brook no additional debate.

She exited the courtroom, slamming the door behind her. In the final analysis, we'd received no leniency credit from the Florida court for our New York cooperation, and may well have received a lesser sentence had we not cooperated in New York at all.

No one knew what to say; the impossible had just happened. Kaufman joined us some twenty minutes later and shared that the Florida United States Attorney had authorized the drafting and filing of motions to reargue the sentences. He added the Attorney General's Office in Washington was going to participate directly in the reargument—a highly unusual undertaking reserved for extraordinary cases involving national policy considerations. He did his best to reassure our group of near-hysterical defendants, family, and attorneys, and to urge us to keep hope alive.

Before returning to the county jail in Orlando for more solitary confinement, Andrew and I agreed to meet with Art Leach. The Atlanta prosecutor, with a pending trial, opened the discussion: "If you two had been sentenced by any judge in my district, we'd be sharing dinner tonight in any restaurant of your choice. My god, you were responsible for the indictment, conviction, and incarceration of dozens of mob members and the head of one of the five families. That would have been enough to set you free in any court in the country except here. In over twenty years as a prosecutor, I've never seen a judge act less professionally or reasonably. I'm so sorry because I feel I'm part of a system that just let you down miserably."

We knew Art was concerned we would end our cooperation in anger. But we quelled his anxiety, agreeing to continue cooperating in Georgia. We were going to do the "right thing," even in the face of betrayal.

We did in fact return to Atlanta and testify in the Gold Club case. The Atlanta press labeled my testimony as "the most damaging," and I was apprised that Kaplan reversed his plea to guilty after I testified and in the middle of the trial. Only Mikey Scars, and one other defendant, were later acquitted by the jury.

Years after, I learned the sad and ironic reason for Scars's escape from justice. Gambino acting captain Craig DePalma was scheduled to be the chief government trial witness against Scars. It had been DePalma's grand jury testimony that led to Scars's indictment in Atlanta in the first place, and it was DePalma's trial testimony that was anticipated to convict him.

However, at the trial, on the witness stand, DePalma refused to answer any questions, instead asserting his Fifth Amendment right not to testify. Apparently, having inwardly hoped in vain that Scars would plead guilty and not proceed to trial, he found he could neither face Scars in the courtroom nor accept a public labeling of him as a mob "rat." After the judge dismissed him from the stand, he was returned to a holding facility where he hung himself. Sadly, DePalma's "sacrifice" was for nothing because, within a year, Scars would be charged in an unrelated murder case in New York and would himself become a federal cooperating witness in major mob prosecutions and a WITSEC participant.

Although brain-dead from that fateful night, Craig DePalma's physical body continued in an unresponsive vegetative state, and his father had his body placed in a Westchester, New York nursing home on life support. As Greg DePalma renewed his illegal activities as a Gambino captain, including the planning and the commission of new crimes, he held weekly meetings in his son's room, with the body present, believing he would be safe from the government's prying eyes and ears. He turned out to be wrong.

The executive prosecutors in the Florida prosecutorial office, humiliated by the results in our case and its national ramifications, quickly moved to prepare and file a motion for reconsideration of our sentences. The final motion was signed, not by Hunt, but by the United States Attorney, the chief legal officer in the district. The stated ground for reconsideration was the government's self-proclaimed failure, the first time around, to sufficiently emphasize the crucial policy considerations involved in the sentencing of "those who undertake at great personal risk, cooperation against organized crime."

What happened next was breathtaking. In what appears to have been a unique act during his tenure as President George W. Bush's attorney general, John Ashcroft authorized his office, represented by Assistant Attorney General Michael Chertoff—Director of the National Crime Division and later to be Director of Homeland Security—to appear in support of the reconsideration motions. Chertoff's support was extraordinary in its force and quality. All the other districts, as well as Delaware, appeared and echoed the position of the Attorney General of the United States, arguing for our immediate release.

Conway denied the motions, pronouncing herself well satisfied with her original sentences. She acknowledged the opinion of the Attorney General, noted the motion signatory as the United States Attorney, as well as the victim's unusual continuing support, but apparently couldn't have cared less.

Additional motions were filed by the government to reduce our sentences; each was denied by Conway. We served every day of the two-hundred-month sentence, minus federal good-time credits, for a total of thirteen-plus years. No nonviolent undercover cooperator, having risked his life at the government's request, has ever served as long.

EPILOGUE
The Aftermath

After my surrender into WITSEC custody, the Delaware Insurance Department filed a motion in the New York federal district court seeking appointment of a Receiver over Scores. The day the motion was to be heard by the court, Blitz Bilzinsky and Harvey Osher, representing Scores, filed the club into formal bankruptcy. That bankruptcy filing had the effect of staying Heritage's Receiver appointment motion, and Delaware next proceeded to file a creditor claim in the case.

Faced with years of litigation, and an uncertain outcome as to where ownership would eventually be awarded by the court, Heritage opted to settle its claim with Scores, realizing a multimillion-dollar recovery.

As a result, ownership of Scores became the undisputed property of Bilzinsky, Osher, and their associates.

Scores remains one of the most successful upscale gentlemen's clubs in the world, with establishments in New York City and around the country.

Anne C. Conway continues to serve as a federal district judge on senior status in Orlando.

Judy Hunt retired as a prosecutor in the Middle District of Florida and is now engaged in the private practice of law.

Mike Sergio, after pleading guilty to conspiracy to commit murder, surrendered into federal witness custody in 1999 and served a total of twenty-two months of imprisonment. His potentially multi-decade sentence was dramatically reduced by his cooperation against high-level mafia defendants. He is now retired.

Steve Sergio pled guilty to reduced charges in an arrangement with New York prosecutors and served thirty-seven months in federal prison. He refused to cooperate with the government.

William "Willie" Marshall entered a witness prison facility and served nine months in custody, also receiving significant credit for his cooperation against major mafia targets.

Acting mafia captain Craig DePalma initially pled guilty in the Scores case and received an eighty-seven-month sentence. While incarcerated, he agreed to testify in Atlanta and became the chief witness leading to the indictment of Michael "Mikey Scars" DiLeonardo. However, at trial, he refused to answer any questions and later hanged himself in a United States Marshals holding facility.

Greg DePalma, who was facing a twelve-year sentence in the Scores case, received a seventy-month term when he succeeded in falsely convincing his sentencing judge that he was extremely ill and on the verge of death. When he was convicted in yet another subsequent case based on recorded telephonic evidence against him, including boasts of the health ruse he'd pulled off on the prior judge, he received an extremely harsh sentence. He died in jail.

Mikey Scars was acquitted in Atlanta, but was subsequently indicted in a murder case in New York. At that time, he became a major cooperator against the mob, going on to testify in multiple major trials, including a case against Gotti Jr. In an extraordinary sentencing proceeding in New York, where he received maximum leniency for his cooperation, he was required to waive double jeopardy, enter a guilty plea to the Atlanta acquitted offenses among other crimes, and admitted he'd been wrongfully found not guilty in the Gold Club trial.

Steve Kaplan, owner of the Gold Club, entered into a plea agreement with Atlanta prosecutors during the Gold Club trial. He stipulated to a three-year prison term, a cash forfeiture of millions of dollars, hundreds of thousands of dollars in restitution, and surrender of the Gold Club real estate, the business, and licenses.

Atlanta AUSA Arthur W. Leach retired from the US Attorney's office after an impressive career in organized crime prosecution. Today he practices criminal and civil law in the federal courts in Georgia and throughout the United States.

AUSA Carol Sipperly retired from government service after the Scores case concluded, but returned and now serves as a federal prosecutor based in Washington, D.C. After the Scores case, I'm told AUSA Marjorie Miller retired from the practice of law.

Special Agents William Ready and Jack Karst remain in distinguished active service in the Federal Bureau of Investigation.

Attorneys Morris "Sandy" Weinberg in Tampa, and Peter Ginsberg in New York, remain highly distinguished practitioners of law. They were never fairly or reasonably compensated for their tireless advocacy and representation in this matter; their work spanning almost twenty years. Our attorney and friend, Myles Malman, died in the spring of 2014, after a ten-month battle with brain cancer. We all mourn his passing.

I have not spoken to Pearlstein since 2001. We each served a total of thirteen-plus years in WITSEC facilities (two hundred months minus full good-time credits). Although the New York prosecutors had promised to use all their influence to keep us housed together while incarcerated, we were separated in the first year by the Bureau of Prisons, and New York refused to intercede on our behalf.

My former law partner, Andrew Cuomo, has been elected, reelected, and serves with distinction as governor of the State of New York, following in the footsteps of his father.

In September 1998, *GQ* published an article about Scores, mafia infiltration at the club, and the FBI investigation into the Gambinos.

Playboy published an article by A. J. Benza in 1999 titled "The Naked and the Dead," lamenting the decline of Scores after my ownership ended; remembering the good old days.

Maxim magazine published a history of Scores' celebrity magnetism in December 2009 titled "Savanna to the Champagne Room," and *Stuff* magazine joined the parade with a pictorial: "Scores Scoreboard: Living in the lap dance of luxury," featuring photographs and stories about star regulars at the club.

Law and Order presented an episode based, in part, on our Scores story. It was called "Ambitious," actor Joe Piscopo played me, and it aired in May 1999, almost one year after our surrender.

The undercover recordings from the Gold Club case are still aired on television programs exploring the risks of undercover cooperation.

Since 1998, I have continuously cooperated with the Delaware Department of Insurance in the recovery of fraud proceeds. Working in conjunction with the National Heritage Life Insurance Receiver, I testified and submitted affidavits in multiple civil trials and other proceedings and also participated in ongoing debriefings, all of which resulted in multimillion-dollar recoveries. My efforts were lauded as particularly distinguished and significant in court submissions by Delaware seeking leniency on my behalf.

Originally promised a few months in witness jail, followed by life in the Witness Protection Program, I was released from a WITSEC facility after thirteen-plus years and given not a new identity, but a bus ticket to Brooklyn. (But that's a story for another day.)

I appeared on *60 Minutes* in 2015, interviewed by correspondent Anderson Cooper. The segment featured a reunion with Agent Ready, retired Atlanta prosecutor Art Leach, and Steve Sergio. I managed to refrain from calling him "Sigmund the Sea Monster."

Oh, and I wrote a book.

acknowledgments

This book began its road to life in the year 2000, in a Federal Witness Security Program facility, on a manual typewriter, using ribbons purchased at commissary. The work kept me sane and provided an outlet for my frustration, fear, and bitterness.

During those years, my amazing nieces, Sheri and Kim, kept the wheels of progress spinning by talking to me every day, putting up with my incessant complaints, typing my drafts into the computer, and correcting my errors; along with my angels, Angela and Patricia, they were always always there for me. Without my devoted friends, no book—nor sane person—would have emerged from the ordeal.

I was kept alive by the steadfast friendship and amazing support of those who never left me in their rearview mirrors—Keith, Julie, Marissa, Harvey, Mark, Ted.

It was celebrated filmmaker Marcos Zurinaga from Puerto Rico who read my 1,000-plus page manuscript and, finding merit and meaning within its pages, first encouraged and nurtured me through the experience of sharing it.

All my respect and gratitude to Joel Gotler of Intellectual Property Group, my agent, advisor, friend, and confessor. He keeps my head on straight (not easy with a gay man). My love to Joel's right-hand woman, Rachel Levine, who has more patience than Job; and my sincere appreciation to IPG's affiliated literary agent, Murray Weiss of Catalyst Literary Management, who taught me so much.

I owe everything about this book to the gang at BenBella Books out of Dallas. But for its impressive publisher, Glenn Yeffeth, I seriously doubt my story would ever have seen the light of day. He has become the "soul" and "guiding light" of my story, and his staff of enthusiastic and talented folks has infused me with excitement and anticipation. Special thanks to Erin Kelley, who started me on this creative journey with Skype calls from Europe.

No words can express my feelings of complete gratitude to my editor, Alexa Stevenson. How lucky I am to have found a kindred soul who understands me, my life, my sense of humor, and my desire to express my innermost feelings. You have made me a better writer and a better person, and you are always there for me. I will never forget your tremendous contribution.

To my fantastic lawyers, Jon Moonves and Tom Greenberg, at Del, Shaw, Moonves, Tanaka, Finkelstein & Lezcano. They taught me that I am not the easiest client to handle.

To everyone at Goldcrest Films and Gaumont International Television, especially Nick Quested, David Kennedy, Robyn Meisinger, and Sharon Hall, for believing in me and filling me with dreams of a bright and exciting future in a new life.

And to all the friends who took me back when I came home and supported and cherished me, and the new friends who gave me back my old confidence and hope for long-awaited redemption: Keith, Julie, Steve, Harvey, Mark, Angela, Ted, Adam, Alex, Peter, Carol, Greg, Sam, Bruce, Mark, Sabrina, Blue, Bentley; to my dear ones, Jamie, Mike, Daniel, Lew, Harry, Jacob, Kyle, Nick, Drew; and to my hearts, Adam and Claudio.

To my family of all families: Carole, Sheri, Kim, Joe, Robert, Nina, Parker, Brooklyn. I love you all so much. More than you know.

And to all those I have failed to honor here under the pressure of writing these acknowledgments: Forgive me. I owe you.